THE RADICAL LEFT
IN BRITAIN 1931-1941

The Radical Left in Britain

1931-1941

JAMES JUPP

Principal Lecturer, Canberra College of Advanced Education
and Visiting Fellow, Australian National University

FRANK CASS

First published 1982 in Great Britain by
FRANK CASS AND COMPANY LIMITED
Gainsborough House, 11 Gainsborough Road,
London, E11 1RS, England

and in the United States of America by
FRANK CASS AND COMPANY LIMITED
c/o Biblio Distribution Centre
81 Adams Drive, P. O. Box 327, Totowa, N. J. 07511

British Library Cataloguing in Publication Data

Jupp, James
    The radical left in Britain 1931–1941
    1. Radicalism – Great Britain – History
    2. Political parties – Great Britain – History
    I. Title
    320.5′3′0941   HX243

ISBN 0-7146-3123-X

*Typeset by Saildean Ltd.,
Printed in Great Britain by
Page Bros (Norwich) Ltd.,
Norwich, Norfolk.*

Contents

Preface

The past ten years have seen a revival of interest in the recent history of the British labour movement, and particularly in the alleged 'lost opportunity' for a British revolution at some stage between 1900 and 1926. What is attempted here is a reassessment of the radical politics of the 1930s, a decade also mythologised in the recent past as one in which British intellectuals were either 'fellow-travelling' with Stalin or 'moving towards Marxism', depending on your point of view. My concern is not centrally with those poets, writers and scientists whose memoirs of the 'Red Thirties' are readily available. Their politics were a reaction against two outstanding and connected features of the 1930s, the collapse of the world economy and the rise of Fascism. What is presented here is an analysis of the politics of the Radical Left – descendants of the pioneering socialists who failed to make the revolution at the beginning of the century, but, equally, the forerunners of the radicals of today. I am particularly concerned to argue that the Labour Left of the 1970s is in the same tradition as the Left of the 1930s. Even the 'New Left', which is based on a generation which knows nothing of the pre-war years, might see some of its origins in that decade even while it rejects so much of the tactics and outlook of the Popular Front.

The initial research on which this book is based was undertaken at the London School of Economics in the 1950s under the supervision of Professors R. T. McKenzie and Donald G. MacRae. Since then I have seen no reason to alter my basic proposition that the Left has a useful function in enlivening the Labour Party but has no future as an independent force in British politics. Despite the student radicalism of the 1960s or the current myths of trade union dominance over British politics, the Radical Left has always been peripheral to the centres of power in British political life. That is not to say that its intellectual influence has not been substantial, although a hard look at much of the work produced in the 1930s might suggest that it is often ephemeral. Nor do I argue that the million or more who have passed through the Radical Left in the past forty or fifty years have not been important and influential in Labour Party and trade union politics. On the contrary, the dilemma of the Left has always been that it has trained and inspired activists only to see them pass into the broader stream of national life which the Left has always been unable to control.

It is difficult to write about labour politics without a personal acquaintance with the labour movement. Without my experiences in the British and Australian labour parties, in student politics at the LSE or as a University teacher during the student militancy of a few years ago, it would have been impossible for me to follow and understand much of what has happened on the Left. Equally, without the experience of canvassing, organizing and running for party and local office, I might have overlooked the limited impact which the Left has always had on the average working class voter, trade unionist or Labour supporter. Particular thanks are due to all those with whom I have worked over the past thirty years. This book, at least, could not have been written from a University study alone.

Many of those who helped me with my original research have now died, although happily some have lived on into their eighties and nineties. Particular thanks are due to Fenner Brockway, Harry McShane, J.T. Murphy, John McNair, Jock Haston and many others active on the Left, including some who would rather not be named in a book which questions the value of their life work. Academic colleagues who have discussed these issues with me most fruitfully in the past have included David Coates, Lewis Minkin and Bob Looker, not to mention a whole generation of York University students (many of them Trotskyists of various persuasions) with whom I argued for a living and for the hell of it.

The libraries consulted have been many and various, some of them little more than dusty collections in party back rooms. Most important were the Transport House library of the Labour Party and the Trades Union Congress, the London School of Economics, the British Museum and the Colindale newspaper library, the offices of the Independent Labour Party and of *Forward*, and the University libraries of York, Leeds, Canberra and Waterloo (Ontario). My particular thanks are due to my wife, Marian, whose editing and assistance were appreciated because they were offered by a Marxist scholar who can also write English. Most of those who helped me will probably disagree with my conclusions. Like my mistakes, these are entirely my own responsibility.

James Jupp
Canberra

CHAPTER 1

The Origins of the Left

The period between the wars was an unhappy one for the British people in general, and particularly for the majority who belonged to the industrial working class. Between 1914 and 1918 almost 900,000 British Empire soldiers had died in the trenches, most of them from the working class. In the 1920s the basic industries of coal, textiles and heavy engineering went into long-term decline. Major industrial centres such as Glasgow, South Wales, Lancashire and the Northeast coast collapsed inexorably. Eight years after the end of the war Britain experienced its only general strike,. in defence of the miners. It was a dismal failure, and was followed by restrictive legislation against the unions and by victimization of many union activists. Fourteen years after the war there were almost three million unemployed, and in the North-East and South Wales at least one-third of all breadwinners were out of work and being steadily pushed onto the meagre relief provided by the Poor Law.

Twenty-one years after the end of the First World War the British people were subjected to a second war, which, while it produced only half as many British military casualties as the first, struck more radically at the lives of ordinary civilians. Throughout the whole period Britain remained 'Great' in the sense of ruling over the largest empire in human history. Its parliament, most of its ministers and nearly all of its higher civil servants, continued to be chosen from a narrow social class, which had drawn its income from industrial areas now derelict, from agriculture now unable to support its labourers and from an empire which was even more depressed than the 'Mother Country'. The ruling class was clearly visible in terms of its life-style, attitudes, accents and political and

1

social dominance. It was also surprisingly incompetent and reactionary, and it was unable to comprehend what was happening within Britain or what was happening to Britain's relationship with the rest of the world. The recent ancestors of those who ruled Britain had been innovative, adventurous, intelligent, sometimes radical, always thrusting. Their descendants were none of these. The only politically important area of British life which was not dominated by these less than adequate children of the Victorians was the labour movement. But that movement itself, despite rapid expansion, was also a child of the Victorians and of Liberal radicalism.

The British labour movement, the Labour Party and the trade unions, emerged from the First World War greatly strengthened. The extension of the franchise in 1918 gave rise to a rapid expansion of the Labour vote accompanied by a rapid decline in Liberal support and organization.[1] Labour Party members had taken part in government for the first time under the wartime coalition of Lloyd George and with the support of the party's National Executive Committee. Parts of the labour movement, however, remained or became hostile to the war. This was particularly true of the Independent Labour Party, which was the dominant influence on local political organizations sponsoring Labour candidates. The ILP's opposition to the war was the major element aggravating existing tension with the trade-union officials who dominated the federalized machine of the Labour Party. The Trades Union Congress and most union officials supported the coalition government but there was strong and growing antipathy towards it, particularly among miners and engineers in Scotland and Wales. The years immediately preceding the war had seen massive industrial unrest and propaganda for syndicalism, which seriously challenged the constitutionalism of established union leaders. In South Wales and Clydeside a radical tradition established itself which emphasized direct action as an alternative to labour representation in parliament. Much of this was spontaneous, although a number of small syndicalist and Marxist parties were able to exert some influence.[2] The Glasgow 'rent strikes' of 1916, the engineers' strikes led by the Clyde Workers Committee and the political agitations of John Maclean marked a growing radicalism in Scotland which was largely outside established parties, although it was a major factor in the electoral sweep of Glasgow seats for Labour and the ILP in 1922.[3]

The Russian and Irish revolutions stimulated this radicalism still further and the period between 1910 and 1926 has been extensively treated as a potentially revolutionary period.[4] Certainly there was a revolution, but it created the Irish Free State rather than the Socialist Commonwealth. Much of the support for syndicalism and for self-styled revolutionary and Marxist parties was concentrated outside England in the increasingly 'depressed' areas of central Scotland and South Wales. They were remote from the centre of political power in London and were even regarded as peripheral by many of the leaders of the labour movement. The Miners' Federation, possibly because it was the largest and most militant component of the Trades Union Congress, gradually found itself isolated from the TUC General Council and its full-time officials in London. Miners were represented by elderly and fairly conservative MPs who had worked their way up the union hierarchy in the days when mining areas were controlled by the Liberal Party. Engineers were dominated by craft unionism which divided them by organization and levels of skill even within the newly created Amalgamated Engineering Union. Those who were employed in expanding industries like motor and electrical engineering had a diminishing common interest with those in the depressed shipbuilding and railway engineering industries. Thus when the General Strike came in 1926 it marked the end of a period of working-class militancy and collective resistance to industrial decay and stagnation. The enthusiasm and militancy of 1919 no longer existed in the areas and industries where it had mattered most. Working-class voters had already elected one Labour government in 1923 and following the General Strike they elected another one at the first opportunity in 1929.

The General Strike ended a major epoch in the history of the labour movement.[5] It destroyed the myth that a nationwide work stoppage could lead to a fairly bloodless revolution in which the system simply 'collapsed'. It showed how firmly union officials had become embedded in the governing structure and how reluctant Labour politicians were to jeopardize the chances of gaining office. The notion of 'betrayal' took hold on militants in the labour movement and partly accounts for the bitter resentment between the Left and most union officials during the 1930s. The initative in the TUC and, increasingly, in the Labour Party passed from the miners and engineers to the general workers' unions with less tradition of direct action and less membership participation in the making of decisions.

The Labour Party in parliament did not immediately suffer from the reaction against the General Strike. The first Labour government of 1924 had been ineffective and supported by the Liberals. Nonetheless, despite its defeat, a shift continued towards the Labour Party of millions of former Liberal voters or new voters who were put off by the factionalism of the Liberal Party.[6] Between 1918 and 1929 the Labour vote rose by over six million to the total of 8,364,883 on which a Labour government with Liberal support was returned in 1929. But this too marked a climax and the end of a political epoch. The collapse of the MacDonald government in August 1931 weakened and divided the Labour Party as effectively as the General Strike had demoralized the trade unions.[7] Two major 'betrayals' in five years were more than enough and created the permanent attitude of mistrust towards leadership which characterized radicals in the labour movement from then onwards. Like other party leaders before and since, Ramsay MacDonald had been regarded as on the Left before his election, particularly because of his opposition to the war and his domination of the Independent Labour Party after Keir Hardie's death in 1915. In fact MacDonald was as much a 'gradualist' as the Fabians or as the cautious trade-union officials who initially regarded him with much suspicion. His leadership of the party, although seldom challenged, took it far away from the radicalism which had encouraged the adoption of a socialist objective in 1918.

The fall of the Labour government in 1931 and MacDonald's defection to lead an essentially Conservative National Government, marked the lowest point ever reached in the morale of the Labour Party. It completed the disillusionment begun by the failure of the General Strike. The ten years which followed had certain peculiar characteristics. There was a noticeable discontent with parliamentary practices and institutions. New problems had arisen which the old parties, with their controversies over free trade or the gold standard seemed unable to solve. The world depression further demoralized the labour movement, as it had begun in Britain under a Labour government and struck hardest at the major centres of unionism and Labour support. Even the Labour

Party, a new and self-consciously 'progressive' party, had shown that its solution to economic problems was both ineffective and unoriginal. In Europe new movements were arising which were totally different from previous political parties, and the conventaional wisdom of British foreign policy was quite irrelevant in dealing with them. To all who had looked for a 'new world after the war' the 1930s proved particularly depressing. In an attempt to find the causes for their disappointment many who would normally have been content with everyday party politics turned to more radical solutions.

Many short-lived groups appeared with formulae for fundamental change.[8] All failed because they were unable to gain either electoral backing or the support of sections of the existing parties. During the 1930s a strong pacifist movement came into being which was not tied to a major party although most of its supporters were Labour or Liberal voters.[9] Pacifism and support for the League of Nations (which were not always compatible) appeared to have mass support, particularly in 1934 when the 'Peace Ballot'[10] was launched. Even the National government and the Conservative Party leadership felt obliged to pay some attention to a movement with which they had little sympathy; they frequently referred to pacifist feeling as a reason for slow rearmament and later for 'appeasement' of Germany and Italy. But pacifism did not convert itself into an electorally oriented party and its position in the Labour Party was seriously eroded when George Lansbury resigned from the pary leadership in 1935 (see below, pp. 163 – 72).

The Labour Party was not immune to the new ideas and movements which were springing up. Most trade unionists had been indifferent to any political theory beyond an instinctive syndicalism which was itself largely confined to industrial disputes. The parliamentary Labour leaders were inhibited by their acceptance of the conventions and habits of British democracy.[11] The individual member of the Labour Party was, however, particularly susceptible to all movements of protest. In the peculiar circumstances of the 1930s vague feelings of unrest with the Party crystallized into something more concrete.

The Labour Party was developing from the federation of industrial and political organizations set up in 1900. The various socialist minorities in the party were being eliminated as autonomous bodies and their members forced into the less independent but more electorally effective local labour parties. The constituency parties formed in 1918 were directly under the control of the Party's National Executive and professional organizers. Unlike affiliated unions or socialist societies they had no collective voice but were regarded as subsidiary units. This did not stop them from associating together nor did it stop the spread of a vague common ideology. Many members of the Party saw the rapid growth in the constituencies as providing the basis for a new form of unitary political party growing out of the political wing and resembling the mass socialist parties of Europe.[12]

Both within the political wing of Labour and in outside groups within the broader labour movement an identifiable 'Left' began to emerge as a major influence. 'Leftism' suggests opposition to existing policies or institutions, and within the labour movement it had come to mean dedication to rapid socialization of the economy whether through parliamentary or revolutionary methods (see below, chapters 12, 13, and 15). There had always been a 'Left' within the Labour movement. Before the formation of the Labour Party it had been represented by the Independent Labour Party and the Social Democratic Federation working within the unions for the formation of a party representing labour. During the 1920s there had been a 'Left' opposition to MacDonald centred around *Lansbury's Weekly*, an unofficial Labour paper, and later around the Independent Labour Party from which MacDonald eventually resigned. Outside the party the syndicalists had formed a 'Left' of the unions and this had been taken over to some extent by the Communist Party of Great Britain, founded in 1920. The fluid political situation in the 1930s made it inevitable that the 'Left' was strengthened as it was in all other democratic societies. 'Leftism' came to mean opposition to the National government and criticism of the Labour Party's failure to express that opposition more strongly. Among the politically active the appeals of the Left were often more attractive than those of the Labour, Liberal or Conservative Parties. All the major parties were committed to some extent to discredited policies and persons.

The Left never formed a unified whole. It was kept together by basic ideas held in common, by joint activity between the many Left minorities and by traditions of 'united action'. Despite this apparent vagueness there came into existence a body of individuals who may be referred to collectively as 'the Left', who were described as such by themselves and by their opponents and who acted together during the 1930s on most political issues. By the end of the decade this tendency was firmly established in the political wing of the Labour Party and had done much through its propaganda to discredit the National governments, which ruled the country from 1931 until 1940.

CHAPTER 2

The Depression: 1931 – 1934

British politics in the 1930s were often disillusioning for the labour movement, starting with the defection of the Labour Party's leadership and the Party's electoral eclipse, and ending with the Second World War, which destroyed the party's hope of peace through disarmament and the League of Nations. At no time in the intervening period was there any possibility of the Labour Party replacing the National, predominantly Conservative, government. The defections of MacDonald and Snowden were to harden an already present suspicion of powerful personalities in the Labour Party, and to confirm trade-union suspicion of 'intellectuals'.[1] Union leaders reacted by taking a more constructive role in the policy discussions of the party. The Left now completely rejected MacDonald's concept of 'gradualism' which had not been subjected to searching criticism until some three or four years before he left the party.[2] There was a tendency to radicalism in the labour movement.[3]

In the general election of 1931 Labour Party representation was reduced to forty-six. All the former Cabinet Ministers who remained with Labour were defeated except for George Lansbury, who became party leader by default in place of Arthur Henderson. The latter was not re-elected until 1933. Although the Labour vote was still six million, its numbers were lower than at any time since 1910. Consequently, until 1935 the labour movement is of more interest when studied in its extra-parliamentary role, which centred largely around the issue of unemployment. Not until after the general election of 1935 was the Labour Party able to take a decisive stand in parliament, and by that time foreign rather than domestic policy had become the main consideration of the political parties. Before that Labour was a vocal if ineffectual Opposition under the leadership of George Lansbury, C. R. Attlee and Sir Stafford Cripps. Nearly all its remaining MPs were from the coalfields and it looked once more like the Labour Representation Committee of the pre-war period.

Unemployment was the most important problem facing the labour movement. During 1930 the total of unemployed had more than doubled to 2,600,000. The financial crisis which brought down the Labour government caused a rapid increase in the cost of unemployment assistance, an increase which pre-Keynesian economic theory held to be highly undesirable. The 'Anomalies Act' passed in July 1931 was the first major attempt to reduce such expenditure.[4] Under the National government this was followed by the 'means test', a deeply resented measure which was operated with a lack of compassion by many local Public Assistance Committees.[5] Over one million claimants were denied further guaranteed payments and the amount of relief was fixed by Public Assistance Committees on the basis of family resources. What had been a right to receive benefit was replaced by grudgingly distributed charity with all that implied in the era before the abolition of the workhouse. The majority of insured unemployed were subject to the means test and there was naturally widespread resentment of this. In 1932 there were violent demonstrations, several of them leading to serious riots. The TUC, though deploring such activities, urged a return to the system operating in 1930.

Unemployment reached a peak of just under three million in January 1933 and the total number of unemployed did not fall below one million until the outbreak of war. In 1934 a new Unemployment Act was passed which went some way towards relieving a gradually diminishing problem. The level of benefit was restored and the Unemployment Assistance Board created to administer the work previously done by PACs in distributing relief. Locally elected authorities subject to local political pressure were thus by-passed, limiting localized agitation by the National Unemployed Workers Movement. The latter had grown rapidly and become well known for its imaginative if sometimes desperate tactics. The Labour Party and the TUC remained 'against any form of Means Test at all',[6] but they discouraged association with the NUWM which was under the control of Communists, particularly of Wal Hannington and Harry McShane.[7]

As unemployment receded it left behind the problem of the Distressed Areas whose situation often worsened as the general employment position improved. Real wages were rising for those in work, and living standards improved markedly in the Midlands and the South-East, serving both to diminish the political impact of unemployment and to increase the differentiation of the country. In South Wales, the North-East, Lancashire, Cumberland and central Scotland permanent unemployment and steady dereliction became characteristic of once-prosperous mining and industrial areas, most of which were represented by Labour MPs after 1935. The Labour Party published the result of its own enquiries in 1936 and began a campaign for more effective measures, but the compulsory control of industrial location had to wait until the war and the post-war Labour government.

Public reaction to unemployment was largely one of stunned submission. Labour kept the issue alive in parliament to the extent possible with its small numbers. The NUWM was at the centre of most of the violent clashes with the police in the early 1930s, though this tactic was later changed to the more peaceful and probably more effective 'hunger march' which took the unemployed through the countryside and down to London rather than leaving them isolated in the Distressed Areas. The centres of militancy of the previous decade were among the hardest hit, Labour MPs nearly all came from constituencies with massive unemployment, and the unions were faced with the protection of their employed members through organizations weakened by declining funds and membership. Industrial militancy naturally declined, and the problem of the unemployed almost completely preoccupied the labour movement until 1934. There was no disagreement in accusing the National government of callousness and indifference. But most Labour leaders were moving towards the adoption of Keynesian solutions and the improvement of existing unemployment benefits: the Left, on the other hand, saw in the situation final proof of the collapse of capitalism and the failure of all amelioration.

After the initial shock of the 1931 election had been overcome, the Labour Party tried to revise its programme and to improve its organization. A policy committee of the National Executive Committee, established in December 1931, was responsible for preparing reports embodying the programme of a future Labour government. The 1932 Conference reflected a radical reaction to the defeat of 1931 and particularly to bankers, who were held responsible for the financial collapse in Britain and throughout the Western world. Conference decisions were taken out of the hands of the National Executive on several major issues, indicating a spirit of defiant independence which was rare in the Party as a whole. The Conference decided 'that the leaders of the next Labour Government and the Parliamentary Labour Party be instructed by the National Conference that, on assuming office, either with or without power, definite Socialist legislation must be immediately promulgated, and the Party shall stand or fall in the House of Commons on the principles in which it has faith'.[8] Despite the opposition of Arthur Henderson, a series of resolutions bound the Parliamentary Party to Conference decisions and to extra-parliamentary guidance.[9] Discussions on workers' control and the general strike to stop war also showed that an important section of the trade unions had reacted against gradualism, at least in words, and was returning to the syndicalist notions fashionable some ten years before. However the industrial basis for syndicalism was lying in ruins as a result of the Depression and in later years the unions strongly opposed the idea of industrial action for political ends.

Trade-union membership remained low for some time, affected by unemployment and by the movement of industry to less highly unionized areas in the South of England. Union affiliations to the Labour Party had been confined to those 'contracting in' under the Trades Disputes Act of 1927, and the total of affiliated unionists stood at two million throughout the 1930s. In consequence the numerical significance of the unions within the Labour Party structure was declining in contrast to that of the expanding constituency Labour Parties. By 1937 there was one individual Party member for every five affiliated from the unions. This apparent weakening of trade-union domination of the party machine was, however, somewhat illusory. After 1937 the centre of power in the Party appeared to be moving towards the individual membership, but in 1939 the union leaders showed their strength in ensuring the expulsion of Sir Stafford Cripps and his supporters. Despite appearances of a 'Leftward swing' after 1931, or of a lessening of trade-union influence, there was little real change in the underlying gradualism and stolidity of the Labour Party.

It was in the elaboration of its programme rather than in its parliamentary Opposition or in campaigns in the country, that the Labour Party made the greatest advances in recovering from its collapse. *Socialism and the Condition of the People*, the new programme presented to the Hastings Conference of 1933, initiated the controversy which was to drive Sir Stafford Cripps and the newly formed Socialist League into opposition to the official policy of the Party. Cripps and his supporters objected that the Labour leadership had failed to absorb the lessons of 1931 and were not prepared to deal with the inevitable 'sabotage' of the Labour programme by capitalist interests. At Hastings and at Southport in 1934, controversy centred around the issue of 'Emergency Powers'; i.e. the granting to a future Labour government of 'authority to take over or regulate the financial machine, and to put into force any measures that the situation may require for the immediate control or socialization of industry'.[10] By 1934 the Labour Party was preparing for the next election and the delegates at Southport resisted the attempts of the Socialist League to change the programme *For Socialism and Peace* into a radical appeal for a rapid transformation to socialism. The Left of the Labour Party found itself in an increasingly unfavourable position. Ernest Bevin, leader of the new force in the unions, the general workers, resented the attempts of intellectuals like Cripps to elaborate a new Party policy which ignored decisions taken by the Trades Union Congress. The unions were not prepared to support any form of 'direct action', despite the resolutions carried at earlier Congresses in favour of the use of strikes for political ends. By 1935 the dominant force in the unions led by Bevin and Walter Citrine, the TUC secretary, was tired of Cripps's radicalism and of Lansbury's pacifism and decided to demolish Cripps and Lansbury politically.

An important change in the balance within the industrial movement, and hence within the Labour Party, was brought about by the decline in numbers and influence of the Miners' Federation of Great Britain. With the decline of the mining industry and the isolation of the MFGB after the General Strike, it could no longer retain its dominant position and was replaced by the Transport and General Workers Union. Through the TGWU, Ernest Bevin became the leading figure at the Labour Party Conference, using his influence increasingly against the Communists and the Left and in favour of rearmament against Germany. For after 1933 the labour movement internationally was faced with a problem which was to preoccupy it and to change its focus from domestic to international affairs. The Labour Party was a member of the Labour and Socialist International and the TUC was affiliated to the International Federation of Trade Unions at Amsterdam. But the heart of European Socialism lay with the German Social Democratic Party and the largest Communist Party outside the Soviet Union had also been in Germany. Although the Soviet Union had become the major influence on revolutionary socialist movements since 1917, the Communist International had always looked upon Germany as the next most likely centre for a proletarian revolution. In 1928 the Sixth World Congress of the Communist International began a violent onslaught against Social Democracy, the main representative of which was the German Social Democratic Party. At the same time the small National Socialist Party began to win a growing following for its attacks on the Weimar Republic, the maintenance of which was a prime aim of German Social Democracy.

Thus the Communists and the Nazis had a common interest in the destruction of the Social Democrats and this fact was frequently referred to by the Labour Party and the TUC in the early 1930s as a reason for opposing both movements with equal vigour. The German Communists believed that, after a temporary victory for Hitler, they would be able to gain power in the ensuing confusion.[11] This was an illusion and the Communists were forced into semi-legality after Hitler's appointment as Chancellor in January 1933. The Nazis polled over seventeen million votes on 5 March 1933 and began the transformation of Germany into a totalitarian state.[12] The European labour movement lost its heartland, and no distinction was made between Communists and Social Democrats, between workers or intellectuals. The German Communist Party had not only failed to carry out the revolution but had vanished as rapidly as the Social Democrats. Apart from underestimating the strength of the Nazis and overestimating their own, the Communists had directed their main attacks since 1928 against the Social Democrats. British Communists continued to blame the Social Democrats for Hitler's victory while at the same time trying to organize common anti-Fascist activities between Communists and the Left of the Labour movement. This merely confirmed the distaste for Communists which Bevin and other union officials had acquired in the 1920s.

In the following year it became clear that fascism was not confined to Germany and Italy but was a development common to all European countries. This was underlined by the transformation of Sir Oswald Mosley's New Party into the British Union of Fascists and its organization of a bloody and violent rally at Olympia in London in June.[13] Previously existing fascist groups, which had been oriented towards Italy, were bullied or out-organized by the BUF which followed German Nazi example in becoming increasingly anti-Semitic. The mass circulation *Daily Mail*, encouraged by its owner Lord Rothermere, gave support to fascism and the BUF until discouraged from doing so by a marked drop in readership. The event which finally drew the attention of the labour movement to the threat posed by fascism was the overthrow of democracy in Austria in February 1934. It is evident that the defeat of the Austrian Socialists was felt more strongly in Britain than that of the Germans, who had failed to put up an armed resistance and who were divided by the struggle between the Communists and the Social Democrats. The British TUC had given £10,000 to the Austrian Socialists as a contribution to their defence. Hundreds of Labour Party members had gone to 'Red Vienna' in the past and all were distressed at the news of its bombardment.

Fascism and Communism were both foreign creeds with very limited followings in Britain before 1929. The experiences of 1933 and 1934 suggested to many that European politics was likely to intrude increasingly into a previously insular British labour movement. The politically active came to see Britain's problems in international rather than exclusively domestic terms, an important change for many in the Labour Party. To some extent there was an unwarranted transfer of European analogies to the British situation. The battles between Fascists and the Left which began in 1934 looked superficially like those which had marked the last years of the Weimar republic. But they did not presage the same collapse of democracy nor the rise of the BUF and the Communists as mass parties.

Nevertheless, a major lesson was drawn from the German and Austrian situation by many in the British labour movement. Communists and Socialists had been equally suppressed and imprisoned. It was fatal for them to emphasize their differences in the face of armed attack from the German Nazi or Austrian Christian Social autocracies. It was foolish to attack parliamentary democracy when the real alternative being offered in Europe was not the Socialist Commonwealth but the Third Reich. The leaders of the labour movement concluded from this that the British government had a responsibility to defend democracy against fascism and were increasingly bitter about the apparent indifference or even acceptance which characterized the response of many Conservatives to dictatorship in central Europe. The Left drew the less tenable if understandable conclusion that all socialists should unite in a single organization to oppose the threat of fascism, without placing any reliance on the British state to protect domestic political institutions. Thus there was no substantial difference in the labour movement about the nature of fascism, but much disagreement about how to deal with it.

CHAPTER 3

A Sectarian Left

Despite its shattering defeat in 1931 the Labour Party had established itself as the dominant political force opposed to the Conservative Party, as the unchallenged controller of local government on the major coalfields and as the Party to which the great majority of trade-union officials gave their loyalty. All this had been achieved at the expense of the Liberal Party which had monopolized all three areas before 1910. In another sense the domination of the Labour Party had also been achieved at the expense of other claimants to the leadership of the socialist movement and the working class. Prior to 1910 it was by no means clear either that Labour would replace the Liberals or that it would move so far ahead of these rivals as to reduce them to marginal sects. Between 1910 and 1914 the whole concept of parliamentary Labourism was seriously threatened by syndicalism in those areas such as South Wales where the parliamentary representation of unionized workers had first been pioneered. The Liberal loyalties of the older generation of miners' officials had been challenged not merely by the idea of independent labour representation but also by the notion of direct action, based on industrial power and leading to a system of 'workers' control' which would supplant parliamentary institutions. Such ideas had their major influence in South Wales where nearly all men were engaged in mining and could envisage a pure 'class struggle' between themselves and the coalowners which would at the same time be a political struggle between the great majority and the rich minority.[1] In other parts of Britain such ideas were more difficult to put across except to relatively small minorities or in the predominantly proletarian areas of central Scotland where miners, engineers and shipbuilders also constituted the majority of wage earners.

Apart from syndicalism, whose appeal was thus confined to limited and peculiarly class-conscious districts, the total domination of the Labour Party had been challenged before 1914 by a variety of organizations representing two important traditions, ILP 'independent socialism' and Marxism. When the ILP had been a founding organization of the Labour Representation Committee in 1900, its opposition to the 'Liberal-Labour' position separated it from many trade-union officials and earned their suspicion. The ILP founder, Keir Hardie, although a miner, had not entered parliament as the nominee of the Miners' Federation and most ILP Members were nominated by local Party branches or Trades Councils rather than through the national trade unions. Thus the ILP was both 'in the Labour Party' and 'apart from the Labour Party' even before 1914. With the outbreak of war the ILP put itself in opposition to the trade-union leaders by its refusal to support the war and by its criticism of those Labour Party members who either joined the government after 1916 or gave it their loyal parliamentary support. By 1918 there were many Labour Party parliamentarians and trade unionists who would willingly have excluded the ILP from the party, were it not that opposition to the war had spread quite widely and had partly justified the ILP position. An essential ideological difference remained. The ILP was specifically 'socialist' while many Labour unionists and politicians were essentially 'labour' in that they regarded the protection of living standards and of trade unions as their primary reason for entering parliament.

The socialism of the ILP was based partly on egalitarian and pacifist beliefs of Nonconformist religious origin. These were based on a faith in the rationality and co-operative character of man and in the possibility of building a more harmonious society once inequality and exploitation were removed through state action. They stood much closer to the mainstream of political thinking in the working-class movement than the Marxists and were able to tap a tradition of radicalism which extended back to the Chartists of the previous century and further. After 1918 the ILP was also able to recruit Liberal radicals from the middle classes to what had always been a predominantly working-class party. The Marxists, by contrast, had only been able to build a viable organization, under the name of the British Socialist Party, for a few years before 1914 and were always bedevilled by sectarianism and schism. Unlike the ILP, Marxists tended to be ambivalent about parliamentary socialism although most of them accepted the combination of revolutionary and democratic ideas which had been formulated in the German Social Democratic Party by Kautsky and Bebel. The Marxists never quite reconciled themselves either to the policies, the leadership or the tactics of the Labour Party. They joined it, left it, joined it again, but only to oppose its acceptance of the war. During the upsurge of industrial militancy between 1910 and 1914 Marxism and syndicalism became closely intermingled, a development influenced by the writings of Daniel de Leon. This tradition was clearly counterposed to that of the founder of British Marxism, H.M. Hyndman, who became a patriotic supporter of a war to which most British Marxists were opposed.[2]

Until the Bolshevik revolution the question of whether Marxists should be inside or outside the Labout Party was very much a matter for themselves, as for all other radical and socialist groups. The Labour Party was a federation of autonomous organizations, all of them older than the party itself. Until 1918 it was a 'movement' in the sense of having little central discipline and being bound together by an agreement to accept all ideological positions critical of existing society and postulated on social change through political action. It had no orthodoxy, unlike the European social-democratic parties. It had no individual membership within a centrally-controlled structure and thus no means, or desire, to exclude those who wished to join. Only within the Parliamentary Labour Party was there an attempt at collective discipline and that was so loose that the Independent Labour Party was to maintain its right to direct its own members within the PLP as late as 1931. The strength of the Labour Party lay in its ability to win votes, which became increasingly clear in relation to the Liberals after the granting of manhood suffrage in 1918 and had been clear in relation to other socialist groups ever since 1900. As trade-union officials came to recognize this ability they swung their organizations behind the only Party which has ever secured any significant working-class representation in the British parliament. They did so all the more readily because they were not expected to adopt any ideological formula but, rather, were able to put the stamp of their own opinions on the policy of a Party which had no set position of its own.

After the Bolshevik revolution and the creation of the Communist International in 1919, most British Marxists were put into a situation which had never previously existed for any part of the British labour movement. The Second International had been intellectually dominated by the German Social Democratic Party and the small British Socialist Party and Independent Labour Party seem to have accepted this without feeling bound to follow the directives of a single foreign party, let alone a government. The Communist International quite deliberately set out to create 'sections' under its detailed control, which would be more easily disciplined than the Second International parties which in Lenin's eyes had been too independent to act together on the outbreak of war. The collapse of the previous International was also attributed by Lenin to the deviant ideology of its leaders and the Comintern was consequently designed to see that orthodoxy was imposed centrally upon all sections. Moreover the Communist International was located in Moscow, the capital of a Communist state, derived its funds from a governing party, and could not have functioned without the help of its largest member, the Soviet Communist Party. Many British Labour leaders were already hostile to radical Marxists for their opposition to the war and their encouragement of syndicalist movements challenging existing trade-union practices. The creation of the Comintern gave them an opportunity to exclude from the Labour Party, for the first time, Marxists who wished to join it. As those Marxists were receiving guidance and money from a party and government which declared their dedication to the destruction of 'the MacDonalds and the Hendersons' (as already of 'the Kerenskys and the Martovs') this exclusion was hardly surprising. It hastened the process by which the Labour Party developed into a unitary political party in alliance with the trade unions and with a commitment to parliamentary socialism and against authoritarian socialism.

The Communist Party of Great Britain, which was thus excluded from the Labour Party on its foundation, was by far the most important Left minority in existence in the 1930s although it had to compete with the ILP for that position at least until 1935. The Party's formative years were marked by controversy over its relations with the Labour Party, over its internal reorganization along 'Bolshevik' lines, over its attitudes towards parliamentary democracy, but not significantly over its allegiance to the Communist International and the Soviet Union. Its attitudes towards and behaviour within the broad labour movement steadily antagonized activists, officials and leaders, including those calling themselves 'socialist' who were sympathetic to the Soviet revolution.[3] Until 1925 it had been possible for Communists to be represented in all sections of the Labour Party but at the Liverpool Conference it was decided to exclude them from membership. In 1926 over a dozen Constituency Labour Parties were disbanded for accepting Communists into individual membership and for being controlled by the Leftwing Movement, the aim of which was to reverse the Liverpool decisions and to recruit Communist support within the Labour Party. The Trades Union Congress of 1927 enforced the disaffiliation of local Trades Councils from the Minority Movement, formed in 1924 as the British branch of the Red International of Labour Unions.[4] In the following year the TUC General Council was authorized to conduct an enquiry into the activities of 'disruptive elements', a category which included the Minority Movement and other subsidiaries of the Communist Party. While Communists had taken an active part in the 1926 General Strike and earned some support within the Miners' Federation, most trade-union officials looked upon them as enemies trying to control the movement in the interests of a foreign organization.

At this moment of crisis the Communist International began an onslaught on Social Democracy, despite the strenuous opposition of the leadership of the British Party.[5] The Comintern described Social Democracy as 'social fascism' and forced its constituent sections to break off all relations with the official labour movement. The Central Committee of the British Party showed no enthusiasm for the new policy and were reluctant to declare 'all-out war' on their comrades in the unions and local Labour parties. While the Comintern policy was nominally accepted in Britain it was only vocal extremists, backed by the Comintern, who wished to see it rigorously enforced. After a disappointing vote of 50,622 in the 1929 general election this group was able to blame the 'reformist' Central Committee for the weak following and small membership of the Party. At the Eleventh Congress, held in December 1929, a completely reformed Central Committee was elected with Harry Pollitt, an upholder of the Comintern's policy, elected as General Secretary.[6] It became increasingly clear in the next two years that the change in leaders and policy had served only to weaken the

Party still further. The rigid application of the 'social fascist' line did more to alienate the Communists from the labour movement than any previous actions.

If the Communists were steadily driven out of the Labour Party and expedited the process by withdrawing themselves from the official levels of the labour movement, the Independent Labour Party drifted uncertainly into opposition to the Labour leadership and finally expelled itself from the party it had helped to found. A separate political party within the federation created in 1900, the ILP remained the most important avenue for taking an active role in the Labour Party as an individual socialist. The new constitution of the Labour Party made it possible in 1918 for members to join local labour parties without being enrolled in an affiliated organization. Ten years later there were 215,000 such members, dwarfing numerically the 30,000 members of the ILP. Within the Labour Party the ILP remained more important than its size would indicate. Campbell Stephen prophesied as late as 1932 that the Labour Party would not function if the ILP disaffiliated from it.[7] Exaggerated though this proved to be, the ILP was still providing much of the enthusiasm in the Labour Party. As Attlee wrote in 1937, 'its influence lay not in its numbers, but in the intensity of the work done and in its political consciousness.'[8]

After its opposition to the war the ILP had become deeply influenced by the political currents produced by the Russian revolution. For a short time entry was considered into the Communist International which the Left in the ILP saw as a continuation of the Second International of which the ILP had been an affiliate. On receiving the Twenty-one Conditions for entry the ILP decided instead to link with the Vienna or 'Two-and-a-Half' International which included various Left Socialist groups in Europe. The ILP Left, led by S. Saklatvala and C. L'Estrange Malone MP, joined the Communist Party and represented it in parliament in the 1920s. There were few Marxists in the ILP but it was disproportionately strong in Scotland and came under the domination of the 'Clydesider' MPs returned in 1922, from acutely overcrowded and poor constituencies which seemed to call for extreme social measures. Feeling themselves isolated from Ramsay MacDonald, who had been helped into Labour leadership by the 'Clydesiders', the ILP became receptive to the radical socialism of the Scottish MPs. James Maxton, Member for

Bridgeton, became chairman of the ILP in 1926 and was its
leading figure until his death twenty years later.[9] In 1928 Maxton
started a campaign with A.J. Cook, secretary of the Miners'
Federation, to arouse Left activity within the Labour Party.[10] The
ILP also subscribed to the *Socialism in our Time* (or 'living wage')
programme which MacDonald and the parliamentary Labour
leaders found too radical.

The 1929 Carlisle conference of the ILP adopted conditions
for membership of the Parliamentary ILP Group which, in effect,
would have turned it into a distinct party separate from the
Parliamentary Labour Party of which it formed nearly a half.
Candidates were asked to avoid 'commitments with other organisa-
tions of such a nature as to militate against their effectiveness as
ILP Members of Parliament'. A further step was taken at
Birmingham in 1930 when the Conference instructed the National
Administrative Council:

> to reconstruct the ILP Parliamentary Group on the basis of
> acceptance of the policy of the ILP as laid down by decisions of
> Annual Conference and as interpreted by the NAC, and to limit
> endorsements of future ILP Parliamentary candidates to nomin-
> ees who accept this basis.[11]

In a letter sent to all ILP Members of Parliament on 30 July 1930,
the general secretary, John Paton, defined ILP policy as being
based on the *Socialism in our Time* programme.

Throughout the summer of 1930 attempts were made by Maxton
and Henderson, secretary of the Labour Party, to reach an agreement
which would leave the ILP free to declare its principles without
endangering the majority of the Labour government. These negotiations were unfruitful and the ILP continued to press its Members for
acceptance of the conditions for group membership laid down at
Birmingham. Written acceptance was made a condition of membership in a circular of 27 October 1930 and only twenty-seven MPs
conformed. Membership of the ILP had been largely a formality for
the remaining four-fifths of the original group, though some active
ILP members like Dr Alfred Salter and Emanuel Shinwell were
among those severing their connections with the party.

Tension between the ILP and the Labour Party had increased in
June 1930 when the National Executive refused to endorse John
McGovern as Labour candidate for Shettleston, Glasgow. This

seat, which had been held by John Wheatley, was an ILP
stronghold and McGovern was elected as an unendorsed candidate. At the end of November the Executive took similar action
against the ILP candidate in East Renfrew who had declined to
accept the new Standing Orders of the Parliamentary Labour
Party. These would have bound him to support majority decisions,
even where these decisions were not accepted by the ILP Group.
Maxton, writing to Henderson on December 30, felt that the ILP
could not accept these Standing Orders, 'without substantial
qualifications and reservation'.[12] Realizing the serious implications
of further disagreement, the ILP National Administrative Council
appointed a sub-committee in February 1931 to consider the
Party's relationship with the Labour Party.[13]

The conflict between 'practical' and 'idealist' politics had become
too bitter for it to be abandoned on the collapse of the Labour
Government. Despite the vindication of much of its criticism, the
ILP refused to see its opposition to Labour 'gradualism' as in any
way affected by the new situation. The Labour Party, on the other
hand, continued to press for the acceptance of its Parliamentary
Standing Orders. A fruitless correspondence between Paton and
Henderson was carried on throughout July 1931. It revealed an
inability to compromise which remained unaltered after the fall of
the Government in August. The Labour Party settled the issue to
its own satisfaction at the Scarborough Conference in October. An
alteration to the Party Constitution forbade selection as a candidate to anyone who 'does not undertake to accept and act in
harmony with the Standing Orders of the Parliamentary Party'.[14]
The Independent Labour Party was thus forced to accept full
responsibility for continuing the dispute.

Twenty-two Labour candidates lost their endorsement in the
General Election of October 1931 for refusing to accept Parliamen-
tary Standing Orders. They secured 285,462 votes and five ILP
Members were returned, Maxton (Bridgeton), McGovern (Shettles-
ton) and Wallhead (Merthyr) under the Party's auspices, and
Buchanan (Gorbals) and Kirkwood (Dumbarton Burghs) as Trade
Union nominees. The National Administrative Council met on the
following weekend to discuss the situation which had arisen.
George Lansbury had approached the ILP Members after their
election to suggest negotiations for uniting the greatly reduced
Opposition. But he would not countenance a 'Party within a Party,'

and the NAC had to face up to the consequences of maintaining a separate party in Parliament. The diversity of views within the ILP on future relations with the Labour Party was fully represented in its leadership. A majority believed that the ILP should remain within the Labour Party until forced to withdraw. John Paton, as General Secretary, pointed to the organizational hazards of withdrawing from the Labour Party:

> The practical difficulties of maintaining and developing the organisation outside the Labour Party were enormous and it might be that it would involve a risk of the complete disintegration of the ILP.[15]

Maxton led the opposition to this view, claiming not that the Party should disaffiliate immediately, but that it should not hesitate to do so if its freedom to advocate the *Socialism in Our Time* policy were limited. No definite decision could be reached. The special November Conference which had been proposed was abandoned, again in the hope that the ILP would not yet have to commit itself.[16]

The two major traditions represented by the Communist Party and the ILP had become enshrined in increasingly sectarian parties. Consequently their influence on the Left of the Labour Party was greatly diminished and for several years after the departure of MacDonald the Labour Left was mainly represented by small groups based on defectors from the ILP and, to a lesser extent, from the Communist Party. The Communists had abandoned the Leftwing Movement in 1929 and it had immediately collapsed. Communist influence within the Labour Party was probably less between 1929 and 1934 than at any time before or since. The Communist Party was engaged in a campaign of abuse and violence against the leadership of the unions. Communists continued to have some success among the unemployed, many of whom felt betrayed by the Labour government and ignored by the TUC. Not only was a large proportion of Communist Party membership unemployed but it was in the shattered heavy industrial areas that there seemed some possibility of gaining support in the 'revolutionary' phase through which the Party was passing. The National Unemployed Workers Movement, under the leadership of Wal Hannington and Harry McShane, was comparatively influential, particularly in the depressed areas of South

Wales, Lancashire and Scotland.[17] The sudden increase in unemployment after 1930 gave it further importance. Unemployed workers were encouraged to look on the NUWM as a 'trade union of the unemployed' acting as far as possible as their representative. From 1923 to 1925 the TUC had maintained a Joint Committee with it, but had discontinued its co-operation and attacked the Movement as Communist-dominated. Partly to counteract its influence the TUC created official Unemployed Associations in 1930.

The NUWM was essentially a political movement, unlike the TUC Associations or the Social Service Centres which were largely educational and recreational. The Movement 'looked upon these associations with hostility and opposed them. Later, under the influence of the Communist Party, this attitude changed and there began a movement for unity and common action.'[18] All the spectacular demonstrations of the unemployed were organized by the NUWM, including the Hunger Marches of 1932, 1934, and 1936. In 1932, at the peak of unemployment, it claimed 386 branches and 50,000 members. Conflict with the police led to serious riots at Birkenhead and Belfast during the campaign against the Means Test in 1932.[19] The Movement put up municipal candidates and worked with the Communist Party and the ILP for the 'immediate demands' of the unemployed. It took an active part in the National Charter Campaign of 1931 and in the Bermondsey Unity Congress of 1934. In those areas where unemployment was endemic, the NUWM was able to establish roots in the community and to establish a legitimacy as a political movement which usually evaded the Communist Party. This was particularly true in Lancashire and the North-East, where the Communist Party was weakly organized.

The Communist Party undoubtedly regarded the NUWM as its subsidiary. Tom Bell wrote that 'its leading comrades were Party members and worked in the closest collaboration with the Party Central Committee. The Party indeed was the main inspirer of the whole of this movement.'[20] Despite this liaison, the NUWM was organizationally more successful than the parent Party and reached a much wider audience during the 'social fascist' phase of the early 1930s. The founder of the Movement, and consequently one of the best-known Communist leaders, Wal Hannington had constantly to assert the autonomy of the NUWM. At the Prague conference on unemployment, organized by the Comintern in August 1931, he complained:

> The unemployed movement has been regarded as a section of the Minority Movement and there have been tendencies in the Minority Movement towards disbanding the existing unemployed movement and substituting it by a special section of the Minority Movement. That is why we have not become a stronger mass movement.[21]

Hannington clearly resented this domination by the almost defunct and hopelessly sectarian Minority Movement which was currently antagonizing union officials by supporting 'breakaway Red unions'. The constant complaint of the British Party against the NUWM was that it had failed to use its influence with employed workers and trade unionists. The Movement increased its membership from 5,000 in 1929 to 40,000 two years later at a time when the Communist Party was at its lowest ebb. It was hoped that by using the NUWM prestige the Communists would be able to regain their lost influence in the unions. The Minority Movement had not only failed to increase Communist support in the unions but was itself fading away.[22]

In general the tactic of maintaining a parallel organization within the unions was a failure. The Communist Party Central Committee complained in February 1932:

> The Minority Movement is a small self-absorbed organization of leaders who have nothing to do with the real struggle of the workers and who instead of going to the workers, working among them and fighting against the reformist leaders in the Trade Unions, simply approach the workers with the invitation to take part in a highly elaborate organisational structure.[23]

The Battersea Congress of the Party, to which this complaint was later addressed, gave official backing to a scheme which had been projected for some time, a Revolutionary Trade Union Opposition to unite the various unofficial movements which had been growing up in many important unions.[24] While this did not expressly exclude the Minority Movement, the growth of Communist-led 'rank and file movements' did in effect bring an end to the MM and to all formal Party subsidiaries within the unions. Communist fractions, of course, remained in being but they did not breach the

basic principle of British trade unionism that there should be no
separate organizations based on ideology or religion and standing
in opposition to the TUC.

At the Seventh Congress of the Comintern in 1935 the trade
union policy pursued since 1928 was tacitly admitted to have been
a blunder. It had been particularly disastrous in Germany and
Britain, the countries for which it had been designed. Wilhelm
Pieck said of the Minority Movement:

> The most striking example of sectarianism in the trade union
> movement was provided in Great Britain where ... the Com-
> munists adopted such unfortunate and sectarian tactics that the
> Minority Movement actually fell to pieces.[25]

The failure to recruit for 'reformist trade unions' and the attempt to
use the MM as the nucleus for Red Trade Unions had greatly
reduced Communist influence, argued Pieck. In fairness to the
much maligned British Communists it might be added that
Lozovsky, the RILU leader chiefly responsible for the discarded
policy, had to admit to its failure throughout the world.[26]

The unemployed movement served to increase Communist
influence, but was attacked for not doing so fast enough. The
Minority Movement undeniably limited Communist influence in
the Labour movement and earned the undying hostility of most
trade-union officials. In October 1934 the TUC issued Circular 16
(called 'Black Circular' by the Communists) banning Communists
as members of Trades Councils. Encouragement of 'unofficial
movements' only strengthened TUC hostility to the Communists
and this was, of course, reflected at Labour Party conferences and
on the Labour National Executive, both of which were dominated
by full-time union officials. TUC opposition also limited the
effectiveness of the NUWM, which became an embarrassment to
the Communist Party once it left its sectarianism behind it. Pollitt
reported in January 1936:

> The Central Committee believe that whilst everything possible
> should be done to suppport and strengthen the NUWM we must
> now open up the wider perspective of one united unemployed
> organisation identified with, and part of, the Trades Councils
> and the Trade Union Congress.[27]

As the TUC would not negotiate with the NUWM this logically

implied an end to the Movement which finally dissolved on the outbreak of war in 1939. Apart from the South Wales Miners' Federation, it had been almost the only major working class organization through which the Communists had consistently exercised influence.

The Communists were busily isolating themselves from the labour movement; the Independent Labour Party was about to do the same. The Labour Party, in August 1931, suffered the most severe blow to its pride, solidarity and sense of mission ever experienced in its history. The spectacular rise to power throughout the 1920s suddenly came to a halt, betrayed by the leaders who had inspired it. The trade unions were disillusioned by the General Strike, shackled by the Trades Disputes Act and demoralized by the Depression. Of the three component political groups which had founded the Labour Representation Committee thirty years before, the Marxists had mostly isolated themselves within the Communist Party, the ILP was ready to depart and the Fabian Society was moribund. If the Labour Party was to recover intellectually from the collapse of MacDonald's 'biological gradualism' and to build its local organisation it needed support from radical intellectuals and from the youth. In June 1931 G. D. H. Cole and several of the younger Fabians founded a Society for Socialist Inquiry and Propaganda which, it was hoped, would have a more popular appeal than the Fabian Society.[28]

The Labour Left was to centre around the Socialist League, a successor to SSIP formed in October 1932. It was also to attract increasing support from youth and students. Youthful enthusiasm was welcomed by many of the older members of the Labour Party but it was difficult to control within the constitutional and political limitations of the Party organization. Youth sections of the Labour Party had been formed in 1924, but not until the ILP had created a successful national organization, the Guild of Youth, did the Labour Party reorganize the 150 youth sections into the Labour Party League of Youth.[29] After the collapse of the MacDonald government and the dispute with the ILP, the Labour Party made a concerted effort to increase the strength of the League.

CHAPTER 4

The United Front From Below

At the depths of the Depression, when the case for radical working-class action in favour of a socialist programme seemed incontrovertible, the labour movement was divided and demoralized. The militant socialist minorities were at each other's throats and were completely disillusioned with the Labour Party. The Party itself had lost its leaders and its parliamentary strength. It was looking for a new programme and trying to consolidate its confused followers. Thus during the worst crisis in British industrial history neither the labour movement nor its radical Left were able to take advantage of the situation. The Conservatives were supreme, even in many of the worst hit of the Distressed Areas.[1]

The Labour Party, with considerable justification, saw itself as the 'united front of the working class' and found little reason for joint activity with sectarian minorities on the Left. Within the Left however there were strong practical reasons in favour of some co-operation with others. In isolation the Left minority could have little influence. It had to combine with others, to 'capture' larger organizations or to assume leadership of wider groups. Moreover, despite the ideological differences on the Left, which were most acute between 1929 and 1934, there were strong sentiments in favour of 'working-class unity' in the abstract. The Communists, who were most active in stressing their differences with others were also most active in calling for unity. The Communist Party had most to gain by combination with other groups, for with its strong discipline it could always hope to attract supporters from allied groups without losing many of its own members. In combination with other less tightly controlled groups the Party always had the great advantage of internal unity, coupled with an elaborate scheme of infiltration which had been designed to take advantage of the United Front tactic.

Throughout the 1920s the Communist Party leaders remained intent on affiliating to the Labour Party and on working with Labour Party members. By 1928 some of the Party was prepared for the radical change of tactics authorized by the Sixth Comintern Congress. The group around Harry Pollitt and Palme Dutt was able to take over from the older leaders, Inkpin, Bell, and MacManus and to commit the Party to the new tactic of the 'United Front from Below'.[2] Palme Dutt and Pollitt, presenting a minority report to the Comintern Congress, argued that the Labour Party, by its restrictions on Communist membership, affiliation and co-operation, had transformed itself into a typical 'social fascist' organisation. In the discussion which followed J. T. Murphy characterized the Labour Party as 'the third party of the bourgeoisie', and as a party which had completely defeated Communist attempts to influence it. R. Page Arnot, another delegate, held that the Communist Party had every prospect of becoming the new mass working-class party.[3] These were the attitudes which were to gain official acceptance after the change in British Communist leadership in December 1929.

The Comintern policy was applied in Britain on the theoretical grounds that the Labour Party had ceased to be a federation and that 'the Labour Party was in the process of being transformed from a federal organisation to a party of the social democratic type'.[4] It was necessary to resist the Labour Party's discipline and to attack its structure and policy, rather than to attempt to become part of it. Under the slogan 'Class against Class' the Party was to 'bring out more markedly its independent line and to fight against the bureaucratic discipline'.[5] This was the 'United Front from Below'; the attempt to separate Labour Party members from their leaders and eventually to recruit them into the Communist Party.

In Britain there remained many common ties between Communists and Labour Party members and many Communists were still working within the trade unions. The Party's most important trade unionist, Arthur Horner of the South Wales Miners' Federation, was repeatedly criticized for 'trade union legalism', and their most important supporter, A. J. Cook, national Miners' Federation Secretary, broke with them completely over their support for 'Red

Unions'.[6] The Party's increasing isolation from its natural constituency in the broad labour movement was threatening its viability.

In early 1931 Party membership dropped to 2,500, the lowest
level in its history. The collapse of the Labour government had
little effect on the Party's isolation. It had claimed that 'the Social
Democratic leaders are the conscious enemies of the working class,
the conscious agents of a foreign class, of a hostile class in the workers
midst'.[7] Although the MacDonald defection did much to justify this
claim it did not lessen the resentment created by the Communists'
verbal and physical attacks on the rest of the Left. The Eleventh
Plenum of the Comintern, early in 1931, made it clear that social
democracy was to be regarded as the main enemy. The Comintern
charged that 'the Social Democratic Parties play a direct leading role'
in preparing war against the USSR. Because of this:

> the exposure of the Social Democrats, the exposure of the
> Second International, the liberation of the working masses from
> the influence of Social Democracy, the isolation and overcoming
> of Social Democracy, is the immediate task for the Communist
> Parties.[8]

The Comintern policy had three levels of application in Britain. On
the grandiose plane of a general strike or revolution against a
Labour government it was sheer nonsense, though much more
dangerous in Germany, the country for which the new strategy had
apparently been devised. The Communists largely ignored the
differences between the German and British situations. There was
no Fascist or Communist Party of any significance within British
politics. The entire labour movement was under the control of
'social fascism'. Communist influence in the Distressed Areas was
growing slightly, but on the basis of 'immediate economic
demands' rather than 'the open fight against the Labour Party'.
The industrial aspect of this new strategy, the creation of new,
revolutionary 'Red' unions, was a complete failure in Britain. The
United Mineworkers of Scotland had enrolled about 4,000 Fife
miners, but otherwise there was nothing comparable with the
Communist-led unions of Germany or France.

The second level of application was the forming of the 'United
Front from Below'. Even here the Communists had little success,
their activity remaining on the third level of faction fighting and
street corner abuse of the rest of the labour movement.

But even during the most bitter quarrels of the 'social fascist' period, the United Front was proclaimed and, to a limited extent, practised. The 'United Front from Below' was to be based primarily on 'the immediate demands of the workers' and was to take the form of joint agitation at local level, rather than of organizational unity on a national scale. The National Unemployed Workers Movement and the less successful Minority Movement were the main instruments in the campaign for 'immediate demands' which was organized around the 'National Charter' of 1931. The Communist Party naturally supported the campaign which had been officially sponsored by its subsidiary, the Minority Movement. Its supporting declaration called for the creation of 'independent organs of struggle based on the factories',[9] and this was taken up at the Workers Charter Convention held in Bermondsey on 12 April 1931. Proposals were carried for the creation of 'broad committees', 'Leagues of Young Chartists' and similar groups to attract those 'who will not go all the way with the Minority Movement'.[10] This was the 'United Front from Below' in its purest form, an organized attempt to replace the official sections of the Labour movement by bodies under Communist domination. The Labour Party promptly declared participation in such committees as 'incompatible with membership of the Party'. This proscription, together with the unrepresentative nature of the Minority Movement, prevented the Charter Campaign from arousing any strong feelings or action. The campaign was fought on such issues as increased winter relief and unemployment benefit, though with implicit recognition of the ultimate necessity of revolution. As with all subsequent 'Unity' campaigns, the Communists stressed temporary grievances and short-term aims in the hope of attracting those to whom Communist ideology did not normally appeal.

It was still incumbent on the Party to avoid the impression that ILP co-operation in the campaign for 'immediate demands' had redeemed the ILP from further attack. A meeting between the Communists, the ILP and the NUWM on 23 September 1931, was criticized as abandoning the 'United Front from Below' for top-level negotiations. So strong was the fear that a 'united front from above' would reflect credit on the ILP that Communists were warned that 'the ILP must not be looked upon as a potential ally of the CP.'[11] Harry Pollitt defined the aim of the United Front in October 1932 as the recruitment of Communists from the Left of the ILP. 'We must make a determined effort to win the rank and file of the ILP,' he wrote, 'at the same time to avoid creating the impression that there are no fundamental differences between our Party and the ILP'.[12]

The Communist leaders were desperately trying to establish contacts with the rest of the labour movement, despite their continued adherence to the 'social fascist' line. The only important advance made by the Party was the founding of the *Daily Worker* in January 1930, and that had reached a circulation of only 18,000 by the end of the following year. Nearly 80 per cent of Party membership was unemployed, with serious effects on Party finance and organization. Total membership fluctuated widely around 5,000 and it is clear that many members only stayed with the Party for a short time. With such a small proportion of employed industrial workers in its ranks, the Party had great difficulty in carrying out its work in factory cells and trade-union groups. To widen its support the Communist Party sent representatives to a meeting with the National Unemployed Workers Movement and the ILP. It was attempting to reach agreement on a campaign for improving wages and hours, for combating unemployment and repealing the Trades Disputes Act.[13]

Communists were interested in the ILP only because it was possible to secure recruits from what seemed to be a disintegrating party. In electoral terms the ILP remained much stronger than the Communist Party, as the results of the general election in October 1931 underlined. Communists improved only slightly on the vote of 1929, when they had fought under less favourable conditions but had been less fully committed to the 'social fascist' position. Twenty-six candidates polled 74,824 votes, all but five of them forfeiting their deposits. Nearly half the vote was secured in the eight Scottish seats contested.[14] The ILP, in contrast, returned five MPs without official Labour Party endorsement, four of whom remained loyal after the final break with Labour.

While the Communists were engaged in manoeuvres on the fringe of labour politics, the Independent Labour Party was about to abandon its position within the Labour Party and to give up its effective role as an alternative Left party. Despite their consistent and eventually justified opposition to MacDonald, ILP disaffiliation from the Labour Party was regarded as an extreme measure to be adopted only if the Labour National Executive refused to make any concessions. At its 1931 annual conference the ILP heavily defeated a proposal to disaffiliate, by 173 votes to 37. Divisional Conferences held in January and February 1932, though recording greater support for disaffiliation, nevertheless gave a two to one vote in favour of staying inside the Labour Party.[15] In the Scottish Division, containing nearly one third of the membership, disaffiliation was defeated by 88 votes to 49. It was supported only in London and the South-West. In considering these results the NAC decided to allow resolutions on disaffiliation to be considered at the Easter Conference, but declined to make any recommendation on the issue by seven votes to five.[16]

The Easter Conference, held in Blackpool, did little to solve the problem. Dr Cullen of Poplar, who had been leading the disaffiliation campaign in London, moved to instruct the NAC:

> to take immediate steps to discontinue the affiliation of the ILP to the Labour Party.[17]

Although defeated by 144 votes to 183 Cullen nevertheless gained more support than Dollan of Govan, whose resolution for a return of the ILP to its propagandist role within the Labour Party received only 93 votes. Majority opinion in the ILP was best expressed in the resolution moved on behalf of the Rugby Branch, which argued for continued affiliation on the basis of a satisfactory revision of Parliamentary Standing Orders. The NAC was instructed to continue negotiations with the Labour Party to this effect. When it met after the Conference it set up a subcommittee to draft acceptable Standing Orders with which it could approach the Labour Party National Executive.[18]

The Parliamentary Labour Party, despite its greatly reduced numbers, was not prepared to return to the previous Standing Orders which had allowed the ILP to put forward a distinct policy in Parliament while still remaining within the Labour Group. The ILP leadership, feeling it had a mandate from the Easter Conference, made preparations for a Special Conference at which it would make:

> a recommendation for disaffiliation, and for the re-organisation of the ILP as an independent Socialist Party with a programme aiming at a decisive change from Capitalism to Socialism.[19]

For over two years the ILP had been moving towards a position where it could no longer work within the limitations of Parliamentary discipline and electoral necessity. Two sections of the Party now openly advocated disaffiliation. Some felt with Maxton that Socialists should be inside a socialist organization,[20] not committed to the policy of a trade-union Party. Others, influenced by Cullen's Revolutionary Policy Committee, had accepted the Communist attack on the Labour Party as the 'third party of the bourgeoisie'. But it was only after the persistent refusal of the Labour Party to concede complete autonomy to the ILP that the majority of members were forced to accept disaffiliation. The Bradford Special Conference of 29 July 1932 ended affiliation by 241 votes to 142 and created an independent party with a disunited membership and with an organization which was in serious difficulties.

Resignations and the formation of dissident minorities began immediately after the Bradford decision. ILP membership had already dropped by one third in the past four years, and three months after disaffiliation the NAC estimated a loss of 10 per cent of the remaining branches in protest.[21] Of the 653 branches only 288 had given definite support to disaffiliation, some by small majorities. Patrick Dollan led a considerable reaffiliation movement in Scotland, which, on its expulsion, formed the nucleus of the Scottish Socialist Party. In England an associated group was later to help form the Socialist League. It is unlikely that the ILP retained more than half its membership one year after it had left the Labour Party.[22] The Independent Labour Party had drawn most of its strength from its connection with the larger Party. The Bradford decisions were to prove so effective in isolating the Party that the prophecies of disaster made by the opponents of disaffiliation seemed about to be fulfilled. Not only were connections with the Labour Party broken but the Bradford Conference, against the advice of the NAC, decided to discontinue paying the Trade Union political levy; to withdraw from membership of the Co-operative Party; and to forbid ILP Members from holding any position in the Labour movement which involved giving support to the policies of the Labour Party. Consequently ILP members on local authorities or in Trade Union positions refused to remain in the Party. Ten ILP Councillors remained on Glasgow City Council out of a previous total of over sixty. The Party had decided to make a decisive break with the 'reformist' Labour movement. In the words of John Paton, 'the clean break seemed to be making a clean sweep of the Party members'.[23]

The ILP had opened negotiations with the Communist Party for joint agitation on 'immediate demands' while still affiliated to the Labour Party. Now that it had disaffiliated it recognized the necessity of strengthening this co-operation. The Communist Party had continually attacked the ILP regarding the disaffiliation issue as a temporary manoeuvre 'to hold back the British workers from the revolutionary policy of the Communist International'.[24] Despite this constant criticism the ILP was working with the Communist controlled National Unemployed Workers Movement, and co-operated in the Hunger Marches and Means Test agitation organized by them in November 1932.

The Communist Party had welcomed ILP disaffiliation as indicating the break-up of the Labour Party. Yet it was anxious lest the ILP usurp Communism's already weakened hold on the Left. There were those in the ILP like John Paton who saw this as the only possibility of success for the disaffiliated party.

The 'Front from Below' was based on the totally unrealistic view that the Parliamentary collapse of 1931 would lead to the replacement of the Labour Party by some other form of Left party. Palme Dutt prophesied that 'the Labour movement, the old Labour movement is dying. The workers movement, the independent workers movement is rising.'[25] Whether or not the Communist leaders really believed this or any other of the sweeping statements made at the time is questionable. Nevertheless there was some hope that the rifts in the Labour Party would produce some new combinations on the Left. The Communists expected that if militants were drawn into united demonstrations their allegiance to the official Labour movement would be lessened. 'The revolutionary differentiation of the militant workers will have to take place against the leadership of both the Labour Party and the Independent Labour Party, will have to take place from below.'[26]

At this early stage the Communists persisted in repudiating national negotiation with the ILP leaders, despite the willingness of the latter to take part in such negotiations. William Warbey of the ILP Revolutionary Policy Committee suggested early in 1932 that a joint party should be formed. Despite later Communist acceptance of this policy it was rejected at this time by William Rust for the Party. 'The united front is not a question of the relation of the ILP and the CP,' he wrote, 'but the building up of the workers unity in the struggle against the capitalist offensive on the basis of demands that will unite the widest masses of workers.'[27] A similar repudiation was made by Palme Dutt later in the year. He repeated the Comintern formula that 'the united front can only be built up from below, by the workers themselves, not as a corrupt bargain of the reformist leaders and disorganisers of the struggle endeavouring to buy off the criticism of the revolutionaries, but as the solid class front of the workers'.[28] So the ideological epithets passed back and forth, largely ignored by the workers with whose future they dealt. It was true that many of the unemployed willingly accepted Communist leadership of their demonstrations. Yet they were totally unwilling to join the Party or even to vote for its national and local candidates. The battle between the Communists and the ILP was almost totally confined to the Labour movement, a conflict of organizational loyalties with little relation to the outside world.

The Comintern had not confined its attacks to the Right Social Democrats alone. In its view Left groups like the ILP were even more dangerous enemies, as their intentions were disguised. In Britain this attitude led to a bitter struggle between the Communists and the ILP, with each declaring itself to be the revolutionary leadership of the Left. Sensing the dangers of such rivalry, the Communists intensified their attack on the ILP, going so far as to declare that disaffiliation was but a temporary manoeuvre.

Some ILP leaders undoubtedly believed in the possibility of maintaining an independent Left party distinct from the Labour Party or the Communists. Fear of such a development had motivated Communist attacks on Left Socialism. *Pravda* had commented late in 1931:

> In England, as elsewhere, the task of the 'Lefts' consists in hindering the workers who are becoming revolutionised from abandoning the Labour Party and going over to the revolutionary fight, to Communism.[29]

The Communist Party, reduced to a low level, had good reason to be concerned at the threat of a new Left party. However it was clearly aware of the tensions inside the ILP and was ready to take advantage of them. The Communists saw themselves as the only alternative to the Labour, Liberal and Conservative Parties. Any new development of another Left party could only be an attempt 'to reach for the Leftward workers and draw them back to the basic Labour line'.[30] The belief that the Depression had resulted in a 'leftward swing' in working class opinion was central to Communist strategy. They saw a potential danger in the ILP releasing itself from responsibility for the failings of the late Labour Government. For the ILP had six times the membership of the Communist Party, and although its contacts with the unemployed were not as strong, it had a much larger electoral following than the Communists in predominantly industrial areas.

The Communist Party made a number of charges against the ILP. In the early period of uncertainty, when many prominent leaders of the ILP were clearly wary of forming an independent party, the Communists favoured the suggestion that disaffiliation was a temporary manoeuvre. For many years the Party had attacked the ILP as providing an insincere alternative to Communism. It was still convenient to hold that the Labour Party relied on a 'left' Party 'which will stand between the Communist Party and the Labour Party and hold back the British workers from following the revolutionary policy of the Communist International'.[31] With the break complete, and the ILP intent on remaining separate, it became increasingly implausible that its leaders were 'manoeuvring' the Party in the interests of Labour. The Communist Party began to speak of the ILP membership as having forced the leaders into disaffiliation. Although this was the exact opposite of what they had been saying in the previous year, it was consistent in suggesting that there was a conflict between leaders and members. If the ILP members were 'to the Left' of their leaders, then it was logical that they should advance still further and join the Communist Party. This kind of 'unity' obviously involved the break-up of the ILP and the transfer of its radical membership to the Communist Party. For the next three years the Communists worked towards this aim, though with little concrete success. The ILP certainly broke up, but most of its members went back into the Labour Party.

Communist influence in the ILP began to increase rapidly, largely owing to the work of the Revolutionary Policy Committee which began as an independent minority working within the ILP but eventually merged into the Communist Party. Its first conferences were held at Blackfriars and Blackpool early in 1932. At this early stage the Committee's immediate aim was to secure ILP disaffiliation from the Labour Party. After this had been achieved the RPC turned its attention to formulating a revolutionary policy which would replace the gradualism inherited from the Labour Party. At the Bradford Conference it attempted (unsuccessfully) to commit the ILP to the organization of revolutionary militancy in the working class. The RPC wanted to diminish the already weak adherence of the Party membership to the Parliamentary method. The Committee's policy was in many respects akin to that just being abandoned by the Communist Party, but with a greater syndicalist content. The ILP Conference of 1933 made this official Party policy; this gave the NAC the problem of deciding what exactly the RPC had meant.[32]

At this stage the RPC was still an impossibilist minority, well organized and favouring joint action with the Communist Party, but looked on with suspicion by the Communists themselves. Revolutionary Policy Conferences were held by the *Labour Monthly* in 1933, partly no doubt to increase Communist influence in the ILP at the expense of the RPC. J. R. Campbell directed revolutionary comrades in the ILP as follows:

> Fight for a revolutionary policy and work with the Communist Party to carry out that policy; work for coming over en masse into the ranks of the Communist Party.[33]

Many ILP officials were antagonized more by the Committee's effective organization than by its Communist orientation. The NAC decided as early as October 1932 to warn the Committee that it could not countenance an organization or an appeal for funds by any minority within the Party.[34]

As official hostility grew, the RPC drew closer to the Communist Party. In April 1934 it amalgamated with the Comintern Affiliation Committee, an ILP minority much more directly under Communist control. Their interest became centred around sympathetic affiliation to the Comintern and the creation of a United Communist Party, the two main objects of Communist tactics at the time. At the 1935 ILP Annual Conference unofficial groups were declared bad in principle though previous attempts to disband the RPC had been defeated. Finally in November 1935 the Committee decided to withdraw its members from the ILP and to join the Communist Party. Jack Gaster and Dr Cullen, the two leading members, took with them the Poplar, Wood Green and Harrow branches and some 50 members of the Party. The RPC had been successful in getting its policy adopted by the ILP Conference but had become too closely associated with the Communists to receive continued support from the ILP.

The Communists' blatant use of the RPC to influence and later to break up the ILP naturally worsened relations between the ILP leaders and the Communists. Attempts by the CP to identify the ILP with the policies of MacDonald had been particularly annoying. Whatever other motives were responsible for disaffiliation, there is no doubt that the ILP was strongly opposed to Labour 'reformism'. Even the Revolutionary Policy Committee, the section of the ILP most closely identified with the Communists, was dubious of the value of associating with the small and discredited Communist Party. Jack Gaster, a leading member of the RPC, strongly criticized the 'narrow sectarianism'[35] of the Communists and was responsible, with Dr Cullen, for the *Memorandum on the Present Political and Economic Situation and the ILP* which openly condemned the failure of Communist tactics in Britain. There was little enthusiasm in the ILP for a United Front with the Communists, and little affection for the ILP in the Communist Party. Despite this the two parties began almost immediately to undertake joint campaigns.

The reasons for this were practical rather than doctrinal. Maxton, no less than Paton or Brockway, realised the dangers of complete isolation for the ILP. If the disaffiliated Party were to prosper it would have to attract those who had previously turned to the Communist Party. The Left Wing of the ILP took the same view, though eventually it became more sympathetic to the Communists. It preferred to work within a party which still had a certain amount of prestige. Yet both sections realised the futility of trying to be too independent. The Communists were in control of the unemployed demonstrations, they had the reflected glory of the Bolshevik revolution. It was essential to work with the Communists, if only to share some of these advantages. What the ILP leaders failed to realise was that their party lacked the internal discipline of the Communist Party and would inevitably succumb to organized attempts by the Communists to disrupt the larger organization.

Pollitt had declared a 'war to the knife' with the ILP in a debate with Brockway in 1932. For over a year leading Communists had urged ILP members to 'come over en masse into the Communist

Party'. Even before disaffiliation the Communists had urged all ILP 'militants' to 'take the lead in calling upon all revolutionary elements to come out of the ILP in a body, hold a separate conference and decide whether and in what way they can link themselves up with the only revolutionary party in Britain today – the Communist Party'.[36] The Comintern Plenum of 1932 had reappraised the 'Social Fascist' policy and lessened some of the hostility to Left Social Democratic members though the former antagonism against Left Social Democratic leaders was retained. Gradually the ILP and the Communist Party drew together into the United Front. The Communist Party, further modifying its policy, came to advocate the formation of a joint party with the ILP.

In its less dogmatic and more amateur way the ILP had also been giving serious consideration to the United Front. Despite every discouragement, the National Administrative Council seemed determined to work with the Communists where possible, although this was a potentially suicidal policy. If, as they themselves admitted, the Communists aimed at the supersession of the ILP, it was obviously dangerous and foolish to help them in their work. The ILP leadership, particularly Maxton, seemed to believe that the Communists could be beaten with their own tactics. Every critic of disaffiliation had emphasised the danger of getting out of touch with the Labour movement. Fred Jowett, who nevertheless remained with the ILP, 'believed that it was fundamental for the ILP to continue to keep in the main stream of working class life through its mass organisation in the Labour Party and the Trade Union Movement'.[37] After the 'clean break' of 1932 the ILP could only alleviate its isolation by working with the smaller, though more militant, groups on the Left. The Party was particularly concerned with gaining influence among the unemployed and was working with the NUWM as early as 1931. The NUWM, however, was under Communist control, and it was difficult to co-operate with it so long as the ILP was regarded as 'Social Fascist'.

A serious breach occurred as the result of the Hunger March of 18 October and 1 November 1932. A mass demonstration on the Means Test had petered out in confusion and each party blamed the other for its failure.[38] The Communists claimed that the ILP Member, John McGovern, had weakened the demonstration by trying to present its demands to Parliament himself, rather than allowing the leaders of the NUWM to do so. The ILP, for its part, accused the Communists of misusing their influence in the NUWM. For two months the *New Leader* was filled with the controversy. Pat Devine, secretary of the NUWM, summed up the whole Communist objection to the ILP concept of the United Front as meaning a formal alliance between groups. He wrote:

> The big thing in developing the United Front is to agitate and bring the masses into activity around the particular issues and to get organisation (Committees), expressing and representing the actual character of the movement.[39]

Thus, early in 1933, the Communists were still advocating the 'United Front from Below', the formation of action committees rather than the establishment of formal relations between Left leaders. They still regarded these leaders as the main enemy.

The tortured relationship between the Communists and the ILP was almost all that the strategy of the 'United Front from Below' had to show by the middle of 1933. The rest of the Left was still divided into small groups which for various reasons did not wish to be involved in these narrow manouevres. Several of these groups were offshoots from the ILP which had disagreed with its decision to leave the Labour Party. Members of the Society for Socialist Inquiry and Propaganda had combined with the ILP Affiliation Committee (dissentients from the Bradford decision) in founding the Socialist League. An inaugural conference was held during the Leicester Conference of the Labour Party in October 1932 to establish a Socialist educational and propaganda organization affiliated to the Labour Party. At a further conference held in London a fortnight later former leading members of the ILP, including H. N. Brailsford and E. F. Wise were prominent among the speakers.[40] Naturally the ILP remained hostile to the League, commenting that:

> The only groups which will participate in this effort are the insignificant number which have already put themselves outside the ILP.[41]

The Socialist League defended itself against any suggestion that it was exceeding its limited aims. In 1933 the Labour Party acknowledged these aims by accepting the affiliation of the Socialist League, giving its 2,000 members the same opportunities for submitting policy resolutions as the largest Trade Unions. Inevitably the League began to acquire the characteristics of a political party, rejecting the 'self-denying ordinance' which prevented the Fabians from submitting political resolutions to the Party.

J. T. Murphy, who had resigned from a leading position in the Communist Party in 1932, became the Secretary of the League on the death of E. F. Wise. His interpretation of its aims as 'working for the transformation of the Labour Party into the Party of the working class revolution'[42] came to be accepted in a modified form by most members of the League. The policy at which the League had arrived reflected the discontent with Parliamentary methods which dominated the ILP and the Communist Party, though it was expressed in less revolutionary and more 'managerial' terms. The League's policy was 'Fabianism for the 1930s', a radical version of the idea of efficient administration based on accumulated knowledge. Despite this the Labour Party found it distasteful. Herbert Morrison wrote shortly before the 1933 Labour Party Conference:

> If the Socialist League point of view were approved by the Party it would drive us to defend ourselves for the greater part of our time against Tory allegations of Bolshevism and dictatorship.[43]

The Socialist League submitted detailed amendments to the Party's policy at the Hastings Conference where they were supported by Sir Stafford Cripps. The alterations to the National Executive report, *Socialism and the Condition of the People*, which he advocated were finally left to the Executive to consider, and were moved again at the Southport Conference of 1934.

CHAPTER 5

The Reaction Against Hitler

Before 1933 a United Front of any kind had been largely fictitious. The United Front was openly being used to gain converts to Communism from the ILP and the Labour Party and, if possible, to split these organizations. The labour movement in Britain had not paid much attention to the revolutionary propaganda of the Communists. 'Unity against the capitalist offensive' had remained an empty phrase, while the agitation for 'immediate demands' was conducted almost solely among the unemployed. The victory of the German Nazi Party in the 1933 elections changed all this. Despite the recriminations surrounding the collapse of German socialism, the British Left became increasingly willing to work together against fascism; the willingness increased when the British Union of Fascists emerged in 1934.

The Left Socialist Bureau, which included the ILP, the Italian Socialist Party, Norwegian Labour Party and various small European groups, cabled the Second and Third Internationals from its Paris conference of 4 February 1933:

> We strongly urge the immediate summoning of a conference between the Labour and Socialist International, the Communist International and the Independent revolutionary Socialist Parties. The purpose of this conference would be to establish a plan of action to assist the workers who are now opposed by Fascism in its various forms and to break the power of the counter-revolution everywhere.[1]

The Communist International was in a difficult position after Hitler's election victory. It was taken by surprise by his success and appears to have accepted Thaelmann's slogan: 'After Hitler, Us!'

On 9 March, fully one month after the Paris telegram, the Comintern took up the slogan of 'the United Front against Fascism'. It did so with only grudging recognition of the need for national consultations with Social Democratic leaders. The Labour and Socialist International had issued a declaration on 19 February calling for joint action between the German Social Democrats and Communists to defeat Hitler. It concluded: 'The Labour and Socialist International has always been ready to negotiate with the Communist International with a view to common action as soon as this body is also ready.'[2]

The Comintern response was that there could be 'no faith in the sincerity of the declaration of the LSI Bureau'.[3] The Comintern suggestion that Communists should approach the official national committees of their respective Social Democratic Parties was, however, a significant departure. Should this approach receive no response they were to form joint anti-Fascist committees at a lower level 'despite the leadership'. The Comintern, completely disregarding their past policy, called upon 'all Communist Parties to make yet another attempt to set up the united front of struggle with the social democratic workers through the medium of the social democratic parties'.[4] The Labour and Socialist International was not prepared to recommend the formation of United Fronts in individual countries but issued the following reply to the Comintern:

> We feel it to be our duty to call upon the Parties affiliated to the LSI to hold their hands if possible and not to deal with Communist offers of this kind in the individual countries until the Executive of the Labour and Socialist International has defined its attitude towards the new platform of the Comintern.[5]

In Britain the ILP and the Communist Party were naturally the first to take up the call for united action. Following on the resolution of the Paris Left Bureau, the National Administrative Council of the ILP adopted a statement on Germany at its meeting of 5 March. It announced that:

> The National Council has decided immediately to approach with concrete proposals the British Labour Party, the Trades Union Congress, the Co-operative Party, the C.P.G.B. and all other working class bodies.[6]

Thus the ILP advanced at the same time as the Comintern the

necessity of the 'United Front against Fascism'. Five days later the
Communist Party of Great Britain sent a letter to the same
organizations approached by the ILP.[7] Not surprisingly, the two
parties were the only ones to accept each other's invitations. Each
was conscious of its isolation, each felt the necessity of maintaining
contact with the Labour movement. Despite intense and continuing
rivalry, the Communists and the ILP could not afford to remain
apart.

The Labour Party had no incentive to accept the United Front
proposals. The National Joint Council of Labour unanimously
rejected the United Front on 21 March. Its reply took the form of a
detailed statement, *Democracy versus Dictatorship*, which stated the
case against Communism and Fascism with equal vigour. It took as
its theme part of the statement made by the Labour and Socialist
International with regard to national United Fronts:

> Past experience goes to show that such negotiations in individual
> countries may unfortunately only too easily be turned into
> manoeuvres by the Communists, with the result that they help to
> poison the situation and increase the mistrust in the Labour
> Movement instead of diminishing it.[8]

The statement was circulated by the Labour Party and endorsed at
the Hastings Conference in October where resolutions in favour of
the United Front were defeated. Herbert Morrison, in opposing the
resolutions, recalled the Communist attacks on the Labour Party in
recent years. At the Southport Conference in 1934 it was agreed:

> That united action with the Communist Party or organisations
> ancillary or subsidiary thereto without the sanction of the
> National Executive Committee is incompatible with member-
> ship of the Labour Party, and that the N.E.C. seeks full
> disciplinary powers to deal with any case or cases that may
> arise.[9]

The Labour Party refused to consider the United Front proposals,
and for over two years the only form of 'Unity' was that established
with some difficulty between the ILP and the Communist Party.

The Left elements in the new Socialist League were not too
enthusiastic about joining their former ILP colleagues in collaborating with the Communists. The National Council of the League
passed a resolution in March 1933 urging the Labour Party and

TUC to arrange 'a meeting with the representatives of the Co-op movement, the ILP and the CP for the purpose of proposing to them a basis for United Action'. After the publication of *Democracy versus Dictatorship* the League decided to modify its policy in conformity with the Labour Party attitude. The League's National Council submitted a drastically revised statement to its Derby Conference at Whitsun, calling on the TUC and the Labour Party 'to formulate a policy which would rally the whole working class movement against Fascism and Capitalism'.[10] A resolution from the Hendon branch favouring joint action with the Communists and the ILP was defeated. The idea of a United Front was slowly gaining favour on the Left, despite the intransigence of the Communists. However, the Labour Party, in recovering from the defeat of 1931, seemed to be adopting a more radical policy. The great majority of its members were more attracted to this than to the abuse from the Communists or to the dissensions of the ILP.

The readiness of the ILP to co-operate with the Communists did not lessen the tension between the two parties to any important extent. Having failed in their attempt to attract individuals or sections from the ILP into their Party, the Communists were now advocating a 'United Working Class Party', a combination with the ILP which would inevitably come under Communist leadership. In a *Labour Monthly* article, 'The United Front and Revolutionary Unity', Palme Dutt developed the theme that the United Front created on 17 March 1933 was merely a preliminary to the creation of a new Left party.[11] Communist influence in the ILP was growing, and although the ILP leadership remained hostile to Communism, there seemed to be opportunities for greatly expanding the Communist Party at the expense of the older and larger party. The National Administrative Council of the ILP decided on 14 April to continue and expand the United Front. The Party Conference had accepted this recommendation, despite the opposition of two if its MPs, McGovern and Wallhead. So strong had sympathy with the Communists grown among the active membership, that the NAC was instructed, against its wishes, 'to approach the Communist International with a view to ascertaining in what way the ILP may assist in the work of the International'.[12] The Comintern Secretariat cabled a reply on 30 April, welcoming the Conference decision, and expressing its readiness to begin negotiations with the NAC. For the next few weeks it seemed as though a genuine 'United Front' would be established. Brockway, Mann and Pollitt spoke from a joint platform at the May Day Rally in Hyde Park. It was not long, however, before squabbles broke out between the temporary allies. There were three attitudes to the United Front within the ILP. Some like McGovern and Wallhead were opposed to collaboration with the Communists on principle; rather than accept the United Front, Wallhead resigned from the Party. Allied with these two MPs were Paton, the General Secretary, who later resigned, and Elijah Sandham and the Lancashire Division who seceded in 1934. They all felt that the United Front was 'frittering away valuable energy and finance in resultless activity'.[13] The official majority viewpoint on the other hand, was expressed by Brockway and Maxton, who were hostile to the Communist Party and constantly aware of the dangers of isolation. They put little faith in the sincerity of the Communists but were prepared to make concessions in the interests of 'Unity against Fascism'.

On the Left wing was the Revolutionary Policy Committee, which openly favoured the 'United Communist Party' proposals of the Comintern. The ILP was in its usual position of trying to go three ways at once and the Communists took advantage of the situation.

A new dispute was begun by the articles written by Fenner Brockway in the *New Leader*, in which he criticized the failure of the Comintern in Germany and supported the pretensions of the Paris Left Bureau to be a bridge between the Communist and Socialist Internationals. The Communists saw this as a revival of the Vienna International of 1920, which had eventually merged with the Labour and Socialist International. In a letter to the ILP Otto Kuusinen attacked Brockway's articles and outlined the growing split between what he termed the 'left reformist' and 'revolutionary elements' in the ILP.[14] The ILP leadership was trying to avoid close contact with the Comintern. Kuusinen quoted to them the obligations imposed by the Whitsun Conference decision:

We propose that the following questions be raised for discussion in all the organisations of the ILP.
(1) What concrete mass actions on the basis of the united front of the C.P.G.B. and the ILP can and must be carried out in the near future with the aim of a successful struggle for

a 10% wage increase, against the Means Test, and other similar partial demands advanced by the C.P.G.B. and the ILP?

(2) Is it desirable for the ILP to join the Communist International as a Party sympathising with Communism with the right to a consultative vote ...?[15]

Thus after six months of Nazi rule in Germany, the 'United Front' had changed little in its essentials. Kuusinen's report to the XIII Plenum of the ECCI in December 1933 still spoke of 'the hypocritical and treacherous sophistries of social democracy'.[16] It was well over a year before Communist policy changed radically, though it had undergone substantial modification. Throughout that year the feud between the ILP and the Communist Party continued, rather ludicrously disguised under the label of the 'United Front'.

By early 1934 there was convincing evidence that European Fascism was expanding at the expense of Socialists and Communists alike. The ILP wrote to the Labour Party, the TUC and the Co-operative and Communist Parties on 13 February 1934 calling for:

an immediate consultation between representatives of all sections of the working class so that we may plan common action.[17]

On the following day Maxton and Brockway met Arthur Henderson who expressed his sympathy with their request but once again repeated that the Labour Party would not join any United Front which included the Communist Party.[18] The Labour Party officially replied to the ILP on 9 March as follows:

Your suggestion for 'an immediate consultation between representatives of all sections of the working class' is one which, in the considered opinion of the National Executive, would not result in any agreed policy of 'common action', in view of the fundamental differences which exist, for example, between the Labour Party and its associate movements on the one hand and the Communist Party on the other.[19]

The situation remained as before. Indeed the 'United Front' was further restricted by an NAC decision on 16 February 'to limit co-operation with the Communist Party to specific objects as agreed upon by the representatives of the two parties from time to time'.[20] The Labour Party rebuff had impressed the ILP leaders with the difficulties of maintaining contact with the Labour movement while allied with the Communist Party. Rumblings from Lancashire had prompted the NAC to survey the results of the United Front campaign. John Paton reported at the end of 1933:

> The analysis of the reports shows that the policy of isolated co-operation with the Communist Party has completely failed to bring general support from the other organised bodies.[21]

Wrangles with the Comintern continued, despite the growing realization by Communists that genuine Fascism had rendered the concept of 'Social Fascism' out of date. At the beginning of 1934 the ILP had written to the Comintern, criticizing the rigidity of Comintern control over constituents. The ILP wanted international discussion to precede important decisions of the Comintern. The most provocative demand was that the monopolistic position of the Communist Party of the Soviet Union should be replaced 'by a real collective international leadership based upon the class relations in their countries'.[22] The Comintern expressed righteous indignation at such an attack, although eighteen months later it tacitly accepted all these points. The Political Secretariat of the ECCI replied on 20 February, repeating its suggestions for a United Communist Party and accused the ILP leadership of attempting to escape the decisions of its 1933 Conference. The ILP leaders felt that 'the whole tone of the Comintern letter is deplorable in view of the need for working class unity'.[23]

The refusal of the ILP leaders to follow up 'sympathetic affiliation' to the Comintern was endorsed at the York Conference of Easter 1934 by a four-to-one majority. Enthusiasm for an approach to the Comintern had largely evaporated as it became clear that the Communists were intent on superseding the ILP. William Rust, for instance, had stated openly that sympathetic affiliation had been suggested 'in order that it could facilitate the movement of the ILP workers towards Communism'.[24] Internal dissension in the ILP caused by Communist sympathizers came to a head in August 1934. The Communist Party had written to Divisional Councils and branches of the ILP inviting them to send representatives to the forthcoming Seventh World Congress of the Communist International. This was done without consulting or indeed informing the National Administrative Council. The NAC meeting of 7 November called on the Communist Party to give guarantees of non-interference in ILP affairs as a condition for continuing the United Front. The leading members of the Comintern Affiliation Committee, who eventually went to Moscow in 1935, were suspended from membership of the ILP.

The negative aspects of the United Front were still dominant at the end of 1934 but several positive steps had been taken. The 'Great United Front National Congress of Action' was held in Bermondsey on 24 February 1934. It was organized mainly by the National Unemployed Workers Movement, and was characterized by criticism of the official Labour movement. Indeed so bitter were Communist attacks on the Labour Party and TUC as 'saboteurs' of the Congress and its accompanying march, that the ILP was forced to defend them.[25] By October the Communist attitude had softened in the light of the Pact of Unity between the Socialists and Communists in France. The Communist Party was preparing to take advantage of the strong reaction to Nazism which was sweeping the Left. Local Communist Parties were authorized to approach their Labour Parties in an attempt to make electoral agreements, and in the November 1934 Municipal elections the bulk of Communist candidates were withdrawn in favour of the Labour Party. The negotiations between representatives of the two Internationals had made top-level agreements acceptable tactics. The Communists were realizing the possibility of forming alliances with the national leadership of other Left-Wing parties. Piatnitsky wrote, early in November:

> The united front from below must remain the basic form of the Communist united front tactics. However this must not mean that the application of the united front from above is thereby excluded from our activities. It may possibly be seen that in some cases the application of the united front from below is the only possible tactic, but it can never be the case that the application of the united front from above is the only possible tactic.[26]

While this may appear a grudging recognition of negotiation between Party leaders, it was as significant as the breakdown of the anti-Communism of the LSI. The British Labour Party, after its stern admonitions at Southport, showed no signs of abandoning its decision that collaboration with Communists was out of the question. However there was some hope that proposals for 'Unity' put forward by a self-effacing and co-operative Communist Party might be accepted by the Left of the Labour Party. The ILP, despite the endless trouble which the United Front had caused, was still prepared to work with the Communists. A meeting at the House of Commons between Maxton, Brockway, Campbell Stephen and McGovern of the ILP, and Pollitt, Gallacher, Kerrigan and Springhall of the Communist Party, laid down conditions for the continuance of the United Front. The ILP was able to get assurances that the Communist Party would stop interfering in its affairs.[27]

Co-operation with the Communist Party did not, however, seem to be helping the ILP. In June 1934, despite the United Front, a Communist candidate opposed the ILP nominee at Merthyr, a seat formerly held by the ILP Member, Dick Wallhead. Communist influence in the ILP Guild of Youth led to its virtual disruption at the end of 1934 and the Revolutionary Policy Committee was becoming a Communist instrument. Unrest at these tendencies had caused the resignation of John Paton from the position of General Secretary in August 1933. His repeated warnings of the effect of the United Front on the ILP had been ignored by the National Administrative Council and he eventually left the party altogether and returned to the Labour Party.

The ILP Guild of Youth, like its counterpart the Labour Party League of Youth, was in conflict with the senior party. The National Committee of the Guild decided to apply for 'sympathetic affiliation' to the Young Communist International and at the Norwich conference of May 1934, the Guild ratified this decision by 18 votes to 12. Representatives of the NAC met the Guild Council on 21 October and made it quite clear that the NAC could not continue to recognize the Guild as the youth section of the Party if it retained sympathetic affiliation to the Young Communist International.[28] The National Council of the Guild decided by three votes to two to call a special conference to rescind the affiliation decision. At Derby on 18 November, the Guild did so by 21 votes to 11 in order to prevent a split.[29] In an attempt to curb the Guild the ILP reduced its age limit to 21 at the 1935 annual conference, thus removing many of the advocates of YCI affiliation from the Guild's leadership.

The ILP's troubles were by no means confined to its youth

section. It was also subject to Trotskyist penetration, to the loss of many Scottish members and to the defection of most of its followers in Lancashire. Trotsky's final expulsion from the Soviet Union had left him free to encourage groups of supporters elsewhere, though his main concern remained the policies of the Soviet state and Party. A 'Left Opposition' was already in existence in several European Communist Parties and by 1932 the 12-man 'Balham Group' had emerged from the British Communists.[30] The January resolution of the Communist Party Central Committee in 1932 criticized 'Left and Right sectarianism' within the Party, warning particularly against the dangers of Trotskyism.[31] The 'Balham Group' was expelled and formed itself into a Communist League. After two years the Communist League decided to merge with the Independent Labour Party in accordance with the 'entrist' tactic of those French and American Trotskyists who had joined their respective socialist parties. On 23 March 1934, members of the Communist League informed the ILP that the International Communist League had disbanded its British section and advised its members to join the Independent Labour Party. The statement by former members of the League outlined their aims with disarming frankness:

> The building of a new party would be painfully slow. The possibility of a speedier way of establishing an effective revolutionary party is provided by the ILP, which, despite its past mistakes, represents a potentially revolutionary force.[32]

This appeal presaged two years of uncomfortable relations, which were to disturb the ILP without adding much to the strength of Trotskyism.

The Independent Labour Party in its rapid decline gave rise to several minorities besides those going to make up the Socialist League. Immediately after disaffiliation from the Labour Party an important body of members in Scotland organized together to reverse the decision. On 14 August 1932, the NAC agreed to the expulsion from the ILP of members of the Scottish ILP Affiliation Committee, among whom were Patrick Dollan, David Kirkwood MP and Tom Johnston. The Committee formed a Scottish Socialist Party at the end of August which was accepted for affiliation to the Labour Party on a total of 1,000 members. By November 1932 the new party claimed nearly 2,000 of the original 3,300 Scottish ILP members.[33] The Scottish Socialist Party, like its English counterpart the Socialist League, aimed at fulfilling the original function of the ILP. Patrick Dollan stated at Motherwell, soon after the party's foundation, that the aim of the SSP was to be the missionary society for socialism, in full co-operation with the trade union and co-operative movement.[34] The SSP's policy was close to that of the Socialist League although it had a strong pacifist section and remained hostile to Communism. Its most important asset was the Glasgow weekly *Forward* which became the party's official paper in 1934.

Dissension over disaffiliation was soon followed by a revolt against co-operation between the ILP and the Communist Party. In Lancashire, where the ILP had been well represented on local authorities and in the Trade Union movement, co-operation with the small and sectarian Communist Party was held to be damaging the ILP's local influence. In July 1933, the Lancashire Divisional Council circularized its branches, proposing an end to the United Front. The Lancashire Division publicized this viewpoint through its paper *Northern Voice*, and at the York Annual ILP Conference of 1934 an NAC Report, censuring the Division for its actions, was carried by 135 votes to 31. J. T. Abbott, the Divisional Organiser, resigned from the Party and formed a Unity Committee which set up the Independent Socialist Party in May 1934. Seven of the 32 ILP branches in Lancashire joined the new party which also attracted Middleton Murry, the critic, who had been unsuccessfully urging his own form of democratic Marxism on the ILP for the past two years.

By the end of 1934, then, the Independent Labour Party was falling apart in all directions. The Socialist League and the Scottish Socialist Party had gone back to the Labour Party and many members of the Independent Socialist Party were to do so before long. The ILP itself was rent with dissension between the openly pro-Communist element around the Revolutionary Policy Committee, the parliamentary leadership and the Trotskyists. The Communist Party still had less than 6,000 members at the end of 1934 but the balance within the Left was beginning to move towards it and away from the disintegrating ILP. Within the Labour Party the Left was naturally wary about both the parties in the fractious 'United Front'. Some of the Left had just defected from the ILP and had no desire to join with it again. Others had quit the

Communist Party in reaction against its 'social fascist' line. All remembered and periodically still experienced the vicious attacks on them which the Communists were only just beginning to abandon. The Labour Party leadership did all it could to limit any appeal which the Left outside the Party might exercise over its members. The National Executive increased its powers to discourage contact between local Labour parties and outside minorities and extended the list of 'proscribed organizations' (begun in 1930 to name Communist fronts). Hence the Left was not merely confined to two small and quarrelsome groups outside the Labour Party but the Party itself was quite satisfied to keep things that way. However the Labour Party was not the decisive element in the situation and events in Europe were to change everything almost overnight.

CHAPTER 6

The Spread of Fascism: 1934–37

During 1934 the emphasis in Left politics began to shift from domestic to international affairs. Although unemployment remained and the problems of the Distressed Areas grew worse, the politically active were increasingly forced to consider the implications of European fascism. The relatively puny Fascist and Communist movements in Britain gained attention because they were seen as projections of much more important European counterparts. Extra-parliamentary agitation began to shift from the unemployed movement to opposition to fascism, despite the fact that the unemployed demonstrations continued to attract popular attention. Regular Hunger Marches from the Distressed Areas to London, of which the most famous was the Jarrow March of 1936, helped to emphasize to the more prosperous areas that unemployment had not been abolished but had merely receded. On most occasions when mass demonstrations took place there were clashes with the police and it was primarily for this reason that the Labour Party and the TUC tried to discourage such a form of protest.[1] The demonstrations had some effect, however, notably in 1935 when the new Unemployment Assistance Board scales were withdrawn. The public was kept aware of the problem and intelligent opinion was roused by the conditions revealed.

Violence on the streets increasingly moved from the Distressed Areas to London, Manchester and other major cities in reaction to the rise of the British Union of Fascists. Sir Oswald Mosley's movement was associated with street battles, violence and anti-Semitism on the model of the Nazi Party.[2] Metropolitan Police regulations restricted the holding of rival meetings in close proximity, while in Manchester the police had banned the wearing

56

of political uniforms. Both measures were later incorporated in the Public Order Act. In October 1936 the 'battle of Cable Street' broke out to prevent an attempt by the Fascists to march through Stepney.[3] After this riot, which involved 100,000 people, political processions were banned in the Metropolitan Police area for six months. In 1937 there was a further riot when the BUF tried to march through Bermondsey.

The Blackshirts deliberately concentrated on those areas where there were liable to be violent counter-demonstrations. The Left, seeing the European situation repeated in Britain, made every attempt to prevent the BUF from marching, even though the BUF never showed any evidence of becoming an effective political force.[4] The Left claimed that the government and police were prejudiced in favour of Mosley, and were convinced that the National Government was favourable to fascism. The BUF claimed the opposite.[5] Mosley undoubtedly had admirers in important social positions, including for a period Lord Rothermere, and had access to a wide range of the politically influential. But the violent character of the BUF and its unashamed adoption of foreign symbols made it unattractive to many who might otherwise have agreed with some of its policies, and made it doubly obnoxious to the Left.

One reaction against fascism, and the threat of warfare which it was beginning to present, was a revival of the pacifist movement. On 27 March 1934, a National Declaration Committee was set up to organize a ballot on the British attitude to the League of Nations.[6] Although the 'Peace Ballot' was ostensibly an investigation, it was regarded by its opponents and by many of its supporters as an attempt to bring pressure to bear upon the government.[7] The ballot showed substantial support for the attitude of the Labour and Liberal Parties towards foreign policy. Even more importantly it showed that millions of electors could be made to take a stand in favour of the League of Nations, towards which many Conservatives were cynical or even hostile. Those who voted showed themselves not ready for rearmament but, at the same time, in favour of strengthening the League of Nations. The General Election of 1935 was largely conducted in response to this attitude.[8]

There was considerable disagreement about foreign policy both within the Conservative Party and among the Opposition. Until

1935 the Labour Party was led in parliament by an avowed Christian pacifist, George Lansbury. The National Labour Prime Minister, Ramsay MacDonald, had campaigned against conscription in the First World War. But within the Labour Party Ernest Bevin, Walter Citrine and Hugh Dalton began to urge rearmament against Germany and support for League of Nations sanctions against Italy for its invasion of Abyssinia in 1935. In the Conservative Party Churchill consistently called for effective rearmament. Throughout the 1930s the parliamentary situation was complicated by these divisions within the major parties and by the aftermath of the disintegration of the Liberals and the defection of MacDonald in 1931. The parliaments of 1931 and 1935 contained an unprecedented number of groups and remnants, apart from the solid bloc of Conservatives who always constituted a majority. These groups included National Labour, three Liberal Parties, the ILP, Independents, a Communist and, later, a 'Progressive'. Among these moved Lloyd George and Winston Churchill, unacceptable for office, yet suspect to the Opposition. The only hope of forming an alternative government lay in the combination of these diverse elements with the Labour Party and with a body of defectors from the Conservatives. By 1937, in the face of the rapid spread of fascism, many who were active in politics began to be attracted to the idea of such a combination.

Although the general elections of 1931 and 1935 resulted in a large Conservative majority in the Commons, electioneering was not totally meaningless. The East Fulham by-election in October 1933 proved a significant pointer to the strength of pacifist sentiment. The Labour candidate advocating a pacifist programme, reversed a large Conservative majority in a seat never before held by Labour.[9] In the following year the Labour Party gained control of the London County Council for the first time. This emphasized the shift in Labour support out of the Distressed Areas. But these successes were not repeated, and the general election of 1935 was a disappointment; the Labour Party returned only 154 MPs on a vote slightly below that of 1929. The National government, now led by Stanley Baldwin, continued in office and was more Conservative than ever. The National Labour group was diminishing; Ramsay MacDonald was heavily defeated by Emanuel Shinwell at Seaham in the general election. The election was also notable for the return of the first Communist to be elected since Shapurji Saklatvala lost

Battersea North in 1929. The Communist vote was growing stronger in Fife and the Rhondda, though in the rest of Britain its record at by-elections was no better than that of the Independent Labour Party or other fringe groups.

The Peace Ballot and the East Fulham by-election suggested a strong sentiment against war but few established politicians were prepared to argue that the rise of fascism made a future war probable. The contradictions within the Labour Party were quite marked; many supported a boycott of German goods but were unprepared to consider any international action against fascism if this were to create a danger of war. This contradictory attitude was clearly revealed in October 1935 when Fascist Italy invaded Abyssinia, an act of open aggression by one League of Nations member against another. Such overt aggression turned the Labour Party away from pacifism and towards the acceptance of a degree of force to implement collective security. The change in the Party's outlook was not completed without the loss of its leader, George Lansbury, and the resignation from its National Executive Committee of Sir Stafford Cripps. The Left was torn between the pacifists and the dominant group in the Labour Party which urged support for League sanctions. The Communists and some within the Socialist League and the ILP asserted the need for defending small nations against fascism and aggression, by sanctions and force if necessary, while others condemned Abyssinia and Italy as equally reactionary and unworthy of support. Cripps, in particular, became associated with the notion of 'working-class sanctions'; that is the use of union power to prevent arms delivery and the avoidance of reliance on either the National Government or on the League of Nations.

The 'Peace Ballot' had shown considerable support for the use of economic and even military sanctions against an aggressor and this popular attitude was reflected in the policy adopted by the Trades Union Congress and the dominant block of union officials within the Labour Party. On this issue Lansbury and the pacifist element in the Party were unable to compromise with the rest of the party. Cripps' objection to sanctions was based on distrust of the National Government rather than on complete opposition to force in any form. The National Executive of the Labour Party, on the other hand, had supported League of Nations sanctions against Italy and Cripps resigned from it rather than accept this decision. When the

Party conference began at Brighton in October 1935, opinion in the Party had hardened against Lansbury and Cripps. Lansbury's support for pacifism received only 102,000 votes and he resigned from the parliamentary leadership. The vicious personal attack on him by Ernest Bevin and his humiliating defeat made it impossible for him to remain as leader. He was replaced by Clement Attlee, the party's first public-school educated middle-class leader who was widely but wrongly regarded as a temporary appointment.

The debate about 'physical' and 'moral' methods of obstructing fascism was largely terminated by the outbreak of the Spanish civil war in the middle of 1936. In February a Left coalition was elected to office in Spain; later in the year a similar coalition was elected in France. Both elections were taken as further proof that if Socialists, Communists and Liberals worked together they could defeat fascism. The Communist International at its Seventh (and final) Congress in 1935 had called for the formation of such an alliance and this object was being pursued by all national Communist Parties including the British. The Spanish *Frente Popular* relied on Liberal and Socialist support in the Cortes and on toleration by the syndicalist unions and anarchist peasant movement in the country-side. The strength of these movements was greater than that of the Communists and made anti-clericalism and radical land reform essential ingredients in the politics of the Spanish Left. The Socialist trade-union movement, the *Union General de Trabaja-dores*, had drawn closer to the syndicalist CNT after the suppression of the Asturias miners in 1934. The combination behind the new government was certain to clash with long-established religious and military interests in Spain and with the landowning aristocracy.[10]

In July a military rising broke out in Spanish Morocco, was supported by many of the garrisons in Spain, and came under the leadership of Generals Mola and Franco. The major European powers, including initially the Soviet Union, formed a Non-Intervention Committee, designed to prevent foreign involvement in and the isolation of the civil war. The policy of non-intervention was adopted by the Labour Party Annual Conference at Edinburgh in October 1936 after consultations with the Trades Union Congress and the French Socialist Party. 'The official resolution was so drafted as to assume that non-intervention could be made a reality, ...'[11] This was a false assumption as later speeches from the representatives of the Spanish Socialist Party showed. Clement Attlee and Arthur Greenwood immediately caught the train to London to interview the Prime Minister. They advised him that the Spanish government had evidence of Italian and German intervention and urged him to supervise the non-intervention agreement more effectively. On their return the Conference passed a stronger resolution. The Labour Party remained in an ambiguous position. Its members organized aid for the Republican government while its leaders felt unable to do so until the following year when it became clear that neither Germany nor Italy had the slightest intention of discouraging aid to Franco.

The proven fact of German and Italian intervention made the Spanish Republic a symbol of resistance to fascism. The Labour Party, the Communists, most Liberals and a few Conservatives actively worked for the Republic, while many more Conservatives, many Catholics and the BUF supported Franco. In answer to foreign arming of the Spanish Fascists the European Left, led by the Communists, organized voluntary aid and recruited an International Brigade. The German and Italian support restored the strength of the rebels and was eventually decisive, while Soviet intervention led to a rapid expansion of the previously weak Spanish Communist Party. Communist influence was strong in the police and army and they controlled the International Brigade. By advocating the building of a national coalition the Communists were able to attract sections of the Socialist Party. In 1937 the Socialist Unity Party of Catalonia was created by an amalgamation which was in keeping with the United Front tactic of the eventual creation of a single Left party. By the following year the Communist and Socialist youth movements combined, an amalgamation which was often quoted by Young Communist League Leaders in Britain during their overtures to the Labour League of Youth.

The growing strength of Spanish Communism and its identification with the international movement to aid the Republic, underline the increasing influence which the Soviet Union was exercising over the European Left. The Soviet Union had remained a Utopian ideal to the Left even during the vicissitudes of the late 1920s and the collectivization and famine during the First Five Year Plan. 'Who shall say what the Soviet Union has been to us?', wrote André Gide in 1936. 'More than a chosen land – an example, a guide. What we have dreamt of, what we have hardly dared to hope, but towards which we were straining all our will and all our strength, was coming into being over there.'[12] Gide, like many, returned from the Soviet Union disillusioned, and renounced Communism. Many more were inspired, while the great majority of Soviet disciples never went there at all and saw it through the propaganda of the Friends of the Soviet Union or the *Daily Worker*. Sidney and Beatrice Webb surprised the labour movement in 1935 when they added to their earlier works an exhaustive and largely favourable account of the working of Soviet society.[13] The good name of the Soviet Union, marred by the Menshevik Trials of 1930 and the Metro-Vickers Trial of 1933, had been regained by 1936. The Soviet Union had entered the League of Nations in 1934, reached an agreement with France obviously directed against Germany and introduced the Stalin Constitution. But no sooner had this been achieved than the arrests and trials of leading Bolsheviks began, destroying most of the goodwill created among Western sympathizers. Communists and their supporters worked hard to justify the prosecutors' case and the penalties imposed.[14] Western liberals and the Left once again found their credulity stretched in defence of the one state which most of them saw as the only bulwark against Nazi Germany.

Within the labour movement, the emphasis of political discussion moved away from domestic problems to the international scene, although states like the Soviet Union or Nazi Germany were often used as symbols for forces existing in British politics. Many Conservatives supported Hitler or Franco without being fascists, for the same psychological reason as many on the Left cheered loudly whenever the Soviet government executed its enemies. Both sides were translating foreign affairs into domestic battles and acting out the conflicts between classes and parties through the use of international substitutes. However within the Labour Party there was still such confusion between the traditional pacifism of many local parties, the new-found aggressiveness of the Communists and the movement towards rearmament among union leaders, that the party had entered the general election of 1935 with all the outward signs of disunity. The Brighton conference had forced Lansbury out. For over a year the press had been presenting Cripps as a dangerous radical, if not a republican.[15] His resignation from the National Executive had drawn attention to the differences within the Labour Party on foreign policy. Labour lost the 1935 election because of its confusion over foreign policy, just as it had lost in 1931 because of its domestic failure. The parliamentary party was once more an effective opposition under the continued leadership of Clement Attlee, but with no prospect of reaching power for at least another five years.

Rather than ending divisions in the Labour Party, the controversies of 1935 mark the beginning of a new period of prolonged disunity. There had always been a radical element in the local Labour parties and this was now augmented by former members of the ILP who were returning to the Labour Party in large numbers. Moreover, at the end of 1935 the Communist Party began its campaign for a United Front against Fascism. Until 1939 the Labour Party was bedevilled by internal dissensions on this issue. The central theme of the dispute was that the Labour Party had neither the following nor the enthusiasm to oppose the National Government in isolation. The Left of the Party held that the government was little better than fascist and was encouraging Germany and Italy. Consequently, they argued, the Labour Party should refuse to co-operate in any way with the government. In contrast, the official leadership was moving towards agreement with the government on the question of rearmament, though continually critical of the foreign policy being pursued. The trade unions, after the Congresses of 1935 and 1936, were committed to military sanctions against aggression and to that level of rearmament necessary to make sanctions effective. For over three years the Labour Party's foreign policy was an attempt, only partially successful, to accommodate this view with the Party's traditional pacifism and distrust of Conservative governments.

Members of the Labour Party were paying more attention to the Communist Party than for many years, largely as a result of the unique impact of foreign affairs. While Communism in Britain was not very important, it was significant in Europe where the Communist and Socialist Parties faced with active Fascism were working together. Many Labour Party members drew the conclusion that only by building a United Front with the small British Communist Party could the Labour Party be strengthened. At the Edinburgh Conference of the Labour Party in 1936 a request for affiliation from the Communist Party was refused. This decision started rather than ended the controversy about united action.

Until 1939 internal dissension remained characteristic of the Labour Party, with agitations against Fascism and the National Government's foreign policy occupying much of the time and energy of the active Party member. If the Labour Party were to build up an effective electoral machine, its leaders argued, such controversial activities would have to be abandoned in the interests of widening popular support. The gap between these different approaches, basic to all mass radical parties in an electoral situation, was not closed until the outbreak of war. As it turned out this continuing disunity did not have the damaging electoral effects in 1940 that the Party's leaders feared. There was no 1940 general election and by 1945 the voters remembered both that the Labour Party had shared responsibility for winning the war and that it had opposed the Conservative policies which led to the war.

The Labour Party was not deterred from developing a domestic programme despite the growing concentration on foreign affairs. In the years after the defeat of 1935 the Party formulated many of the policies on which it was to be returned in 1945. After the Edinburgh Conference a series of Party enquiries investigated the problems of the Distressed Areas, for although unemployment had declined there was still no solution for the decay of the older, heavy industrial areas from which most Labour MPs were elected. In *Labour's Immediate Programme*, produced early in 1937, the Party suggested state control of the location of industry coupled with a policy of equalizing local rates. *Labour's Immediate Programme* summarized the discussions of the previous five years in a form which appealed even to the Left of the Party and to the Communists. Control of investment was seen as the key to central direction of the economy. Co-ordination of transport, nationalization of coal, gas and electricity, in short the basic measures carried out between 1945 and 1950 were treated in the new programme as the 'four vital measures of reconstruction'. The concept of the public corporation as the controlling body for nationalized industry was finally accepted in the *Immediate Programme*. The syndicalist idea of 'workers control' was finding much less favour than in 1932, when Ernest Bevin had forced through the Party Conference 'the claim of organised labour that it shall have its place in the control and direction of publicly owned industries'.[16] Finally, the *Immediate Programme* reasserted Labour's adherence to the principle of collective security through the League of

Nations. By now Labour was fully committed 'to maintain such
armed forces as are necessary to defend our country and to fulfil
our obligations as a member of the British Commonwealth and of
the League of Nations'.[17]

The Labour Party had traditionally concentrated on 'gas and
water' socialism, but it could not avoid the revision of its foreign
policy which events made necessary. After the death of Henderson
in 1935 and the removal of Lansbury from the leadership,
disarmament and pacifism were less universally accepted among
the Party's members. In 1936 the National Council of Labour,
representing the Labour Party, the Trades Union Congress and the
Co-operative Union, emphasized that collective security against
aggression must rely on a degree of rearmament. Despite the
opposition of many of the Party's leaders, the parliamentary party
agreed in the following year to abstain from any division against
the Estimates for the Fighting Services. Hugh Dalton, returned to
parliament in 1935, had taken a leading part in reconciling the
Party to rearmament and in this he was backed by Bevin, Citrine
and the TUC.[18]

Despite the recovery of the Labour Party after 1931, its electoral
successes were unspectacular. The Labour victory in the London
County Council election of 1934, repeated three years later, was the
most important single achievement of the decade, increasing the
personal prestige of Herbert Morrison and emphasizing the shifting
southwards of Labour influence. The 1935 general election was a
disappointment and it was a major part of Cripps's case for the
Labour Left that the election due in 1940 would not lead to a
Labour victory either. In local government elections, to which
much importance was attached, the Labour Party made little
advance after the victories of 1934, actually losing seats in 1936.[19]
Despite strong condemnation of the National Government by the
Left, there is little evidence that the voters regarded the Labour
Party as a suitable alternative. However, the Party organization
was increasing its effectiveness and recruiting members in areas
which had previously been weakly organized. The local Labour
parties were growing significantly, leading to changes in the Party
constitution and in the relative importance of the Left. By 1936 the
individual Party membership had risen to 430,000, constituting 20
per cent of Labour's nominal strength and the great bulk of its
active supporters. In the following year membership reached a

peak, before dropping away in 1938 and 1939. The local Parties, growing in strength, began to ask for a greater voice in decisions than was allowed under the 1918 constitution. After an agitation lasting several years the Constituency Parties won the right in 1937 to exclusive choice of their representatives on the National Executive Committee.[20] Real power remained in the hands of the union delegations but it now became possible for the local parties to ensure that their opinions were more effectively voiced. Something like a collective opinion was growing in the individual section under the influence of the Left. It was never true that the majority of local parties were under the control of the Left but the more active and vocal Constituencies were becoming so by 1939.

The balance of power within the Party Conference and on the National Executive moved in favour of the local parties after 1937. The Labour Party was ceasing to be a loose federation of political and industrial groups. It was becoming an alliance of the trade-union movement with a unitary political party. There was less scope in the individual section for the organized expression of minority views than in the political affiliates of the past. Local Labour parties were subject to a centralized control which had never been exerted over the ILP or over individual unions. As the number of local agents increased and the Party adopted a regional structure directly answerable to London, so the central authority became more effective. There was no device comparable to the annual conferences of individual unions or affiliated socialist societies at which Constituency Labour opinion could be expressed. Neither the new regional conferences nor the revived Labour League of Youth were allowed to debate national policy. With the disaffiliation of the Socialist League in 1937 and of the University Labour Federation in 1940, the Party ended the possibility of a political affiliate being able to oppose official policy within the Labour Party. Party members were further prohibited from joining or affiliating to the 'proscribed organizations' (groups listed by the National Executive and almost always under Communist Party control).

Domestically the Labour Party was improving its organization and developing its programme after 1934, with its focus on the general election of 1940 which never took place. The world, however, was not moving in the desired direction and the Left often annoyed Labour leaders by pointing this out in public. The

Left became increasingly cosmopolitan in its outlook and concerns while the Labour Party and the union leaders were still firmly rooted in the conditions and outlook of the Distressed Areas. Moreover, Labour politicians and full-time union officials were much more sensitive to the conservatism of a working-class electorate which was just weaned from Liberalism and, in many important areas, continued to return Conservative MPs. The Left, even in the local Labour parties, tended to move in a world of the politically involved and to be far more responsive to what was happening in Europe than were most British voters. By 1937 this was helping to bring into the orbit of Left politics an increasing number of younger, better educated middle-class activists, who found themselves confronting a leadership which still belonged to the 1920s intellectually and was socially based on the older industrial areas and occupations. As Fascism became the central concern and unemployment a secondary issue, the social differentiation between the Left and the labour movement became more marked.

The Communist Party, which was largely working-class in its leadership and electoral following, was able to bridge this gap precisely because the Soviet Union was also centrally concerned with the rise of Nazi Germany. This gave it an influence among the middle classes which it had never previously enjoyed, while allowing it to maintain the tenuous but important industrial base which it had been creating in the 1920s. It, too, was able to expand its following in London and among new working-class sections like the London busmen, while still able to benefit from its loyal followings in South Wales and Central Scotland. It was further able to influence important sections of the expanding local Labour parties, which grew most rapidly away from the Distressed Areas.

CHAPTER 7

The Recovery of the Communist Party

On the extreme Left the Communist Party began to emerge as the dominant group although throughout the decade the ILP had more electoral and parliamentary influence. By November 1934 the conciliatory attitude of the Communist International had caused the Labour and Socialist International to modify its earlier warning against entering into United Front agreements with national Communist Parties.[1] The 'Pact for Unity of Action' had already been signed between the Communist and Socialist Parties of France. In Britain the Communist Party returned to its attempts to work with sections of the Labour Party. Pollitt, speaking in October 1934, proposed an electoral agreement with the Labour Party and the ILP in the approaching municipal elections.[2] The ILP leadership continued to regard co-operation with the Communists as a preliminary to the extension of the United Front to the rest of the labour and trade-union movement. At a meeting with Communist leaders on 12 December 1934, Fenner Brockway laid down three conditions for continued co-operation:

(a) Neither Party was to interfere in the internal affairs of the other

(b) The Communist Party should state clearly whether it would oppose Labour Party or ILP candidates at elections

(c) There should be no attempt to unify the ILP and the Communist Party into a single organisation until the next Annual Conference had discussed the matter.[3]

Despite its participation in the United Front, the ILP was fully aware of the danger of its complete submersion. Both Parties had some 6,000 members in 1934, but the Communists were on the increase, while the ILP was declining, in financial difficulties and riddled with unofficial groups, two of them directly encouraged by the Communist Party.

At the Derby ILP conference in 1935 Harry Pollitt, acting as fraternal delegate from the Communist Party, suggested 'the holding of a joint congress for the formation of a United Communist Party'.[4] Maxton, in reply, foresaw the formation of a new working-class party, but would not agree that unification was opportune at the time. Throughout 1935 joint activities between the two Parties virtually ceased. Three years after disaffiliation and the beginning of the United Front the ILP had less than one third of the membership on which it had last affiliated to the Labour Party. The General Election was to show where the strength of the ILP lay. Fifteen candidates secured 139,517 votes, four-fifths of them in Scotland, and in the four successful contests the official Labour candidates forfeited their deposits. Bridgeton, Gorbals, Camlachie and Shettleston in the East End and South Side of Glasgow returned a solid bloc of ILP Members and City Councillors. The Party position in the area remained far stronger than that of the Labour Party, which hardly existed. Though small in numbers, the ILP had four vociferous Members of Parliament who were assured a hearing in the House and in the country. However remote their political views remained from the rest of the electorate, the 'Clyde group' remained as secure in their own area as they had ever been.

Internally, however, the ILP was in confusion. The Revolution-ary Policy Committee members in the London Division resigned to join the Communist Party in November 1935. The NAC was severely criticized for its policy towards the Abyssinian war. It had given its support to League sanctions against Italy, putting this view forward to its international contacts in the 'Left Bureau'. However the Party Inner Executive, consisting of Maxton, McGovern and Campbell Stephen, disagreed with what appeared to them as support for Abyssinia and the League of Nations. After the NAC had reluctantly accepted this view the Keighley Confer-ence of 1936 censured it, declaring its support for sanctions. The Parliamentary Group declared itself 'unable conscientiously to carry out the Conference decision'. Faced with the threat of losing its Parliamentary representatives the NAC had to agree to a plebiscite of the membership on the issue. This vindicated the refusal of the Inner Executive to support either Italy, Abyssinia or the League of Nations. Such vacillation still further reduced the political influence of the Party.

By 1935 the Trotskyists had succeeded in organizing an effective group within the ILP. They advocated a less sectarian approach to relations with the Labour Party, favouring work for a third Labour Government, rather than the virtually syndicalist policy being put forward by the ILP. The National Administrative Council continued to support the loose federation of European 'Left' Socialist Parties, described as 'renegades from Communism, Brandlerites and counter-revolutionary Trotskyists' by the Communist Party. The Trotskyist branches, on the other hand, wanted the formation of a Fourth International with the centralizing and directing power which the NAC refused to countenance in the Comintern, or encourage in the Left Socialist Bureau. As a reaction against the Trotskyist agitation and the existence of groups favouring the Communist Party, the Conference ruled that unofficial groups were 'bad in principle' by the narrow margin of 63 votes to 60.[5]

As a recognizable group the Trotskyists disbanded in April, but continued to work within the Party until the end of November 1936. C. L. R. James, their leader, then wrote to Brockway, the ILP Secretary, declaring the intention of all Trotskyists to withdraw from the Party to form a separate organization. In a circular sent to branches on 5 December, Brockway estimated that only 30 members would be involved, mostly in the London Division, but possibly in Liverpool also.[6]

While the ILP was in confusion, its 'loyal' successor, the Socialist League, was beginning to reconsider its role. The League had presented a full programme to the Labour Party Conference at Southport, intended to increase the socialist elements in the official *Socialism and the Condition of the People*.[7] This had been defeated and the League began to move from the elaboration of policy to agitation. A special League conference was called on 25 November 1934, at which its National Council was given executive powers to take action on contemporary political issues. The *Socialist Leaguer* declared:

> A disciplined organisation founded on a common policy and working as part of the Labour movement is what the League conceives itself to be. We have passed out of the realm of programme making into the realm of action.[8]

J. T. Murphy saw this as marking a definite departure from the limited aims of the League. 'It at once sharpened the process of transforming League branches from research groups into active political units', he wrote in the official League journal.[9] Considerable discussion had gone into the Socialist League programme and the debates on Labour Party policy promoted by it at the Hastings and Southport Conferences were undoubtedly the best on domestic policy during the decade. They lacked the bitterness and sterility of the debates on Party discipline, Communist affiliation and the United Front which took place at subsequent Party Conferences. Labour Party leaders, however, did not appreciate the radicalism of the League, nor its increasing domination by Sir Stafford Cripps.

The Socialist League began to find itself in the same critical relationship with the Labour Party which had forced its predecessor, the ILP, to disaffiliate. At its first annual conference in June 1933, the League had been asked to consider the issues raised by the United Front between the ILP and the Communist Party. However the conference had felt it advisable to avoid this and the Labour Party and the TUC were asked instead ot formulate a policy which would rally the whole working-class movement against Fascism and Capitalism.[10] The Socialist League still took the view that only through work in the Labour Party was there any possibility of building a united labour movement.[11] The United Front was not regarded as sufficiently important for the League to abandon its propaganda work in favour of joint agitation with the Communist Party and the ILP. The National Council advised the Bristol conference of the League of 1935:

> We must not allow ourselves to be diverted into activities definitely condemned by the Labour Party which will jeopardise our affiliation to and influence in the Party.[12]

The Socialist League was developing an independent policy in conflict with the official programme of the Labour Party. At its 1935 conference it decided to oppose League of Nations sanctions against Italy, an approach close to that eventually adopted by the ILP and reflecting the influence of Cripps. This led to the resignation from the League of J. T. Murphy and was clearly opposite to the policy of the Labour Party. The League organized Anti-War Conferences and once again found itself drawn into political action on a policy differing from that of the Labour Party in being critical of the League of Nations. Early hostility to the

United Front began to lessen after the departure of J. T. Murphy and Socialist Leaguers were soon involved in the controversies on Spain, the rise of Fascism and the need for 'working class unity'. They were encouraged by Sir Stafford Cripps who was both their president and the unchallenged leader of an emerging Labour Party Left of which the Socialist League was the core.

By the end of 1935, then, the situation on the Left had become increasingly favourable for the Communist Party. The ILP was in decline and the Communist Party was seriously attempting to make amends for its previous abuse of the rest of the labour movement. Within the Labour Party the Socialist League was finding that its attempts to remould policy were resented and rejected and it began to look for allies outside the Party. At the same time both the Constituency Labour Parties and the Labour League of Youth were enjoying a rapid increase in membership and many of their new recruits were more interested in what was happening in Europe than in the traditional problems of unemployment and labour conditions. Newcomers to the Left could be forgiven for not being acquainted with the tactics of the Communists and with the tortuous and unedifying relationships within the United Front. Much of the appeal of official Labour condemnation of the United Front in all its forms stemmed from recollections of these manoeuvrings for power. The advocates of 'Unity' argued, however, that a considerable change had come over the Communist Party and that it had given up its 'social fascist' accusations. The Communist International appeared to substantiate these claims at its Seventh World Congress held in Moscow in the middle of 1935. As a result the change in atmosphere, in tactics and in the whole conception of 'Unity' in the second half of the decade was spectacular.

Alterations in the structure and personnel of the Comintern themselves indicated the adoption of a new approach. Manuilsky and Kuusinen were replaced in the public eye by Dimitrov, the 'Reichstag hero' and new Comintern Chairman. The 'Leftists', who had been in power since 1928, made open or implicit recantations of their policies. On practically every issue the Comintern found itself in the role of an infallible body which had adopted a manifestly fallible policy. In fact the Comintern, with its internecine struggles reflecting Russian politics, and its persistent failures, was increasingly ineffectual. The continuing sessions of the Plenum, and the controlling powers of the Executive Committee were abandoned. The independence of national Parties was enshrined as an organizational principle.[13] Communist Parties throughout the world continued to think and act alike, as the crisis on the outbreak of war was to show. The real significance of the Seventh Congress was, however, that it tried desperately to create the impression of a new approach. It was even prepared publicly to bury the Comintern if 'Social Fascism' could be buried with it.

The United Front was broadened and its aims made defensive. The tactics by which such aims were to be achieved were reformist and not revolutionary. The Comintern still asserted its belief in 'Soviet Power', and the weakness of parliamentary democracy, but despite this the aim of the United Front was to be the formation of an elected coalition Government, which could not achieve 'Soviet Power', but which could educate and encourage the Left towards this distant goal by virtue of its existence. The Comintern Congress was trying to reconcile its revolutionary past with the necessity of gaining support from constitutional parties. The contradictions and misunderstandings which were later to centre around the objects of the Popular Front were, in the main, the product of this attempt to reconcile the defence of parliamentary democracy with the advocacy of eventual revolution. The inconsistency between the broad appeal of the Popular Front and its continued use as a tactic for ultimate Communist control is the central theme in the discussions which occupied the next four years. The Popular Front was, in any case, accepted almost unanimously by national Communist Parties as a relief from the increasing absurdity of the previous policies.

In Britain, as in other countries, the Communist Party had already adopted tactics similar to those officially blessed by the Seventh Congress. Despite the continued indifference of the Labour Party the Communists had made many concessions aimed at attracting support from Labour members. The Party had supported Labour candidates and was calling for the return of a Labour Government. While Pollitt was not satisfied that the United Front was being used sufficiently to the advantage of the Party, he warned at the Thirteenth Congress in February 1935 that the Communists should not be too obviously in control of the campaign for Unity. Similarly he anticipated Dimitrov in calling for a new approach to the middle classes. 'We must also endeavour to recruit the doctor, teacher, student, architect,' he said, 'and thus we will grow stronger and stronger and build a strong united front.'[14]

The Communist Party had not yet abandoned its attempts to gain control of the ILP, despite the assurances made in the previous year. For the first time in its history the 1935 Annual Conference of the ILP was attended by a fraternal delegate from the Communist Party, Harry Pollitt, who put forward the policy of 'organizational unity', that is of merging both Parties, now equal in membership, into a single unit.[15] In its discussion prior to the Seventh World Congress, the Communist Party was asked to consider the position of other Left groups in Britain and, in particular, the experiences with the ILP in the United Front. The Party also considered the place of the Socialist League which 'continues the traditional ILP role in the working-class movement under a pseudo-Marxist cloak'.[16] At its Bristol Conference in April the League had once again refused to become involved in the United Front. It favoured the development of a more radical policy for the Labour Party, a policy which would provide 'a real basis for unity'. The Annual Report made it clear that the League considered its influence within the Labour Party as its most important contribution to Left unity.[17]

The Communist Party could apparently hope for little from the Socialist League and for nothing from the Labour Party. It was forced to maintain its alliance with the ILP, in spite of its growing contempt for that Party. There was still a faint hope that the ILP would accept 'organizational unity', and become submerged in the more unified and efficient Communist Party.[18] Even if 'organizational unity' with the ILP had been carried through, this would at best only have doubled the small membership of the Communist Party. Assuming that all the ILP members acquiesced in the amalgamation, the new Party with less than 12,000 members would certainly have lost two of its three MPs. Even Maxton could not have worked for long with the Communists whose infiltration he had done so much to resist. With this in mind the Communists began to pay increasing attention to the Labour Party. By the end of 1935 they were quite prepared to abandon their former ILP allies in the hope of gaining influence with the 400,000 individual members of the Labour Party.

Limited though the desire for Unity was in the Labour Party, both the Communists and the ILP were anxious to take advantage of it. Speaking at an ILP Summer School, Maxton proposed an electoral agreement:

> The ILP is prepared to consult with the Labour Party, the Co-operative Party and the Communist Party, regarding the General Election, with a view to avoiding conflicting candidatures in order to
>
> (a) defeat the National Government candidates and
> (b) secure the return of candidates nominated by the Parties taking part in the consultations.[19]

Pollitt, at the Seventh World Congress of the Comintern, was prepared to go further than the ILP. He urged that the Communist Party 'should propose a meeting with the Labour Party ... to jointly formulate a united front programme around which the common fight could be organised'.[20] He went on to state that the Party would definitely affiliate to the Labour Party if accepted as a 'revolutionary organisation'. The Communists had decided to pursue a policy which could not be followed by the ILP. Brockway had specifically rejected any proposal to reaffiliate to the Labour Party at the end of 1934: 'The decisive objection to this', he wrote, 'is that a Socialist can now only function through the Labour Party by giving up his Socialism'.[21] The Communist decision to withdraw its candidates in all but two Parliamentary constituencies aggravated the situation still further. Except in the three ILP seats the Communists would support Labour rather than ILP candidates. ILP speakers attacked the Communist 'betrayal' at length but were dismissed contemptuously by Pollitt. Referring to the ILP and the Socialist League, he wrote in November:

> Fortunately for the British working class movement, such organisations, with no mass connections or mass influence, or record of mass struggles in any part of the country, are of little significance at the present time.[22]

Although the Communists were to turn to 'such organisations' in just over a year, they were, for the present, much more intent on wooing the Labour Party.

CHAPTER 8

Towards the Popular Front

The National Conference of the Communist Party, which met in Sheffield in October 1935, passed a resolution which departed considerably from the slogan 'For a Communist Group in Parliament' adopted at the Thirteenth Congress only eight months previously. In the intervening period the decision of the Comintern Congress had become public. The resolution adopted by the National Conference consequently proposed an electoral agreement with the Labour Party and a campaign for affiliation to it.[1] This was a preliminary to withdrawing Communist candidates from all but two of the contests in the General Election. Even in West Fife and Rhondda East, the Central Committee declared that: 'the Party is prepared to, in conjunction with the Trade Unions and Labour bodies in them, convene a selection conference, bring the various working class candidates before it and abide by their decisions'.[2]

At the General Election in November, William Gallacher was successful in West Fife while Pollitt in the Rhondda secured 13,655 votes. After his election Gallacher applied for the Labour Party whip which, as he was not a Party member and had defeated someone who was, could not be granted. Although the Communists had greatly modified their policy they failed to persuade the leadership of the Labour Party to make any concessions on the United Front or affiliation proposals. The Communist Party wrote to the National Executive of the Labour Party on 25 November applying for affiliation; they based their claim on the federal nature of the labour movement and the help which Communists had given to Labour candidates. The letter was far more conciliatory than that which had been rejected in 1921.[3]

Whether or not the Communist Party leaders expected such a

76

letter to have anything more than a propaganda appeal they can hardly have been surprised by the Labour Party reply on 27 January 1936 which rejected the application and outlined the history of relations between the two parties, particularly during the 'social fascist' period. In this reply and in the report *British Labour and Communism* submitted to the 1936 Annual Conference, the Labour Party stressed that acceptance of the application would only serve the Communist Party's ends. These were 'to utilise Party facilities on the platform, in public conference, and in the Party press, to displace their essential democratic and socialist character and substitute a Policy Programme based upon Communist Party principles'.[4] The National Executive also noted 'the proclaimed fact that the present application for affiliation is but an evidence of the deviation in the tactics which have been pursued by the Communist International in recent years'.

The official labour movement remained hostile to the Communists, at the international and national levels. The Executive Committee of the Comintern had cabled the Labour and Socialist International on 25 September 1935, asking for negotiations for the 'defence of peace'. The LSI Executive met in Brussels on 12 October and rejected the suggestions. The LSI had no authority over its constituents but the growing domination of the British and Scandinavian parties was enough to secure this refusal which directly countered the United Fronts established by the Latin parties in the LSI.[5] There was ample evidence that neither the Comintern nor the local Communists had abandoned the aim of changing Labour's programme and capturing its machine. Harry Pollitt reported to the Central Committee of the Party in January 1936 that:

> We fight to affiliate as an organised Party, campaigning for united action on the part of all workers organisations, for a change of policy that corresponds to the desires of the Labour Party members, and that also opens up the perspective of realising at a later stage one united working class political party.[6]

At the lower levels of the movement, however, many were becoming attracted to the prospect of ending the feuds of recent years. In January 1936 the University Labour Federation accepted the amalgamation of the Communist Federation of Student

Societies. The British Youth Peace Assembly, a largely Communist gathering, was held in March 1936, and attracted some support from branches of the Labour League of Youth and from the University Labour Federation. The Young Communist League had already agreed to merge with the Labour League of Youth, if possible. *Advance*, the unofficial League of Youth paper which was growing rapidly in influence, was calling for a 'drawing together of the working class youth Internationals'. Left-wing, and particularly Communist, influence was increasing rapidly among organized youth and students; a symptom of the reaction against European fascism. The annual conference of the Labour League of Youth, meeting in Manchester on 12 April 1936, passed a resolution in favour of a 'United Front of working class youth organisations' by 82 votes to 75, bringing the League into immediate conflict with the Labour Party. This was followed in June by a letter from John Gollan, Secretary of the Young Communist League, to the League's National Advisory Committee asking for joint talks aimed at 'uniting all working class youth organisations into the Labour League of Youth on the basis of the decisions of your recent conference'.[7]

Communist influence on the youth and student organizations of the Labour Party grew markedly during 1936. The Eighth National Conference of the Young Communist League, held at Bermondsey in February 1936, marked the first serious attempt to broaden the appeal of the YCL. Visitors and observers from 26 other organizations were invited to attend. The Labour League of Youth sent observers from thirteen branches and from the London Federation. The rules of the Young Communist League were altered so as to widen its membership 'not only to those who support its stated policy and aims, but also to those who, while not being actively hostile to its policy and aims, wish to study Socialism'.[8] The YCL internal bulletin, *Communist Youth*, was replaced by the weekly *Challenge*; the new paper had a popular appeal which gained it 20,000 regular subscribers within two years. Within the Labour League of Youth the YCL was able to maintain contact with the membership and the National Advisory Committee, particularly through the influence of Ted Willis and the *Advance* group.[9]

The attempt of the Communist Party to implement Comintern decisions naturally gave rise to the most widely publicized of the movements for some kind of co-operation on the Left. Campaigns to involve the Liberal Party in an electoral agreement with the Labour and Communist Parties were less significant, though they were to provide the ultimate form of the 'People's Front'. The idea of such an alliance was based on the *Front Populaire* in France, which included the Radical Party among its members. It was quite unacceptable at the time to the British Communists. A campaign for a People's Front would detract from their attempts to influence the Labour Party, and was felt to be inspired by Lloyd George, with whom the Communists had a long standing feud, dating back to the First World War. An article by Lloyd George in the Co-operative newspaper *Reynolds News*, lending support to such an idea, was attacked by the Communists as a manoeuvre 'to drag Fascism into England behind the popular sign of the "People's Front".'[10] More moderate criticism held that it was essential to ensure Communist affiliation to the Labour Party before appealing to other diverse political elements.

Within two years the Communist Party was to be foremost in advocating co-operation with leading Liberals. The difference was one of timing. Pollitt believed that 'there can be no real and effective People's Front unless there has been already united action within the Labour Movement itself'.[11] As with so many of the apparently unreal differences on the Left it was organizational rather than principled considerations which divided the Communist and non-Communist advocates of Unity. The Communist Party felt that there was still much resentment against the Liberals in the Labour Party for the role they had played in 1931. All supporters of 'Unity' realized that their aims could not be attained without the participation of the Labour Party.

Several leaders of the Liberal Party 'were known to favour a Popular Front to move the Government, but acquiesced in the view that they could do nothing about it unless the Labour Party changed its attitude'.[12] At the end of 1936 G. D. H. Cole, in his *The Peoples Front*, advocated the formation of 'Radical Groups', to work in local Liberal parties and to co-operate with the Labour and Communist Parties.[13] Here again the central place was given to the Labour Party. Early in 1937 a group of prominent Liberals pressed such a policy on the Liberal Party Executive, their appeal for 'Unity' being printed by the Party without comment.[14] The Communists held back from such attempts to draw the Liberal Party into a People's Front. They still believed in influencing the

Labour Party. This caution on the part of the Communists was due to their natural antipathy to the Liberal Party, their desire to concentrate on the campaign for affiliation to the Labour Party, and organizational conflicts with the People's Front Propaganda Committee. Ideologically the Party was committed to creating a 'working class united front' before going on to an alliance on the French or Spanish models. Despite this it was to be less than two years before the Party adopted the idea of the 'People's Front' in its entirety, including the help of Liberals and even of Conservatives who were opposed to the National Government.

The Independent Labour Party, in contrast, had deeply-rooted objections to the Popular Front idea. The suggestion of Communist affiliation to the Labour Party was regarded as an unwarrantable departure from principle.[15] Nevertheless 'working class unity remained a desired end despite all our disappointments in seeking it. Among the general body of workers the urge for unity was wide and deep. There seemed no hope of removing the National Government so long as division continued.'[16] The ILP desire to exert influence on the rest of the Labour movement was tempered by hostility to the Communists and, above all, by an inability to compromise or to sacrifice any of the Party's independence. With its declining membership the ILP tended to adopt a purist attitude to other Left groups. If it was to continue in existence the ILP had to reach some agreement, to find some acceptable compromise between 'Unity' and 'independence'. It turned to federalism for the solution; a solution in keeping with its history.[17] To distinguish its proposal from the variations of the 'United Front' which were current in 1936, the ILP described its own suggested Left federation as the 'Workers Front'. On 7 August 1936 the NAC put its proposals to the Labour Party, the Communist Party and the Co-operative Party, but received no support. The 'Workers Front' hung fire; it was revived in 1938 when the 'People's Front' began to solicit the aid of non-Socialist groups.

The election of Popular Front governments in France and Spain and the outbreak of the Spanish Civil War made 1936 the decisive year for the Left. Any lessening of Fascist activity might well have led to complete confusion among the differing advocates of 'Unity'. As it was the campaign for Communist affiliation continued smoothly and support for 'Unity' grew rapidly in the Labour League of Youth and in local Labour Parties. The central position which the Communists occupied in these campaigns was a result of their international connections, which made them appear as the principal opponents of Fascism. In Britain, their insignificance was overcome by the long agitation for affiliation to the Labour Party. This presented the Communists as a part of the federal Labour movement, and made it necessary for sections of the Labour Party to give serious consideration to Communist aims and activities. Communist sympathizers like John Strachey saw Communist affiliation as 'the indispensable foundation stone upon which a Peoples Front for Britain can alone be built'.[18] Even G. D. H. Cole, far more critical of the Communists than Strachey, could not see 'any sharp line which marks off British Communists from other British Socialists'.[19] The Socialist League, which, it will be remembered, had deliberately kept out of the United Front, accepted the need for Communist affiliation at its Annual Conference on 1 June 1936. Several Trade Unions agreed to support the Communist application, among them the Miners' Federation of Great Britain, whose votes made up the bulk of those recorded for Communist affiliation at the Edinburgh Conference of the Labour Party. Even the Fabian Society Executive made a similar decision, though at a meeting held in the middle of the summer and therefore poorly attended. In the Labour League of Youth leading members were actively negotiating for the formal amalgamation of the Young Communist League. Clearly the Labour Party Executive was finding 'unity' a serious problem.

The Edinburgh Conference[20] was the last to be held under the complete trade-union domination which had been noticeable since 1932. In later years the initiative passed to the political wing of the Party, although decisions were, of course, ultimately decided by the union vote. The Edinburgh Conference decisions, particularly on 'non-intervention' in Spain, were widely resented in the Labour movement. The close identification of C. R. Attlee with the Spanish Republican Government, and Herbert Morrison's part in increasing Constituency representation on the National Executive, indicated dissatisfaction even among the moderate Parliamentary leaders. For these reasons the inevitable defeat of the 'United Front' and of Communist affiliation by a predominantly trade-union vote did little to deter the 'Unity Campaign' which grew in direct defiance of the Edinburgh decisions. The two main resolutions on the 'United Front' and Communist affiliation did, in any case, receive half a million votes each and were backed by such important bodies as the Miners' Federation and the Amalgamated Engineering Union. This in itself was sufficient to encourage the Left to continue with its agitation. Despite a speech by Will Lawther for the MFGB, praising the work of Communists in the unions, the majority of union officials were totally opposed to the Communist Party. It was inevitable that affiliation would be rejected. From the Communist viewpoint their campaign had been justified by the vote of 592,000 for affiliation[21] and by the importance which it had given the Party in the eyes of militant Labour Party members.

The Labour Party conference defeated Communist affiliation at the request of the National Executive and with the approval of most union officials other than some in the Miners' Federation and the Amalgamated Engineering Union. Rather than ending the discussion this decision merely began a period of three years during which the issue of 'Unity' was rarely off the agendas of local Labour parties, trade unions and other sections of the labour movement. The Labour leadership also had to face two revolts from among individual Party members which were tackled in organizational terms but which were largely motivated by ideological sympathy for the Left. The Labour Party National Executive had submitted a memorandum on League of Youth organization to the League's annual conference in Manchester in April 1936. It was suggested that the League should concentrate on recreational and educational activities and that the age limit, which had been raised to 25 in 1926, should be progressively reduced to 21 by 1939. This would have forced the resignation of many of the League's leading members who were closely associated with the Communists. Not only did the Manchester conference reject the memorandum with only one dissenter but it went on to request:

> that Conferences of the Labour Party League of Youth be empowered to freely discuss and record decisions upon policy.[22]

The National Executive submitted a report to the Edinburgh Conference in October including new rules for the League of Youth. These repeated the proposals of the earlier memorandum and in addition recommended the disbanding of the National Advisory Committee, the suspension of the 1937 League conference and the replacement of the *New Nation* by a bulletin for League branches prepared by the National Organizer's office. This would have reduced the League of Youth to a simple ancillary of the Party, entitled to discuss organizational matters but not empowered to formulate any collective view on current issues. The University Labour Federation failed to carry its motion to reject the report.[23] The concessions granted to the League since 1929 were finally withdrawn in 1937 when the League representative on the National Executive was dismissed.

A less obtrusive movement of opinion, which was to have an important effect on the balance of forces within the mass Labour Party, was the demand for organizational changes which would increase the voice of the Constituency Parties on the National Executive. After the Hastings Conference of 1933 an Association of Constituency Labour Parties was projected by members who were dissatisfied with the preponderance of the trade unions.[24] The aim was to separate the individual membership section of the Party from the unions and to set it up in a relationship reminiscent of that with the ILP before 1932. Instead of local Parties being affiliated separately the constituencies as a whole would be able to form a collective opinion in the same way as national trade unions. The Labour Party warned against taking part in any such movement which obviously threatened to disturb the balance maintained at Party Conference by the union block vote.

In 1936 the National Executive Committee rejected a number of proposals to change the party Constitution, most of them inspired by the Constituency Party Association.[25] After the Edinburgh Conference, in November 1936, a Constituency Party Association conference was held in London at which representatives of local Labour parties supported the demand that they should be free to elect the Constituency representatives on the National Executive without the unions being involved. A provisional committee was formed with Stafford Cripps as chairman, to hold unofficial conferences confined to local Party delegates at which this demand would be pressed. This was so successful in London and the South-East that by the middle of 1937 there existed something like a parallel system to the official machinery. Through Cripps the campaign became linked with those favouring 'Unity' of the Left. Thus both in the League of Youth and in the expanding local parties, the Left was able to feed on resentment against organizational restrictions which were largely designed to prevent the expansion of the Left within the Labour Party. The constituency agitation had far-reaching consequences. For the first time local Labour parties were given some sense of common identity, which had been lacking on the political wing since the disaffiliation of the ILP. Although only a minority of parties were favourable to the Left, it was that minority which was most active at Party conferences and in political propaganda in the country. In the South, where Labour was not so deeply influenced by trade-union traditions, the local parties were becoming an increasingly coherent pressure group with a common outlook and a tendency to look outside the Labour Party and towards the Communists for ideological guidance.

CHAPTER 9

Appeasement and the War

There was a perceptible movement of opinion away from the National government in the two years before the outbreak of war, but there was no landslide to the Labour Party. The general election which should have come by 1940 seemed unlikely to lead to the return of a majority Labour government but it was postponed because of the declaration of war on 3 September 1939. Throughout the war there operated a 'political truce' in accordance with which each major party agreed not to contest seats formerly held by any of the others. The few Communists, Fascist and Stop-the War candidates who ignored the truce were badly defeated until towards the end of the war when the newly formed Commonwealth began to win seats which might otherwise have gone to the Labour Party. In some cases the Left opposed the 'electoral truce', causing difficulties within local Labour Parties.[1] While there seems to have been a major but largely unmeasured swing to Labour during the war, the pre-war electoral situation revealed no great reaction against the National government.

Nor was Baldwin troubled with the industrial unrest which culminated in the General Strike during his first administration. The Depression and the decline of the Distressed Areas made a return to such unrest very unlikely. Not until 1937 was there anything like the industrial unrest of the 1920s and this took place mainly outside the traditional centres of militancy. The London Transport strike of 1937 was an unofficial protest by the Communist-led Busmen's Rank and File Movement against agreements reached between London Transport and the busmen's own union, the Transport and General Workers.[2] On the Nottinghamshire coalfield the strike at Harworth against the breakaway 'Spencer Union' was also led by

Communists and ended with the imprisonment of one of their leaders, Mick Kane. After 1932 it was not until 1937 that three million working days were again to be lost in industrial disputes, compared with 162 million days in 1926 and an average of 24 million days per year between 1918 and 1926.

Neither in the industrial nor the electoral sphere, then, was there any measurable and widespread opposition to the National government. On the other hand there was a great surge of Left-wing sentiment in the political and intellectual life of the labour movement. Only gradually was the distaste of the Left for the National government shared by any appreciable section of public opinion.[3] After the war the majority of the electorate reversed its previously favourable attitude to the National government and that process probably began soon after 1941. Yet in the late 1930s there were few signs of it happening. The growing influence of the Left among middle-class intellectuals did not correspond to increasing militancy in the working class nor to growing anti-Conservatism among the voters. Left influence was sustained increasingly by events overseas, events over which most Labour supporters felt they had little control and which most of them probably saw as secondary to their still-lingering economic burdens. The Left became increasingly middle-class and this reinforced the already strong opposition to it among trade union officials. The Communist Party, although still working-class in its leadership, encouraged middle-class radicalism, almost abandoned any claims to be a revolutionary party and dedicated all its energies to supporting the foreign policy aims of the Soviet government. It was thus able to draw on the large reservoir of latent discontent among Liberals and the intellectuals which had been only slightly touched by the problem of unemployment and which was completely cut off from the syndicalist traditions of working class militancy in the previous decade.

The Spanish Civil War and 'appeasement' became symbols of British official weakness and treachery for the intellectuals, as in other Western democracies. The most heavily publicized campaign was that of the Aid Spain Committee which organized the British Section of the International Brigade and the sending of 'food ships' and medical supplies to the Republicans. Although the work of this Committee was almost entirely organized by the Communist Party, it was supported by most of the labour movement. While intellectuals secured most publicity for their support of Spanish Republicanism, the International Brigade drew many of its members from areas which were traditionally Left, particularly Scotland and South Wales.[4] Spain united the Left because it represented a real struggle between Fascism and the Left, more vital than the battles against the British Union of Fascists in the streets of London. Apart from the religious issues which sometimes confused Catholics[5], only one factor weakened British Left support for the Spanish government. This was the growth of Communist influence at the expense of other parties in the *Frente Popular*. In May 1937 street fighting had broken out in Barcelona and was used as an excuse for outlawing the 'Trotskyist' POUM, not in fact Trotskyist but a breakaway from the Spanish Communist Party in close touch with the British ILP.[6] By 1938 the Communist Party had so entrenched itself through the use of Soviet aid and advisers that it was able to force the resignation of Prime Minister Prieto and to improve its position in the Cabinet.[7]

Despite the genuine idealism of those who fought and agitated for the Republicans, the role of the Communist Party aroused some doubts on the Left. The Communists had been the leaders of the Aid to Spain campaign in Britain, raising as much support as the combined efforts of the Labour Party and the TUC. Nevertheless, many on the Left could not fail to notice the consistent attempts of the Party to benefit from the Civil War. Fred Copeman, leader of the British Section of the International Brigade, wrote:

> By allowing Party politics to gain the ascendancy over the popular front, the slogans changed from 'All for Spain' to 'All for the Party'.[8]

Doubts about Communist motives in Spain would have been submerged under the general enthusiasm for the Republic, had not doubts about Soviet Communism been growing at the same time. Bolshevik leaders, tried in Moscow throughout 1937 and 1938, claimed to have been under direct orders from Trotsky and in contact with the German and Japanese governments. The Left watched those they had known as leaders of the 1917 revolution admit to being 'fascist agents', and to 'habitual and base betrayal of military secrets to a certain hostile fascist power'.[9] The effect of the Moscow trials is difficult to gauge from the immediate reaction. D. N. Pritt, at the time a member of the Labour Party National

Executive, gave a pro-Soviet report based on his observations at the 1936 trial.[10] The Friends of the Soviet Union, a Communist organization with some influence, repeated the official charges against the accused. But the Moscow trials dampened a great deal of Left-wing enthusiasm for the Soviet Union. The Moscow trials shattered the notion of a totally good Soviet Union confronting a totally bad Nazi Germany. This had been a central theme of Left propaganda, appealing to a movement which had always tended to think dichotomously. Support within the Labour Party for united action with the Communist Party slackened considerably after the results of the trials become known.[11]

Events moved so rapidly in 1939 that the Left in Britain could do little but point to the complete breakdown of the National government's foreign policy. On 23 August 1939 this feeling was fortified by an event quite unforeseen on the Left and, indeed, by many others. The Soviet Union and Germany signed a non-aggression pact and Soviet propaganda against Fascism completely ceased. Since the end of 1937 the British Left had supported the formation of a triple alliance between Britain, France and the Soviet Union, an object clearly desired by the Soviet government. After the occupation of Czechoslovakia in March 1939, the British government finally accepted the necessity of gaining support from the Soviet Union. But by then the Soviet Union no longer had any faith in the sincerity of a government which it believed had encouraged Fascism for many years. Molotov concluded the parallel negotiations which he had been conducting with German representatives and thus secured two years grace while partitioning Poland with Nazi Germany.

In view of the internal difficulties of the USSR and the apparent indifference of the British government this course was not altogether surprising. But it shocked the Left which had come to regard the Soviet Union as the only genuine opponent of Fascism. Pritt blamed the National government which did 'not desire either an end of Fascism or a genuine reciprocal pact with the USSR'.[12] On the outbreak of war one week later, the Communist Party hesitated and then reversed its support for the war into an appeal for a 'people's peace'. This convinced all but the Party members that the Communists had abandoned their previous opposition to Fascism and simply removed the core of the alliances built up during the Unity campaigns. The Soviet invasion of Finland on 30 November

1939 completed the disillusionment and produced a strong reaction in the Labour Party against Communism and the Soviet Union.[13]

International politics had come to be a formative influence on the thinking of the British labour movement. Pacifist idealism received a permanent setback. It was no longer possible to see the world as developing towards socialism and international harmony. The belief in the inevitability of progress, which had dominated most Labour thinking, disappeared under the impact of Fascism. The Left had always emphasised the influence of power politics and capitalism as forces leading to war and in the 1930s this attitude was revalidated. The Left, like most people in Britain, had been brought up to regard Britain as a world power and had not adjusted to Britain's real weakness. The Left identified the struggle against the National government at home with the world-wide struggle between Fascism and the Left; they saw the Soviet Union as the heart of the 'progressive forces' and the Left at home as its loyal support. This attitude was sustained until August 1939 by the converse attitudes of many on the Right of Conservatism, who clearly sympathized with Hitler and saw him as a bastion against Bolshevism both in Germany and in Spain.

In every respect Britain's foreign policy was a failure: it failed to do anything which would strengthen the declining influence of the League of Nations; it failed to prevent the alliance of Italy and Germany; it failed to stop German expansion, and in the last resort, it failed to prevent the agreement between Germany and the Soviet Union which neutralized the Eastern Front for nearly two years. Most significantly, in terms of British politics, the National government failed to convince informed opinion that it was genuinely concerned about the spread of Fascism. The Labour Party in parliament, most Liberals and, of course, the Left were all opposed to the basic principles behind the government's policy, if such could be said to exist. The failure of the Opposition to provide a constructive alternative in no way exonerates the National Government. Even the consistent opposition to any form of appeasement maintained by Ernest Bevin, Walter Citrine and Hugh Dalton, wavered at the time of the Spanish Civil War in the direction of 'non-intervention'. Everyone quite rightly feared the coming war. The Left was often unrealistic to the point of silliness; it failed to appreciate that the USSR was a power with interests of its own which it would pursue, regardless of the feelings of Soviet supporters in Britain. But the Left did at least sense that Fascism presented an imminent threat to Britain and this is more than can be said for some of those holding the responsibility for Britain's foreign policy and ultimate defence.

Chamberlain's appeasement aroused the concerted attack of such varied elements as the Labour and Liberal Parties, the Left and Churchill's followers among Conservatives. It was taken by the Left as final proof that the National government was, as Cripps had once argued, 'National Fascist'.[14] The Left argued that 'the mere fact of the Chamberlain Government being overthrown and replaced by a Labour or People's Government would be a defeat for Hitler and Mussolini'.[15] This attitude gave further urgency to Left campaigns against the government who were seen as worse than the old-style Conservatives. By 1937 'appeasement' had become a term acceptable to supporters of the National government. While recognising the ultimate necessity of making a stand against German threats to British interests, *The Times* called for 'a supreme effort ... to do what is possible for appeasement before that point is reached'.[16]

The Left suspected that important people in high places were more active in support of Fascism than even the policy of 'appeasement' would suggest. The existence of open support by some Conservative MPs for Franco, the association in the 'Link' and the Anglo-German Fellowship of National supporters with the German Ambassador, Ribbentrop, and the activities of the 'Cliveden set' made such suspicions plausible.[17] The Left believed, and there is little evidence to the contrary even after 30 years of 'revisionist' history, that the National government was willing to make concessions out of all proportion to those necessary and that it was supported by influential people who were quite willing to see Hitler at war with the Soviet Union. After Munich, however, even many Conservatives became disturbed at the failure to halt German expansion and some of the Left, encouraged by the Communists, found themselves seeking alliances with old enemies like Churchill or Lloyd George on the basis of common opposition to Chamberlain's foreign policy. Distrust of the motives of the National government prevented the Labour Party and the Left from supporting measures such as rearmament and conscription which were the logical outcome of the failure of 'appeasement'. Criticism of the illogicality of the Opposition must take into account the complete collapse of faith in the government by the end of 1938. Left agitation against 'appeasement' and rearmament, however contradictory, expressed sentiments widespread in the country by 1939, sentiments which led to the repudiation of the government's foreign policy, either explicitly or implicitly, by leading members of all three major political parties.

When the war finally came in September 1939, the Left had almost burned itself out in frustration at Chamberlain's foreign policy and amazement at the Hitler-Stalin pact. Czechoslovakia, a democratic state with a mass socialist and trade-union movement, had been handed to the Nazis by the National government, which now expected the labour movement to support a war for Poland, a society much less attractive to democrats let alone socialists. It had been argued on the Left that wars were caused by the search for profits, by imperialism, by militarism. On the other hand the pacifist position that war was a consequence of human nature was also still widely held, even though pacifism had been politically defeated within the labour movement on the Left. The great bulk of Liberal and Marxist writing about war had presented it as an activity which no radical could support and which all must fight to prevent. The Left tradition was reinforced by the belief that the war would not have broken out had the Chamberlain government done something to prevent it, a view held by many who had nothing to do with the Left. Thus they blamed Chamberlain as well as Hitler for the war. The dilemma of being forced to support a British government which was hated, against a German government which was hated even more, was not resolved by the formal declaration of war on 3 September 1939. The Left tradition incorporated within it memories of war resistance between 1914 and 1918, in which many leaders of the Labour Party had joined.

In one important respect, however, the situation in 1939 was not the same as in 1914. The Left had fought against fascism since 1933 and had organized support for the Spanish Republican armies since 1936. Pacifism had been abandoned as a means for dealing with fascism and Lansbury was widely ridiculed for his 'mission to the dictators' which some on the Left saw as little better than Chamberlain's visit to Munich. The Left was psychologically equipped for the reality of war, which had not been the case in 1914. Then it had held out against a wave of patriotism among a public which was totally unaware of the reality of modern warfare, never having been touched by it. In 1939 nearly everyone had a direct or indirect memory of mass warfare and mindless patriotism was much less important than a conscious commitment to the idea that aggressive fascism could not be stopped by any method short of war. The Left was ready for war but bound by its tradition to react against it. This dilemma was compounded by the fact that the Soviet Union was not engaged in the war and was also occupying Poland, selling oil to the Nazis and deporting German Communists back to Hitler's concentration camps. The British Communists and the large group of supporters they had built around them could not sidestep the problem.

Between September 1939 and June 1941 the Left almost ceased to exist as a unified force. Its major field of operations, the Labour Party, was restricted by the wartime electoral truce and by the rapid decline in Labour Party individual membership caused by conscription, evacuation, bombing and the virtual suspension of normal electioneering. Its cohesion was shattered by the rift between those who accepted the Communist line that the war was 'imperialist' and should be ended and those who retained their previous belief that fascism could only be defeated by armed opposition. There was little room for compromise between previous allies, especially as the Labour Party took advantage of the situation to discipline and expel all those who publicly sided with the Communists.[18] Within the Miners' Federation and the Amalgamated Engineering Union, which had been centres for anti-war activity in 1916, the Communist position still received some support. Ernest Bevin's entry into the wartime coalition made it even less likely than before that the bulk of trade-union officials would tolerate the Communists let alone support them. After June 1941, however, the Communist Party built a powerful position within the unions on the basis of support for the war, industrial peace and the maximisation of output. Between 1941 and 1945 it created a following for itself which has never been equalled since and certainly did not exist at any time prior to 1941. The Communists were able to benefit from the war, both in the political Left and in the unions. By doing so they tied their fortunes even more firmly to the popularity of the Soviet Union, placing a series of time-bombs under themselves which began exploding in 1947 and 1948.

CHAPTER 10

A Communist-Led Left

Despite official Labour Party opposition, united Left campaigns continued in various forms until 1939. Whatever the consequences for the other participants, there can be little doubt that the Communist Party benefited in strength and influence from these joint activities. At the Party's Fourteenth Congress, held at Battersea on 29 May 1937, Pollitt reported that membership had increased to 12,500, nearly twice that at the previous Congress in 1935.[1] The average circulation of the *Daily Worker* had risen from 30,000 to 70,000 in the same period, while at weekends and on special occasions sales of over 100,000 had been achieved. The 'sectarian mistakes' of the past were being overcome. The Party was even making some slight electoral progress. Fifty-four members had been returned to local councils while in certain local authorities, notably the Rhondda Urban District, the Communist vote had approached that of the Labour Party. While the electoral strength of Communism was still infinitesimal in contrast to that of the Labour Party, it was greater than for the past decade. In the London County Council elections of 1937 the Party 'went all out to secure a Labour victory'.[2] Communist offers of help were accepted by many local Labour Parties, though Herbert Morrison and the London Labour Party made considerable efforts to discourage them. In the November election of 1937 the Communists declared that 'certain seats are being contested independently, but nowhere where so doing would endanger Labour seats'.[3] In this election Phil Piratin secured election to Stepney borough council – the first Communist to be elected in the Metropolitan area since the 'Labour-Communist' candidates of the early 1920s.

The new policy of the Party was reflected not only in its

increased strength but in its composition. Despite electoral concentration in mining South Wales and Scotland, nearly one half of the
Party membership came from the London area. The preponderance of clerical workers, Party officials and students in the Congress
delegation of 1937, though not necessarily representative of
proportions within the Party, indicates the transformation from the
days when over 60 per cent of the members and delegates had been
unemployed. Three thousand members were added in a year.[4]
Even more indicative of the solid support which the Party hoped to
achieve in the future was the weekly circulation of 20,000 copies of
Challenge, paper of the Young Communist League. The Party was
continuing to appeal to those who, in the past, had been regarded
as least sympathetic to the labour movement.[5] The Communist
Party was able to maintain its progress throughout 1939, having
passed through the longest period of continuous growth in its
history. Just as it was consolidating its gains, however, the Party
was forced to make another somersault, which largely destroyed
the advantages it had secured through the various Unity campaigns.

   In contrast to the organizational success of the Communists, the
fate of the Independent Labour Party had already been settled by
1935. It had become a narrow, word-spinning sect. In 1937 its
Annual Conference gave support to the formation of a 'Workers
Front', a coalition of socialist groups for specifically radical
objectives. Three months before, the ILP had signed the Unity
Manifesto with the Communists and the Socialist League. The
resulting Unity Campaign had concentrated on anti-fascism rather
than on a definite programme. The ILP regarded this as a negative
approach and by the middle of 1937 the Communist Party was
complaining of the impossibility of continued co-operation
between the two parties.[6] As it drew away from the Communists,
the ILP leadership became more sympathetic to the Labour Party
which was also criticizing the Popular Front for its inclusion of
non-socialists. At the 1938 ILP conference a resolution was carried
by 55 votes to 49 'to approach the Labour Party for the purpose of
securing the maximum common action against the National
Government, united action on class issues and an electoral
understanding'.[7]

   After discussions in the Divisions and the preparation of a
Report by the NAC, the Easter Conference of 1939 decided by 69

votes to 40 to re-affiliate to the Labour Party, provided certain conditions were accepted. Immediate re-affiliation without conditions was only defeated by 63 votes to 45. The ILP Members of Parliament, with the exception of Maxton, led the movement for re-affiliation. Although the Scottish Division defeated re-affiliation by 88 votes to 6 at its Conference in February 1938[8] the MPs continued to press for a return to the Labour Party. In July, McGovern, supported by Campbell Stephen, had openly stated the necessity of such a return if the ILP were to continue as a significant organization.[9] George Buchanan joined the Parliamentary Labour Party in April 1939. Maxton was faced with the prospect of being the only remaining ILP Member if he did not withdraw his continued opposition to re-affiliation.

The ILP Parliamentary Group had been out of sympathy with the party on two important issues, the Abyssinian War and the Munich agreement. Maxton had surprised the Party by welcoming the agreement, though he made it plain that he did so out of relief that war had been averted. 'Is it not clear that our MPs have flagrantly broken the declared policy of the Party?' asked a London Division statement calling for the disciplining of the Parliamentary representatives. McGovern, too, was involved in a controversy over his attitude to the Spanish Republican Government. The Party had adopted the principle of complete control over its Parliamentary spokesmen, but the stage had been reached where the MPs were prepared to re-enter the Labour Party rather than be instructed on their actions. The original cause of disaffiliation, ILP control over its parliamentary group, was now proving to be disruptive to the Party. Realizing the futility of isolation, many of the Party members were prepared to reverse their earlier decision to leave the Labour Party.[10]

The ILP had shrunk to a small faction by 1940, its only significance being that it was well represented in the Commons. The controversy over affiliation had grown out of all proportion, driving the party into an isolation which neither its leaders nor its members really desired. Similarly, the United Front policy had been pursued despite its damaging effect on the Party. There were only a few realists in the ILP who appreciated that it could not function independently of the Labour Party. Only the Communist Party, with its rigid discipline, could survive alone. By 1939 it had completely replaced the ILP as the dominant minority on the Left.

The spread of Communist ideas and influence among the middle classes and among the steadily expanding constituency Labour parties, was achieved much more rapidly than in the past. The tide of ideas on the Left was flowing in the Communists' favour and they did not have to resort to the often artificial tactics of 'penetration' used since the early 1920s. Many on the Left positively sought out Communists and espoused Communist ideas without being enticed, misled or coerced. The elaborate network of 'sympathizing mass organizations' built up through the Comintern by Willi Muenzenberg was not only maintained but rapidly expanded. Communists joined almost any organization which was prepared to have them and some secretly enrolled in local Labour parties from which they were ostensibly excluded.[11]

The Communists used both direct and indirect methods to contact supporters in other sections of the labour movement, suiting their tactics to the situation. The ultimate aim remained the winning of Party members and their public 'coming over' to Communism. During the Popular Front period it was comparatively simple to attract people to organizations with apparently acceptable aims, later persuading them to become Communists.[12] The Party was able to accommodate the scruples of those who worked with it, while at the same time securing new members with some political experience. This was a primary function of the 'sympathizing mass organizations', which looked like liberal reforming societies, but were invariably managed and funded by the Communist Party. The Communists were also able to take advantage of groups which had leaders only too willing to co-operate with the Party and to draw on its growing network of organizers and activists. Such arrangements were mutually beneficial, although there was always a tendency for the Communist influence to increase at the expense of other less cohesive groups.

The clearest example of a mass organization which voluntarily worked with the Communists, while independently organised and funded, was the Left Book Club. The Left Book Club was primarily an educational body with a political purpose. An introductory leaflet claimed that:

> The aim of the Club is a simple one; it is to help in the terrible urgent struggle for World Peace and a better social and economic order and against Fascism, by giving (to all who are

determined to play their part in this struggle) such knowledge as will greatly increase their efficiency.[13]

The Club was launched in May 1936. Its books were selected by Professor Laski, John Strachey and Victor Gollancz, the publisher.[14] Local Clubs were formed to discuss the topics raised in the monthly selection. Eventually these clubs broadened into miniature 'Unity Committees', bringing together Labour and Communist intellectuals and middle-class people who would not otherwise have exchanged views in such an organized manner.

In assessing the effect of the Left Book Club on the Left it is important to consider the amount of Communist influence in the Club and in its books. The Economic League report on *The Present Trend of Communism in Britain* alleged that 'the Communist Party has made full use of the Left Book Club, enabling it for the first time to make effective contact with some 50,000 members of the middle class'. The Independent Labour Party, critics of Communism from another angle, shared this view. In 1937 Fenner Brockway wrote that 'from the outset the Left Book Club has been recognisable as an instrument of Communist Party policy'.[15] Of the books chosen by the selectors a high proportion were written by Communists. But there were surprisingly few non-Communists capable of writing popular works within the broad limits of the Club's aims. Only *The Labour Party in Perspective* by C. R. Attlee could be held to represent the official views of the Labour Party and Trade Union movement.[16] From August 1937 the Club operated a price-reduction agreement with Lawrence and Wishart, who had a virtual monopoly of Marxist-Leninist publications and of works by the leading members of the British Communist Party. The Left Book Club was serving to publicize Communist ideology. In fairness to its selectors one must stress the virtual absence of any important body of writing expressing an alternative Left viewpoint. The Labour Party began its own Book Service at the end of 1939 in an attempt to provide the alternative, but its efforts were hindered by the war and could not attract a fraction of the readership achieved by the Left Book Club.

Despite its claim to be an educational body, the Club could not escape the charge that it was taking an organized part in politics. Gollancz had indeed proclaimed such an aim at the Club's second Rally in January 1938.

We have to find a way to utilise our fifty thousand members as an educational and propaganda machine.

His aim was 'the drafting through the Clubs, and particularly the groups, of formerly "unpolitical" people into active political work'.[17] By September 1938 the Club had established one thousand local groups which were actively supporting the United Peace Alliance campaign. In the following month it distributed two million leaflets on the Munich crisis, following this up in December with ten million leaflets on the Spanish Civil War. The Club had become of political significance, and as its support for the Peace Alliance was unacceptable to the Labour Party it was inevitable that there should be some conflict between the two. Herbert Morrison attacked the Club in the December 1938 *London News:*

> There is ample evidence that the Left Book Club, through its groups, has become a political movement with substantial money behind it, and that one of its main activities is in the direction of manipulating and controlling local Labour Parties.[18]

The expulsion of Cripps from the Labour Party in 1939 increased the probability that the Labour Executive would take action against the Club, which had publicized his 'Unity Memorandum', though not officially supporting it. G. R. Shepherd, the Labour National Agent, wrote to local Labour Parties in March 1939, warning them against close liaison with the Club:

> Since groups of the Left Book Club are not entitled to affiliation with constituency parties, joint political activities with them should not be entered into, especially when these are in the direction of a so-called 'Popular Front' with any other political party.[19]

The Labour Party took no action against the Club, and with the coming of war the Communist sympathies of the Club's leaders rapidly disappeared. Arthur Woodburn, Secretary of the Scottish Labour Party, articulated the view of many moderate elements in the Party when the Club suspended its activities in 1941:

> It is sad to think that, building its philosophy upon the shifting sands of Communist policy, it was foredoomed to disaster. Had it been broad enough to have included the purpose of the great

organised movement its contribution could have been of historical value.[20]

Nevertheless the Book Club was of great importance in spreading Left ideas. *Left News*, the Club's monthly paper, was an important political journal in its own right. After September 1938 the Club had control over a section of *Tribune*, the weekly paper supporting the Unity Campaign. The Left Book Club was a unique development in Britain, providing a high standard of political literature at a price which ensured its circulation to a wide audience. Nearly three million Left Books were published, providing much of the basic political reading during the war. Undoubtedly this contributed to the Labour electoral victory in 1945 and to the increased participation of middle-class people in the work of the Labour Party.

Communist influence also grew rapidly among the small section of young people organized in political youth and student groups. In 1938 Young Communist League membership stood at 4,500 compared with a total Party membership of 16,000, while at the Birmingham Congress of that year 226 of the 539 delegates were under the YCL age limit of 30.[21] The advance made by the Young Communist League was paralleled in the University Labour Federation. The ULF had been founded in 1920 but remained a small organization affiliated to the Labour Party in 1934 on a membership of only three hundred. In 1932 a number of independent student groups, dominated mainly by the Communist Party, had formed the Federation of Student Societies and this group was accepted into the ULF at its Cardiff conference in January 1936. During that year membership doubled to 3,000, reaching 4,000 by 1939. The University Labour Federation was particularly active in supporting the Spanish Republicans, sending several of its leading members into the International Brigade.[22] Socialist and Communist influence in the universities increased rapidly, one fifth of the undergraduates at Oxford and Cambridge being enrolled in the ULF in 1939. The University Labour Federation was the only socialist society affiliated to the Labour Party which not merely allowed, but encouraged, Communists to become members. On 1 May 1937, the National Executive of the Labour Party warned the Federation that it would be automatically disaffiliated within a month if it did not alter its constitution. The ULF decided to follow the 'contracting in' system of the Trade Unions, allowing non-members of the Labour Party to remain in the Federation without being able to decide the ULF representation at the Party's Conferences. As the National Executive had made its objection on constitutional and not political grounds, it accepted this decision though the support of the ULF for the United Front continued. The Federation was, in any case, the undisputed representative of the Left at the Universities and the Labour Party would have been ill-advised to disaffiliate it while its opinions were so popular and widely accepted.

Youth organizations were making rapid progress, and it was not long before the National Executive decided to re-organize the Labour League of Youth. The majority of branches were still in existence, though without any co-ordinating machinery. The disbanded National Advisory Committee re-formed unofficially in December 1936 as a National Activity Committee, controlling its own journal *Advance* and organizing the League as far as was possible without official Party sanction. It seemed likely that many isolated sections of the League of Youth would merge into the Young Communist League if the national organization were not restored. An unofficial conference of League branches was held in Islington on 8 May 1937 under the Chairmanship of Ted Willis, editor of *Advance*. This called for the withdrawal of the National Executive memorandum abolishing the League's national organization. The Labour Party Conference in October agreed that a meeting of League branches should be held 'to discuss the future of the League' and, early in the following year, most of the national machinery was restored and a Youth Officer appointed. At the official League Conference which met in London in March 1938, policy discussion was allowed on certain topics relating to the problems of young people. In May the National Executive decided to give official recognition to *Advance* which, since its foundation in December 1935, had risen from a local circulation of a few hundred to a sale of 15,000 reaching the entire membership of the League.[23] The National Executive had recognized, temporarily, most of the organizational demands put forward in the paper since its foundation.

The London Conference of the League had been attended by Sir Stafford Cripps representing the National Executive of the Labour Party. His influence as leader of the 'Unity Campaign' increased rapidly in the League. When the National Executive expelled Cripps for his part in the 'United Peace Alliance', it attacked him for his influence in the League. In February 1939 all national and regional committees were disbanded and the League Annual Conference was cancelled after the National Advisory Committee had declared its support for Cripps and his Petition Campaign. In July, Willis and some of his NAC colleagues left the League to join the Young Communist League. The outbreak of war put an end to the possibility of reviving the League of Youth, though a sub-committee of the NEC was created to do so. The ILP Guild of Youth also collapsed at the beginning of the war, the NAC feeling that 'members of the Guild should function through the Party'.[24] The University Labour Federation came into open conflict with the Labour Party at the beginning of 1940 when it was proscribed by the National Executive.

By 1937 the Communists were almost completely dominating the rest of the Left, both organizationally and intellectually. Within the Labour Party and the unions the Communists had still made little progress, and their electoral impact remained negligible. Pacifism was in retreat and the moralistic socialist alternative once favoured by the ILP was largely assimilated into Communist ideology. There was an 'alternative Left' surviving mainly among the ruins of the ILP and in the Labour League of Youth which was generally described as 'Trotskyist' by its opponents in the mainstream of the Left. For such a tiny group, the true Trotskyists had considerable influence. Discontent with the policy of the Communist Party and its tactics in the United Front had grown in the ILP to an extent which caused many of its remaining members to adopt the theoretical arguments of Trotskyism while resenting its organized activities. The Communists reacted by attacking 'the half-Trotskyite ILP, a party that loves to talk of revolution and to shriek out "Left" phrases on every possible occasion'.[25] Even discounting the Communist attacks, however, the attitude of the ILP was now similar to the Trotskyist viewpoint on many issues, particularly on the domestic and foreign policy of the Soviet Government.

Despite their small numbers, the Trotskyists managed to create two organizations in 1937 to work within the Labour Party as they had done within the ILP. The Militant Labour League continued within the Labour Party until its proscription in March 1940 for opposing the war. Through its publication, the *Militant*, it opposed

United Front tactics on the one hand and the policy of the official Labour Party leadership on the other. The Militant Youth League, which was attached to the MLL, followed the same policy within the Labour League of Youth. The group was never strong, but it often provided the only opposition to the pro-Communist *Advance* group in the League. Thus at the unofficial Islington conference of May 1937, the twelve Trotskyist delegates were repeatedly the only opponents of the platform's policy.[26] 'The Youth Militant supporters must be seen in their true light of splitters and disrupters and cleared out of the youth movement,'[27] urged John Gollan, secretary of the Young Communist League, after the Conference. Nevertheless the Trotskyist viewpoint was again presented at the March 1938 Conference of the League of Youth.[28]

The Trotskyist movement reflected the traditions of the pre-Revolutionary Russian Socialist groups, from which it seemed to draw much of its inspiration and terminology. Groups were continually dividing over minor points of doctrine. The most important point at issue was the tactic of infiltration which had led to several splits in the American Socialist Workers' Party, the dominant group in Trotsky's Fourth International. Early in 1938 several Trotskyist groups came together in an attempt to form a unified British section of the Fourth International. So deep was the division on the 'entrist tactic' that the unified body reached the compromise of working within the Labour Party for a period and then withdrawing for a time and continuing independent activity. After six months the group broke up, despite letters from Trotsky and a visit from J. P. Cannon, secretary of the American organization. The Militant Labour League remained within the Labour Party, while the Revolutionary Socialist Party, the Workers' International League and the Revolutionary Socialist League remained independent. New splits came in 1939 when the signing of the Soviet-German Pact and the outbreak of war created a major division in the American Socialist Workers' Party.[29] During the first year of the war most of the Trotskyist groups in Britain collapsed and the Fourth International recognized the Workers' International League as its official section.[30]

The proscription of the Militant Labour League by the Labour Party in 1940 put an end to the 'entrist tactic' (or 'French turn') for a time. Trotskyists drew closer to the ILP again in opposition to the war, making full propaganda use of the Communists' rapid change in policy in September 1939 and June 1941. The policies of the ILP had lost it much support but in its opposition to the war and to conscription it regained some of its influence on the Left. In January 1939, a No Conscription League was formed to oppose the National Registration Bill. By the beginning of 1940 the League had secured the affiliation of nearly seven hundred groups, mainly Co-operative and trade union, with an aggregate membership of 250,000. Its leading officials were Will Ballantine of the National Union of Railwaymen, and Fenner Brockway, both ILP members, and it maintained a close liaison with the Party. The League and the ILP worked jointly to establish the Central Board of Conscientious Objectors, and combined with representatives of the Peace Pledge Union in sponsoring Anti-War candidatures.

The Trotskyist and pacifist groups which continued to oppose the war only had the power to attract Left support between late 1939 and 1941. The Communists were at variance with all their previous allies and there was room for an alternative viewpoint. But there was to be no repeat of the growing anti-war movement of 1916. The Communists became the most active supporters of the war and were able to revive their previous connections on the Left as well as to capitalize on the rapidly increasing resentment against the pre-war Conservative Party. Almost the only significance of Trotskyism in the 1930s was that a tenuous tradition was established which was not to materialize as a significant political influence until the 1960s. By the end of 1941 it looked as though the Communists and their supporters had established the monopoly over the Left for which they had been striving since their foundation. They had done so by being in the right place at the right time, for the first and last time in their history.

CHAPTER 11

From Unity Campaign to Peoples Convention

The Edinburgh Labour Party Conference decision did not deter the supporters of 'Unity', though it ended the campaign for Communist affiliation for the next three years. Despite a Labour Party circular of 12 January 1937, warning against joint activities with the Communists, the Socialist League decided four days later to take part in a Unity Campaign with the Communist Party and the ILP. Stafford Cripps, who had occupied the leading position in the League for the past four years, was particularly enthusiastic about the proposed campaign. However the League conference at which the decision was made was seriously divided. Opposition to the proposed Campaign received 38 votes to the 56 for the successful motion. Opponents were concerned with the future of the League, rather than with the ideological implications of working with the Communists. A Trotskyist group, led by Reg Groves, was particularly afraid of 'sacrificing the Socialist League's position in the Labour Party'[1], thus repeating the objections to working in the United Front which had been made by leaders of the League in past years. To a large extent the Unity Campaign was passing out of the control of the Socialist League into that of the Left Book Club and the weekly *Tribune*, founded by Cripps in January 1937. The formal agreement of the League was, however, necessary as it gave the campaign a much closer connection with the Labour Party than if it had appeared as a personal crusade by Cripps. Without the organization and membership of the three parties to the Unity Agreement, the Campaign could not hope to make any more impression than previous actions of the same sort. Maxton saw the Agreement as 'the answer of the three most politically conscious and informed workers Parties in the country to a very widespread demand for unity that has been felt by every working class spokesman who has faced audiences during the last two years'.[2] By formalizing agreement between 'the three organisations representing the most advanced Socialist workers'[3] it was intended to make clear that the Campaign was a continuation of the United Front on a sounder basis. It was not, as its critics asserted, meant to presage an alliance between the Left and the Liberals.

The Unity Campaign was officially launched at the Free Trade Hall in Manchester on 24 January 1937, when Cripps, Maxton and Pollitt spoke on the points raised in the Unity Manifesto, issued six days before.[4] Although the Unity Manifesto had been signed by Pollitt, Dutt, Gallacher, Tom Mann and Arthur Horner on behalf of the Communists it was essential to stress that there was no intention of setting up a rival to the Labour Party. At the Albert Hall rally of the Left Book Club on 7 February Pollitt assured the audience of seven thousand that the Campaign was 'not directed against the Labour Party', but that its whole aim was to 'strengthen, revivify and revitalise the Labour Party'.[5] The Manifesto had called for 'Unity of all sections of the working class movement' for 'the return of a Labour government', and 'Unity within the framework of the Labour Party and the Trade Unions'. Its signatories were all closely associated with the Communists, the Socialist League and the ILP and, despite the growing interest of some Liberals, the theme of 'working class unity' was deliberately dominant. As Professor Laski wrote:

> The signatories to the manifesto ask that the leadership of the campaign be undertaken by the Labour Party. They seek to fight within its ranks. They believe that with this unity a Labour Government becomes directly into view as the next stage on the road to working class power.[6]

The Unity Campaign could hardly avoid the accusation that it was creating a new organization to invite Labour Party members to work together with Communists, which every Labour Conference decision had forbidden over the previous ten years. Unity Campaign Committees were established after the official launching of the Campaign at Manchester. They were based in the main on constituency Labour parties although Communists and, for a short time, members of the ILP worked within them. A National Unity Campaign Committee was responsible for co-ordinating local efforts and organized the speaking tours of Cripps, Maxton, Pollitt, Bevan and other prominent supporters of united agitation against the National Government and its foreign policy. The Labour Party took immediate action. Its circular of 12 January drawing attention to the decisions against united action taken at Southport, had been ignored. On 27 January, three days after the official launching, the National Executive Committee disaffiliated the Socialist League, making it 'ineligible for affiliation' two months later. The Socialist League was a small organization with only three thousand members. Moreover it was confined to members of the Labour Party, its first rule stating that 'all members are expected to become individual members of their constituency Labour Parties'. The voting at the special January conference of the League had shown considerable disagreement with adherence to the Unity Manifesto.

If the Unity Campaign was to have any effect its links with the Labour Party had constantly to be underlined. The Party had now disaffiliated the Socialist League, announcing on 24 March that its members would be automatically expelled on 1 June. Officially the Labour Party remained hostile to the Campaign, suggesting that it was a Communist-inspired attempt to reach agreement with the Liberals. It further characterized the Campaign as being the personal machine of a few wealthy men, particularly of Strauss, Strachey, Cripps and Gollancz.[7] The Independent Labour Party was also suspicious of what it termed 'the "Popular Front" political line of the Left Book Club'.[8] The ILP had gained two important concessions during the drafting of the Unity Manifesto. A laudatory reference to the foreign policy of the Soviet Union had been excluded and the Manifesto expressed opposition to the National Government's proposals for rearmament. Nevertheless the ILP representatives on the Unity Campaign Committee were constantly in friction with the Communist Party over the tendency to encourage non-Socialists to join the Campaign. Fenner Brockway's conception of the 'Workers Front', limited to 'working class parties', was adopted at the ILP Conference at Easter 1937, and the ILP began to draw away from the other participants in the Unity Campaign. The Communists meanwhile continued to deny that the Campaign Committee was moving towards an understanding with the Liberals. Although Liberals like Sir Richard Acland were becoming identified with the Campaign, the Communists remained hostile to Lloyd George and his Five Point Group.

The Unity Campaign made considerable progress when compared with the old United Front. By the beginning of March 13,000 signed 'Pledge Cards', supporting the Unity Manifesto, had been received by the Campaign Committee. Mass meetings were the central feature of the Campaign, and the Committee was able to draw on the services of Cripps, Maxton, Pollitt, Bevan or Strauss, and virtually every prominent figure on the Left of the Labour movement. The six platforms at the 1937 United May Day Rally in Hyde Park contained, altogether, eleven members of the Labour Party, ten members of the Communist Party, three from the ILP, and a foreign Socialist. Significantly for the future, there were also five religious speakers, including among them the Dean of Canterbury, Hewlett Johnson. Large amounts of money were collected for the Campaign, while the Communist Party was able to supply many full-time workers for the Committee's various activities.

The greatest obstacle to the progress of the Unity Campaign was the opposition of the Labour Party. The placing of the Socialist League on the 'proscribed list' meant the elimination of one of the three sponsoring bodies. Members of the League and supporters of the Unity Manifesto had repeatedly called for 'Unity within the framework of the Labour Party'. The League had little alternative but to disband and thus allow its members to continue their campaign within the Labour Party as individuals. At its Whitsun Conference, therefore, the Socialist League unanimously passed the decision to dissolve itself. Immediately after the disbanding, the Labour Executive turned its attention to the Unity Campaign Committee. Executive circulars on 9 and 22 April had drawn attention to Conference and Executive decisions against Party members co-operating with or speaking from the same platform as members of the Communist Party. A further circular was sent on 26 May 'calling upon all members to refrain from any further joint activities with the Communist Party and the ILP'. In view of the threat of expulsions contained in these circulars, Labour supporters of Unity had to reconsider their position. George Strauss had already been threatened with expulsion for welcoming support from the Communists during the London County Council elections in March. Speaking at Hull on 6 June Stafford Cripps outlined the new tactics which were to be followed by the Unity Campaign Committee. From that date a National Labour Unity Committee was to organize the campaign within the Labour Party, while the Communists and the ILP would carry on separate agitations on their own. Brockway, Dutt, Gallacher, Jowett, Maxton and Pollitt for the Communists and the ILP appealed for support for the new committee. The leadership of the organization within the Labour Party remained with Cripps, Strauss and Mellor, all of them still fully committed to the Unity Manifesto.

The Unity Campaign was officially transformed into the Labour Unity Campaign with committees limiting their members to Labour Party subscribers. As the campaign became more unpopular with the National Executive its organization became less clearly defined and its control by Cripps and his friends more informal. The Labour Unity Campaign Committee statement issued for 'Unity Sunday' on 18 July 1937 called on 'all supporters of unity to put the utmost energy into the work of rousing the Labour Party membership to the need for immediate struggle for the demands listed in the programme and to lead the revival campaign by their example of practical work'.[9] In effect the Unity Campaign was already seriously weakened. Of the three signatories to the Unity Manifesto one had disbanded, the ILP was not too enthusiastic and, as usual, only the Communists remained. The Labour Party National Executive took care to refute the argument put forward by Cripps at Hull that there was no objection to a Unity Campaign within the Labour Party provided it did not involve other groups. An Executive circular of 28 July pointed out that anything in the nature of a campaign for Unity could not be accepted.[10] A crisis within the Labour Party was precipitated in early September when the National Executive refused to endorse William Mellor, editor of *Tribune* and secretary of the Labour Unity campaign committee, as Parliamentary candidate for Stockport. Cripps, Laski and Strauss, who had been booked for a speaking tour in 'Labour's Crusade Week', refused to continue their tour until Mellor had been endorsed. The National Executive consequently arranged for other speakers to take their place.

The Bournemouth Conference of the Labour Party was faced with a serious problem. The Constituency Parties Association, of which Cripps was Chairman, had gained the active support of nearly half the constituency Labour Parties for its proposed revisions of the Party Constitution. On this issue the National Executive reversed its previous attitude, allowing separate voting for

Constituency representatives on the Executive. This concession led
to Cripps and Laski joining D. N. Pritt as 'Unity' supporters on the
Labour NEC. The Party's policy on Spain had also been radically
altered amid the great enthusiasm which was felt over the
resistance of the Republican Government. The Unity Campaign
had been identified with both these changes in Party policy, and,
moreover, had greatly enlivened the Party's activity during the
year. The National Executive issued a statement on the Campaign,
pointing out that 'its object is to bring the Communist Party and
the ILP within the Labour Party. Members of the Labour Party
who are taking part in this Campaign are acting in clear defiance of
repeated and emphatic decisions of the Annual Conference of the
Party'.[11]

Cripps, speaking on behalf of the East Bristol Labour Party,
moved the reference back of this section of the Executive Report
but won only 331,000 votes against the 2,116,000 votes for the
National Executive's condemnation of the Unity Campaign. The
Campaign had not been successful in influencing the Trade
Unions, possibly because it had been officially characterized as an
individual agitation by a few wealthy members. Moreover the
Party had adopted a progressive policy and had made concessions
to the Constituency Parties. The Bournemouth decision made it
clear that the Unity Campaign's success had been more apparent
than real. The leaders of the Campaign, and Cripps in particular,
felt that 'the Unity campaign has played its part. All the energy and
drive which gave to that campaign so electric a character in the first
weeks of this year must find outlets for the same fundamental
objectives in new, and yet familiar channels. We of the Left must
work to make our Party the spearhead of struggle against Fascism,
against War and against the National Government'.[12] This was to
be done through the Constituency Parties, 'the chief instrument of
Socialist propaganda in this country in future'.[13] On 16 October
1937, the National Labour Unity Committee circularized all its
branch committees, winding up the organization. They had concluded that 'a campaign for organisational unity is not, in the light
of the Conference decisions, within the ambit of Party loyalty'.[14]

The aim of the Unity Campaign was propaganda within the
Labour movement. Its appeal to radical Liberals and to the middle
class offered the possibility of forming an electoral alliance between
the main Opposition parties in the General Election which was

due to be held by 1940. The Peoples Front was 'not based primarily on parliamentary or electoral combinations'.[15] Yet its supporters could not fail to realize the possibility of attracting a section of the Liberal Party, which was still a Parliamentary force. The diverse elements which had caused a triple split in the Liberal Party in 1931 were still represented in the official Party. Most Liberals were opposed to the Labour Party let alone to the Communists, but there was an important radical wing of the Party which was attracted by the Peoples Front idea. The original object of the Peoples Front Propaganda Committee had been to attract 'the co-operation of the scientist and artist, the writer, dramatist and philosopher',[16] that is the groups least interested in the industrial aims of Socialism. The Left Book Club had appealed to such people. There was thus a concrete possibility of creating a Peoples Front in Britain which would take advantage of the opposition to the National Government to be found outside the labour movement.

The Communist Party had originally been opposed to such a proposal. But the spread of Communist ideas in the middle class had caused the Party to modify its approach. At the Albert Hall Rally of the Left Book Club in February 1937, 'Mr Harry Pollitt said there was a new awakening among the middle classes and they had to rope these people in rather than keep them out'.[17] The Party was gratified that 'these seekers after peace, democracy and socialism are being brought together'.[18] The Central Committee was already considering the wider implications of the Unity Campaign. Its primary aim was to 'bring to the working class the fundamental idea of their own strength and power'. Eventually it was hoped to attract 'great masses of people now outside the movement who are seriously concerned at the present state of the world ... They would ally themselves with the united Labour forces and afford the possibilities of developing a mighty Peoples Front which will bring down the National Government.'[19]

Four or five years before, the Communist Party would have advocated revolution 'to bring down the National Government'. Now it was accepting the democratic method to the extent of reaching agreement with Liberals or even Conservatives. The Party had become extremely conciliatory, still trying to attract those who were quite opposed to its philosophy. They had been instrumental in ending co-operation with Labour Party members when this had been demanded by the Labour National Executive.[20] When Cripps had abandoned the Unity Campaign to support the Labour Party's *Immediate Programme* his action had been fully endorsed by the Communist Party. They were still interested in affiliating to the Labour Party, though under the Labour Party rules this could not be reconsidered until 1940. 'The Communist Party wants unity in the interests of the Labour movement as a whole', wrote Harry Pollitt. 'Quite concretely the Communist Party wants to discuss with representatives of the Labour Party the difficulties which they consider stand in the way of the realization of this unity and of the Communist Party becoming affiliated to the Labour Party'.[21] For the moment the issue of affiliation was subordinated to that of forming an electoral alliance against the National Government.

'Unity' was redefined by Pollitt at the Second Left Book Club rally on 16 January 1938. The *Daily Worker* described the audience as 'middle class'. It was to this section that Pollitt appealed:

> We believe first of all the shock troops of the Labour Movement, the Radicals within the Liberal Party, the forces who want peace and not to become doormats for Hitler and Chamberlain to walk upon, and the members of the Left Book Club – have all to engage in organised effort to bring about Unity. The interests of the overwhelming majority of professional people, small business men, shopkeepers and farmers are bound up with the social progress of the Labour and Democratic Movements.[22]

This new form of Unity was to be concerned with foreign policy issues, virtually to the exclusion of the domestic policies contained in the original Unity Manifesto. It was to include those who were not within the Labour movement. In all essentials it embodied the proposals put forward by the Peoples Front Propaganda Committee and by G. D. H. Cole in previous years. In a manifesto published in the Co-operative paper *Reynolds News* on 20 March 1938, this projected coalition was referred to as the 'United Peace Alliance'. Its aim was the creation of a triple alliance between Britain, France and the Soviet Union to restrain Nazi Germany. It was implied, rightly as it happened, that such a policy was unlikely to be acceptable to the National Government and that a broad alliance must be formed in Britain to replace the Chamberlain administration. An important body of support was secured to the alliance by the decision taken at the Annual Conference of the Co-operative

Party by 2,343,000 votes to 1,547,000 to endorse the *Reynolds News* manifesto. In addition to that newspaper the idea of an electoral alliance against the government was being canvassed by the *News Chronicle* and the *Manchester Guardian.*

The Labour Party showed some signs of softening in its attitude to the supporters of the new form of Unity. The National Executive Committee reported in favour of reforming the Labour League of Youth, disbanded at Edinburgh for its support of the United Front. The University Labour Federation had been allowed to carry on active propaganda for Unity after being threatened with disaffiliation. The leaders of the Party, particularly C. R. Attlee, were actively campaigning for 'Arms for Spain', a complete reversal of the attitude adopted at Edinburgh. An officially sponsored Labour Party Spain Committee ran an agitation against the Non-Intervention Pact which culminated in a Rally in the Albert Hall at the end of 1937. On 31 March 1938, the Committee issued a Manifesto supporting the right of the Republican Government to purchase arms. The Spanish Civil War was producing a stronger antagonism to Fascism and the National Government than had previously existed in the Opposition.

The apparent trend to the Left in the Labour Party was in keeping with the political atmosphere of the times, but it was not strong enough to force the abandoning of official opposition to any form of the Unity Campaign. The National Executive of the Party circularized its answer to the requests received to join an alliance with the Co-operative, Liberal and Communist Parties, on 12 April 1938. Fear of the Communist 'Trojan horse' was still present in the minds of the Executive, though it was now coupled with a desire to assert the Party's independence from allies on the Right as much as on the Left. From attacking the Communists as undemocratic, the Executive moved to attacking the Liberals as non-socialist. In doing so it probably aroused some sympathy among the Party membership, though it could not prevent a movement which was receiving support from national figures.

The adherents to the Peace Alliance had to undergo a serious reorientation in their political attitudes. Cripps, for instance, admitted that he 'was bitterly opposed to any such alignment a year ago'. He still saw the Alliance 'as a temporary co-operation to save democracy and peace' in which 'the Labour Party should take the lead'.[23] The aim of the United Peace Alliance was deliberately broad, ignoring most of the social and economic demands which were the central feature of all previous 'Unity' campaigns. The Labour Party was still expected to take the leading part, an agitation being started for an emergency Labour Conference to discuss the Alliance. Dissident Conservatives, for instance Churchill or Eden, were not welcomed as prospective allies, because of their expressed hostility to the Soviet Government and their lack of sympathy with the Spanish Republicans. On the other hand, the Duchess of Atholl, a Conservative who had been active in support of the Republicans, took a leading part in the Alliance.

A General Election was expected during the next two years, but already there were signs that the Peace Alliance was preparing to test its strength among the electorate. Though the history and sentiments of the Labour Party were totally against 'Lib-Lab' candidates, it was not long before the idea of formal electoral alliances was being canvassed. R. T. Paget, Labour candidate for Northampton, wrote to *Tribune*, suggesting that the Liberal candidate in the Aylesbury by-election should be given Labour support against the National candidate.[24] In reply the Secretary of the Bucks. Federation of Trades Councils and Labour Parties warned: 'We shall not achieve a Socialist Commonwealth by compromise of this sort.'[25]

The Labour candidate, Reg Groves, went ahead with his campaign, increasing his poll considerably but still not replacing the Liberal as runner-up to the successful National candidate. Peace Alliance supporters, and the Communists in particular, were annoyed that the opportunity for a joint candidature had been lost. A Communist leaflet had painted the terrifying picture of Groves as 'a Trotskyist agent' carrying out 'disruptive policy in Mid-Bucks'.[26] The Labour Party, on the contrary, welcomed the result, feeling that it had been vindicated by the considerable impression made on a difficult seat.

Unrest at 'class collaboration' was an important element in antagonizing many Labour Party members against the latest development in the campaign for Unity. It was to this sentiment that the National Executive appealed in its statement *Labour and the Popular Front*, published in May 1938. The Executive did not believe:

that the proposed combination would afford a better rallying cry, or be more effective electorally against the 'National' Government than the Labour Party itself. Such a view underestimates the growing strength of Labour in the country as indicated by recent by-elections. It fails to take account of the diminishing force of the Liberal Party.[27]

As for the Communist Party, the Executive repeated its belief in the complete inadvisability of associating it with the Labour Party in the public eye. 'The presence of the Communists would bring some few thousand votes to the alliance; but it might well drive millions into Mr Chamberlain's camp.' By associating with the Liberals and the Communists the Labour Party would only split its ranks and disillusion its supporters. Were the Alliance to be successful, the NEC held that it would produce a weak government like that in France. The electoral agreement which Peace Alliance supporters proposed 'would have less electoral appeal than a united and independent Labour Party'. The only circumstances under which it would be possible to remove the National Government were those which actually arose in May 1940: 'A new situation might arise of course, if any considerable number of Members of Parliament now supporting the Government, were to rebel against the Prime Minister's authority'. The Labour Party rejected the United Peace Alliance, though with more reasoned argument than had been used in dismissing the United Front on previous occasions.

Unlike the preceding Unity Campaign the agitation for a United Peace Alliance had no formal organization and only a tenuous connection with the organized Labour movement. Its leading figures remained the same however, though the ILP was replaced by the radical Liberals as the third partner. The intensity of factional dispute had vanished but the Alliance suffered from the weakening of its links with local Labour Parties. Left Book Club groups were capable of immense effort on occasion, but they could not reach as wide an audience as the Local Parties and were unsuited to the work of winning over Labour opinion by consistent effort. Many in the Labour movement were prepared to admit that without a strong combination forcing the National Government out of office 'we may not get a chance for a very long time of putting into effect our ultimate aims'.[28] On the other hand it was difficult for others to see 'where the Alliance would benefit the

Labour Party ... the working class as a whole'.[29] The refusal of the Co-operative Congress to support the campaign indicated diminishing sympathy with the Peace Alliance. The Congress was more representative of the movement as a whole than the Co-operative Party which, despite its vast nominal membership, was in reality much smaller in individual membership than the Labour Party.

The Left Book Club continued throughout 1938 as the unifying force behind the United Peace Alliance. Its rallies on Spain, addressed by Cripps, Gollancz, Kingsley Martin and D. N. Pritt, culminated in a national gathering at the Queens Hall, London, on 17 October. Its mass circulation of leaflets on Munich and Spain surpassed anything undertaken by a political party between elections, while its one thousand local groups worked closely with Constituency Labour Parties. The Club controlled a section of *Tribune*, Gollancz eventually replacing Mellor on its editorial board. Officially the Left Book Club did not favour any specific proposals for a Liberal-Labour alliance, but in effect its influence was directed towards this end. In this activity it was enthusiastically supported by the Communists, who had dropped all their previous objections to the 'class enemy'.

In October 1938, a second attempt was made to secure a united opposition to a National candidate, this time with more success than at Aylesbury. The Constituency Labour Party at Oxford allowed A. D. Lindsay to contest the seat as a 'Progressive', withdrawing its own candidate, apparently under pressure from University Labour opinion. Lindsay was actually a member of the Labour Party, but was not its official candidate. He reduced the Government majority by half, providing an incentive to further 'Progressive' candidatures.[30] At Bridgwater, in the following month, Vernon Bartlett, a Liberal supporter of the 'Peace Alliance', was elected as a 'Progressive' in what had been a National seat. The Labour Party was weak in this rural constituency and had no prospective candidate and hardly any organization. The Left Book Club once again took a leading part, organizing canvassers from surrounding areas, including Cripps' Labour stronghold in East Bristol. Gollancz held that 'had there been no Left Book Club there would have been no Bridgwater'. Although Bartlett's vote was predominantly Liberal the result restored some of the waning popularity of the Peace Alliance. Immediately after the by-election Richard Acland took the responsibility of acting as 'secretary for

Progressive candidates'. It seemed as though the next General Election would see agreements between Labour and the Liberals in several constituencies. Once again, however, the Peace Alliance was out of touch with a strong sentiment within the Labour Party. Acland was a Liberal MP, and in the three attempts to secure a 'Progressive' candidature the official Labour Party machinery had been bypassed.

In normal circumstances 1939 might have been election year. Any electoral agreement with radical Liberals would have produced an embarrassing position for the Labour Party. Stafford Cripps continued to stress that such an alliance was made inevitable as much by the policy of the Labour Party as by the growing danger from Nazi Germany. The Party had modified its opposition to the Government's rearmament programme and the Left felt that this had inhibited the campaign against Chamberlain. 'No one in the Labour Party', wrote Cripps, 'wants to encourage the forming of any sort of combined Opposition if it can be avoided – that is to say, if the Labour Party can show itself strong enough to give the lead to the anti-National Government forces and to be a real and effective Opposition to that Government'.[31] He had become alarmed by the attempts of a group in the Conservative Party to form a New Progressive Group with 100,000 supporters.[32] The group was led ostensibly by Duncan Sandys and the Progressive MP, Vernon Bartlett, but Winston Churchill was widely believed to be behind the movement. The Communists had gone so far towards accepting any ally that the *Daily Worker* expressed hopes that 'this may prove to be a new, broad democratic movement, based primarily on the youth of the country'.[33] However, the tone of the Group meeting in January 1939, although critical of the National Government, was clearly out of sympathy with the pro-Soviet sentiments of 'Unity' supporters. Two days later the Communists saw the new grouping as an 'essentially disruptive organisation which can only hinder the development of unity between existing political parties and organisations against the Chamberlain Government'.[34] Cripps had already taken this view of the New Progressive Group.

The new group did not in fact achieve its target of 100,000 pledged supporters and had faded away by March. Yet its appeal to youth had greatly concerned Cripps, whose influence with the Labour League of Youth had become considerable. He once again submitted his proposals to the Labour National Executive favouring a United Peace Alliance and electoral agreement. His memorandum, delivered on 9 January 1939, repeated previous arguments and drew attention to the weakness of the Labour League of Youth and the difficulty of gaining a majority at the next General Election. The Executive met four days later and rejected the memorandum by 17 votes to three.[35] Cripps had tried to answer the criticism that he was abandoning Socialism by making special reference to the need for the Party to retain its principles should it join any alliance. Despite this the Executive attitude was unchanged, its composition being exactly the same as when Cripps' earlier proposals had been discussed in 1938.

Cripps and his followers were once again in conflict with the National Executive on the familiar topic of the most effective way of opposing the National Government. In contrast to previous campaigns, in which he had kept within the limits imposed by the Executive, Cripps decided to take his proposals direct to the Party membership in defiance of official decisions. On 18 January he circularized all sections of the Labour Party and the Press, and launched into a revived campaign for the Peace Alliance. At its meeting on 25 January the National Executive agreed to a statement surveying Cripps' 'past campaigns waged over a long period', 'his wide departure from the Party's Programme, Principles and Policy', and his 'organised effort fundamentally to change the Party's direction and leadership'.[36] In conclusion the Executive requested Stafford Cripps:

> to reaffirm his allegiance to the Labour Party within the meaning of the Constitution, Programme, Principles and Policy of the Party, and to withdraw his Memorandum by circular to the persons and organisations to whom it was addressed. Failing compliance with these requests Sir Stafford Cripps should be informed that he no longer fulfils the conditions of membership of the Labour Party, and that in consequence he will be excluded therefrom.

Cripps had no alternative but to refuse the conditions laid down by the Executive. To accept them would have meant a complete recantation of all his actions over the past five years. On 28 January he was expelled from the Party, to be followed later by several prominent supporters of his campaign.

The Labour Party leadership was concerned with the prospect of fighting the General Election with an unwelcome and embarrassing group of 'progressives' unofficially allied with its candidates. Cripps had implied in his memorandum that the Party had little chance of gaining a Parliamentary majority without Liberal allies. He had repeated once more that the central position in the Peace Alliance belonged to the Labour Party 'for not only is it the largest opposition party, but it represents the essential core for any progressive alliance – the working class'.[37] The element of continuity with previous Unity campaigns was thus preserved and the Cripps Memorandum received support from basically the same groups and individuals who had supported him on previous occasions. But it no longer seemed possible to capture the imagination of a wide section of the Labour movement. Electoral alliances were not favoured in the Party, and the radicalism of local Labour Parties was of a different character from Liberal radicalism.

The Petition Committee, set up in February to gain support for the memorandum, appealed to the Labour, Liberal and Co-operative Parties, for the 'parties of progress to work together'. Its programme was brief and it was circulated in the form of points from a petition to the three 'progressive' Parties. The Petition called for the defence of democracy, a 'Plan for Plenty', the signing of a Peace Alliance with France and the Soviet Union, the control of vital industries, protection against air attack, and a plan to 'Build for Peace and Justice'.[38] This collection of demands gave the widest scope for an agitation against the government on several issues thought to appeal to radical Liberals and Left Labour alike. Although the Communists actively supported the campaign it was based on markedly less radical demands than the Unity Manifesto of 1937. However it was thought by its sponsors to represent a programme which had some possibility of acceptance by the bodies to which the petition would be presented.

The Labour Party showed no signs of accepting the points made by the Petition Committee. John Marchbanks of the NUR, representing an active Right Wing minority in the Party leadership, saw the campaign as an attempt at 'engineering the break up of the Labour Party, and paving the way to the creation of a new party, in which Liberals and progressives of all political shades will be enrolled'.[39] The majority of the National Executive did not go as far as Marchbanks but warned several of the leading participants in the Petition campaign that disciplinary action would be taken against them (as against Cripps) if they continued in their support for it. As a result of this warning Will Lawther of the Miners' Federation, and C. Poole, Member for Lichfield, withdrew their backing at the beginning of March. Sir Charles Trevelyan refused to withdraw or to curb his activities in any way and was consequently expelled from the Party. Seven Labour MPs, Aneurin Bevan, S. O. Davies, J. Parker, C. Poole, M. Phillips Price, George Strauss and B. Riley had sent a letter to the Executive protesting against Cripps' expulsion and were supported by a number of Parliamentary candidates. The National Executive wrote to the four signatories and supporters who were most closely identified with the Petition campaign, Bevan, Strauss, Cdr Young, and W. Bruce, asking them to discontinue their support for the campaign or face expulsion from the Party. The four wrote to enquire how they could best put forward their views inside the Labour Party. In his reply the National Agent, G. R. Shepherd, summarized five forms of action which 'amount to unpardonable disloyalty against a democratic movement'. The basic objection to any continuation of the campaign was its organized nature, based on the 'creation of machinery with staffs and offices throughout the country'.[40] It was made clear that no campaign of any sort was to be allowed and, on their refusal to accept this decision, the four members were expelled. The Labour Party had now lost two of its most distinguished 'intellectuals', two of its most active Members of Parliament and two prospective candidates, in an effort to suppress the idea of an electoral alliance before the General Election.[41]

Prior to the Party's Annual Conference the National Executive once again disbanded the Labour League of Youth, which had given official support to Cripps' memorandum. The National Advisory Committee of the League had taken part in the 'Youth Pilgrimage' of 18 February, a predominantly Communist demonstration in favour of the Cripps petition. Even after the Committee had been disbanded, the officially sponsored League Conference had called for its re-formation and supported participation in the National Youth Campaign, an offshoot of the Communist-controlled British Youth Peace Assembly. The National Executive had taken rigorous action, reimposing all restrictions imposed in 1936. The Party Conference at Southport at Whitsun was thus presented with the most drastic series of measures taken against the Left since the Edinburgh Conference. Cripps had asked for permission to appeal against his expulsion. The National Executive at first refused this, but eventually left the decision to the Conference delegates. By 1,227,000 votes to 1,083,000 he was allowed to speak, but by general agreement failed to make the most of this opportunity.[42] Cripps dealt with the constitutional rights of Party members, rather than with the items contained in his memorandum. The final result of the debate, in which Cripps was attacked largely on personal grounds, was the confirmation of his expulsion by 2,100,000 votes to 402,000.

The Peace Alliance campaign was virtually dead, lingering on in the remnants of the Labour League of Youth, and in the Communist Party. In the last stages of the drift to war, the United Peace Alliance seemed rather futile. In no circumstances was the bulk of the Labour Party prepared to be allied with groups which were clearly not as influential as they had been in the past. Most of the members clung to the view that 'the Labour Movement is more than an anti-Fascist Party.... It stands for a positive policy – Socialism at home and internationally'.[43] Although the Labour Left may have considered this official conversion to Socialism somewhat belated, it was attracted to the Peace Alliance only in so far as it represented a continuation of previous Unity campaigns. In its last stages the Alliance was essentially a revival of Liberal radicalism emphasizing foreign policy. The Peace Alliance had, as a result, attracted support from a variety of national figures, but had not been so successful in the organized Labour movement. At a Petition meeting in February 1939, the Alliance platform had included Cripps, Strauss, Acland, Paul Robeson and, finally, Lloyd George. Yet less than half a million votes were cast to keep Cripps inside the Labour Party, far fewer than were cast three years earlier to accept the affiliation of the Communist Party.

The various campaigns for 'Unity' after 1936 were increasingly devoted to agitation on foreign policy in the hope that war could be averted. On the outbreak of war the original components of the Peace Alliance and the Unity Campaign scattered in different directions. The ILP and the extreme Left advocated 'war resistance', becoming more sectarian than ever. The most important Labour supporters of 'Unity' gave modified support to the war effort, though they were highly critical of its conduct by Chamber-lain and of the political truce which prevented the running of candidates in previously Conservative seats. When the coalition National Government was formed in May 1940, much of this criticism subsided, except for that maintained by Aneurin Bevan and by *Tribune*. The Liberal radicals and 'Progressives' were eventually brought together by Sir Richard Acland into the Commonwealth Party in 1942, where they provided the only effective electoral opposition to the wartime government.

For their part, the Communists completely reversed their line, earning the permanent hostility of many of their former allies. Just as war began the Communist Party had published a short pamphlet *How to Win the War*, which outlined the Party's continued opposition to fascism and its intention of participating in the war effort. This was the obvious sequel to its policy for the past four years.[44] After communication with the Comintern, however, a majority of the Party leadership decided to reconsider its attitude to the war, which was declared an 'imperialist struggle' to be opposed by the Party. Pollitt and J. R. Campbell were removed from their Party positions on 11 October. On the following day a statement was made in the *Daily Worker* embodying the Comintern declara-tion and correcting the previous statement of policy. On 23 November, Pollitt and Campbell withdrew their support from the initial statement and were readmitted to their positions. For the next eighteen months the Party ran a campaign for a 'People's Government and a People's Peace', setting up a People's Conven-tion to popularize this slogan in the labour movement. Bitter criticism of Communist policy was continually expressed in previously favourable journals like *Tribune*. The principal non-Communist supporters of the Unity Campaign joined in writing a book, *The Betrayal of the Left*,[45] in which they repudiated the Communist attitude to the war. John Strachey, who though not officially in the Communist Party had worked assiduously for it since 1932, was a significant contributor to this volume.[46]

The Communist Party, after its reversal of policy in October 1939, tried to keep the idea of 'Unity' alive through the People's Convention. A People's Vigilance Committee was created in 1940 to fight against the 'imperialist war' and for some of the social measures originally incorporated in the Unity Manifesto. It was a successor to the pre-war campaigns but the central core of anti-fascism had been removed. Formed on the initiative of D. N. Pritt, MP, who had just been expelled from the Labour Party, its main support came from the Communists. Its appeal was to 'the workshops and the mines ... the Trade Union branches and the Co-operative organisations, all groupings and associations of the wider mass of the people'.[47] The Committee's activities culminated in the summoning of a People's Convention on 12 January 1941.

The Communist Party, though it gave full facilities to the People's Vigilance Committee in the *Daily Worker* and *Labour Monthly*, continued to deny that the Convention was entirely inspired by the Party. Neither the Labour Party, the Left contributors to *Tribune* nor the pacifist elements centred around the ILP were prepared to believe these protestations. The Labour Party officially viewed the Convention as 'an attempt to build up a new Political Party',[48] and indeed it is not improbable that the Communists, fearing illegality, were preparing a new organization on United Front lines into which they could merge if necessary. The German invasion of the Soviet Union, however, made the Convention redundant.

The Unity campaigns of the late 1930s ended with a very pathetic whimper indeed. The Labour Party was able to take advantage of current sentiment to settle all its old scores with the Communists; to expel Pritt and the University Labour Federation; to declare the Trotskyist groups 'ineligible for affiliation'; and, by 1944, to make it constitutionally impossible for the Communists ever to affiliate with the Labour Party or for the ILP to reaffiliate. The Unity campaigns therefore failed in their ostensible task, the unification of the diverse elements on the Left. Organizational unity was a remote prospect as long as the minorities refused to merge their identity into that of the Labour Party. What did emerge from the Unity campaigns was a unity of purpose and a common identification. Despite the great differences between the constituents of any Left alliance, they all shared a common fund of ideas and phrases inherited from common radical predecessors. The Communists were linked both historically and ideologically with the Left of the Labour Party. The radical Liberals had certain basic similarities of outlook with the intellectuals in the Labour Party, particularly with those interested in foreign policy. Even the ILP had sufficiently strong links with the past to wish to co-operate with the rest of the labour movement where possible.

'Unity' was essentially an emotional appeal. From the pages of *Tribune* or the *Daily Worker* it is often difficult to see what concrete results its supporters were hoping for. 'Unity' meant far more than Communist affiliation to the Labour Party or even the creation of an electoral alliance. The campaigns appealed particularly to younger and better-educated supporters of the Labour Party who were bored by the squabbles of the past and who saw no clear dividing line between themselves and the Communists with whom they worked on campaigns. For the first time the Left achieved national significance. With three national newspapers and the *Daily Worker* supporting the United Peace Alliance, and with prominent leaders drawn from two of the three major political parties, the Left was transformed from a factional grouping into something resembling a major influence on public opinion. That is not to say that more than two or three 'Progressive' Members were likely to be returned at a General Election. The electorate remained committed to the established parties. But there is little doubt that the propaganda of the Left in the last three years of the decade did much to awaken public opinion to the ineffectiveness of the National Government's foreign policy, and to the implications of the spread of Fascism.

Within the Labour Party the Unity campaigns led to the creation of a unified Left, with a much clearer idea of its strength than in the past. The Unity campaigns helped to gain acceptance for Left ideas in the political wing of the Labour Party. Through the Left Book Club groups, through the joint activities with Communist Party members and the ILP, through every form of participation in the United Front, individual members of the Labour Party assimilated the ideology of the Left. The shift in emphasis to the Constituency Labour Parties which occurred in 1937 under the influence of Cripps gave that section of the Labour Party a sense of its own importance. They suffered from the disadvantage of centralized control by the official Labour bureaucracy, but they enjoyed the advantage of being the recognized representative of a national party in a given area. From being associated with a number of rather odd bodies, the ideas of the Left were now linked with the local work of the Labour Party as a whole. The success of the Unity campaigns was that they developed from skirmishes on the extreme Left to a campaign involving the entire Labour movement in debate on Left ideas and activities. The weakness of the campaigns was that in searching for temporary allies wherever they could be found the Left broke with the tradition of the Labour movement. According to this tradition independence from the other two major parties was the reason for the existence of the Labour Party.

CHAPTER 12

The Ideology of the Left

The diverse minorities on the British Left can be treated as a whole if it is assumed that they possessed a common outlook and ideology. Such an assumption may seem questionable in view of their frequent disputes. Yet many of these disputes were tactical rather than fundamental. Even the ILP and the extremist groups which came to form a 'lunatic fringe' of the Left, disagreed on tactics rather than on the ultimate aim of converting the Labour movement to radical socialism. Many groups on the Left claimed to be Marxist. All believed that society should be fundamentally reorganized. All were in opposition to established policies and institutions. The Left was primarily oppositionist. Its vision of the future society was either Utopian or was based on an abstract notion of the Soviet Union which bore little relation to reality. Even the Socialist League, which inherited the outlook of the Fabians through the Society for Socialist Inquiry and Propaganda, soon succumbed to the more sweeping philosophy of the former ILP members who led it. The Left played a more effective role in focusing opposition to the policies of the National government than in formulating concrete alternatives. While the Left presented few practical programmes for the immediate present, it moulded the general attitudes of a whole generation of activists and kept alive a radical strand in British socialist thought.

Left propaganda

The propaganda of the Left resembled that of the earlier socialist groups in stressing wrongs rather than remedies. Often a penetrating analysis, like Hannington's study of unemployment, ended on

the note that 'a Socialist order of society' could alone 'bring
happiness, security and peace'.[1] Hannington had more concrete
proposals to offer than intellectuals like Strachey or Cripps.
Strachey tended to adopt the 'inevitability of collapse' argument of
Marxism, while Cripps elaborated schemes of parliamentary and
economic reform which were as sweepingly generalized as those of
the most obscure Left faction. It was against such largely destruc-
tive analysis that J. T. Murphy protested on his resignation from
the Communist Party. He replied to Pollitt, who stood for the
'revolutionary way out of the crisis', that 'the workers demand
bread, we give them a propaganda speech'.[2] The manifest impracti-
cality of many Left slogans and the apparently pointless nature of
the Left's analysis of society repelled many practically minded
trade unionists. The ideological elaboration favoured by the Left
did, however, attract educated middle-class followers, who had
been repelled by the mediocre propaganda of the Labour Party.
Arthur Woodburn, secretary of the Scottish Labour Party, summed
up the attitude of many of the middle-class supporters of the Left:

> There are persons holding important places on the Councils of
> the Labour Party who display only contempt for the student and
> reader type of socialist. These people have antagonised and
> driven into the atmosphere of the Communists, valuable young
> minds which sought for deeper discussion than the day-to-day
> politics of the practical politician.[3]

The contrast between Left propaganda and that of the official
labour movement may be summarized not unfairly as that between
outspoken irresponsibility and dull practicality. The former was
undoubtedly more effective. There are few reliable figures of the
circulation of political pamphlets and journals during the 1930s,
but those which exist suggest that the Left provided the bulk of the
propaganda for a socialist philosophy and more than its fair share
of criticism of the National government.[4] Most of this was confined
within the circle of the politically active. The official labour
movement, through the rapidly rising sales of the *Daily Herald*, had
an important medium of mass communication which was committed to the policy of the official labour movement and, where this
was indecisive, favoured the outlook of the TUC rather than that of
the Parliamentary Labour Party.[5] After the launching of the Unity
Campaign in 1937, the *Daily Herald's* place as leading opponent of

the National government was shared by the Liberal dailies, the *News Chronicle* and *Manchester Guardian,* both of which supported the Campaign's proposals. In *Reynold's News,* the official Sunday paper of the Co-operative movement, the United Peace Alliance had its instigator and mainstay. The Co-operative Party served the Left in its extensive publications and well-funded educational activities. Among other journals which were not organizationally controlled by the Left, the *New Statesman and Nation* was, of course, the most influential. Although its readership was not exclusively interested in politics, the journal had been founded by the Webbs and continued in their tradition. As the Unity Campaigns progressed, the *New Statesman* under Kingsley Martin's editorship became identified more with the sentiments of Left intellectuals. At first it was more favourable to the Popular Front suggestions of G. D. H. Cole and the People's Front Propaganda Committee, than to the Communist-sponsored United Front. Eventually, when events made such modifications irrelevant, many writers in the *New Statesman* took the side of the Unity Campaigns against the official Labour Party. Its appeal was to the same general audience as the Left Book Club and its political line was generally similar by the late 1930s.[6]

By the end of the decade there was considerable support for the Left by sections of the mass media which it did not control, and which reached a much wider and more diverse audience than the Left or even the official labour movement could have hoped for. Official Labour publications were few and dull compared with the propaganda of the Left, although it should be said that many Left publications were not of a high standard either. The *Worker,* official paper of the Minority Movement, was as dull as the worst trade union journal. The *New Leader,* founded as the *Labour Leader* by Keir Hardie in 1889, and reaching over 20,000 readers a week, was rather parochial until its reorganization into an illustrated paper in 1934 temporarily increased its sales to 30,000.[7] The early pamphlets of the Communist Party were not only badly printed but were often incomprehensible. However this changed radically after 1935 and the Party's publications eventually became more attractive in presentation than those of any other political party. Communist publications continued to be subsidized by the Comintern after other direct payments ceased. Such a grant made possible the printing of the *Daily Worker,* first published in

January 1930.[8] The paper continued as the official organ of the Communist Party throughout the 1930s though after its suppression by the Home Office in 1941 it was ostensibly controlled by the Peoples Press Printing Society – a change which made no difference to its policy. The original circulation of the *Daily Worker* was only 10,000 and it was very far behind the national dailies in every respect.[9] Under the able editorship of William Rust it increased its sales to over 80,000 a day by the end of the decade. The *Daily Worker* was read almost exclusively by the Left. Its importance in maintaining the ideological supremacy of the Communists over the less well-equipped minorities cannot be overestimated and was fully realized by the Party leadership. Every Communist knew exactly what to think on any issue because he had a regular interpretation supplied by the *Daily Worker*. Even after the founding of *Tribune* in 1937, no other section of the Left could enjoy such regular briefing.

The pamphlets and leaflets of the Communist Party were the most widely circulated on the Left. In the twelve months prior to the outbreak of war the Party sold nearly 400,000 pamphlets under its own name, while its subsidiaries sold a large additional number. This was considerably more than were sold by the Labour Party. In quantity as in quality the propaganda output of the Left excelled that of the official movement. *Labour Monthly*, though its circulation did not rise above 8,000 until 1940, had an influence among intellectuals shared only by the *New Statesman*. The Communist Party also published a number of local and industrial papers.[10] In fact, at every level the Communist Party dominated Left propaganda media. By the time the Unity Campaigns began, the Communists were already established at the centre of the rapidly growing market for political propaganda.

Apart from the publications of the Communists and the ILP, the Left was not well served with propaganda until after 1936. The Left Book Club began circulating its bulletin to all members in that year, while in January 1937 *Tribune* was founded to represent the viewpoint previously served inadequately by the small bulletins of the Socialist League. William Mellor, secretary of the Socialist League, became the editor of *Tribune* and Stafford Cripps, Aneurin Bevan, Harold Laski, Ellen Wilkinson and George Strauss formed the editorial board. The maximum circulation of *Tribune* rose to 30,000 shortly before the war. Its policy was always closely identified with that of Cripps, whether supporting the Unity Campaign, the United Peace Alliance or the petition campaign of 1939. The paper was well produced and its columns provided evidence that it was widely read in local Labour parties throughout the country. It was a major instrument in helping to spread support for Cripps outside the traditional centres of Left activity in London, Scotland and South Wales.[11]

The Left derived great advantage from the rapid expansion of serious political reading in the 1930s, stimulated mainly by Victor Gollancz and by the newly founded Penguin Books. Anyone who wished to study Fascism, Communism, unemployment, international affairs or any of the major issues of the time, was forced to turn to John Strachey, Harold Laski, Palme Dutt, D. N. Pritt, Sir Stafford Cripps and others on the Left. Though the political writings of the 1930s were on a more sophisticated level, they did as much as Robert Blatchford's *Merrie England* in the previous generation to put across socialism to the reading public. Neither the Right Book Club nor the Labour Book Service could attract a fraction of the attention given to the Left Book Club. There was a gap in British socialist ideology which needed to be filled and a sudden desire to learn about problems which had previously been regarded as exlusively European. The Left became dominant in political writing and it was also able to attract literary intellectuals who wished to use their creative abilities to put across a political message. The Writers International and its journal *Left Review*, established in 1934, helped to spread Left and mainly Communist ideas among professional writers and poets. The Left even had its own theatre, Unity, which was founded early in 1936 in London and also had provincial groups. While it is unlikely that much of this affected the traditional labour movement, it was vital in opening up a new audience for the Left which could not be reached through the unions or through the narrow polemics of working-class politics.

The common ideology

Through its expanding literature the Left developed a fairly coherent philosophy and outlook. Marxism was the unifying force, though interpreted in widely differing ways. 'The world of bourgeois thought is discovering Marxism', wrote Palme Dutt in 1937

and this was temporarily true.[12] Marxism had been introduced to
British audiences by H. M. Hyndman whose Social Democratic
Federation had withdrawn support from the Labour Party because
of the latter's refusal to recognize the class war.[13] Hyndman's
doctrinaire attitudes led to the stagnation of the SDF. It was the
partly religious and emotional appeal of the ILP which dominated
the political wing of the newly formed Labour Party. Marxism had
remained an abstract theory, remote from the Labour Party,
though many leaders including Herbert Morrison and Ernest Bevin
had been attracted to it in their youth. While Marxism became the
orthodoxy of the European labour movement, its influence in
Britain was limited by linguistic and cultural barriers as much as by
the sectarianism of the SDF. With the rise of syndicalism before the
First World War a form of Marxism began to have influence
among miners and industrial workers, particularly in South Wales
and central Scotland. It did not come from Europe, however, but
from the United States through the writings of Daniel De Leon
who inspired the foundation of the Socialist Labour Party as a
breakaway from the SDF.[14] British Marxism became identified
with anti-parliamentary and anti-Labour ideas. The bulk of
Marxists in the SLP and the successor to the SDF, the British
Socialist Party, joined together to form the Communist Party and
continued to be isolated from the mainstream of the Labour Party.
While the rump of the Social Democratic Federation remained
affiliated to the Labour Party and advocated 'revisionist Marxism'
it was of no significance and dissolved in 1939.[15]

As Marxism had been characterized by sectarianism and hostility to parliamentary Labour, its intellectual influence in the 1920s
was very limited. The Labour Party was dominated by two streams
of thought, neither of them sufficiently developed to be called a
coherent ideology. One, found mainly in the ILP, was pacifist and
idealist. Society was to be changed without violence in order to
achieve a better life than was available under industrial capitalism.
The second tendency, developed by Ramsay MacDonald, L.
Haden Guest and Sidney Webb, was based on the 'inevitability of
gradualism'. MacDonald believed that society was an organism
evolving through biological processes into another form.[16] In this
process, necessarily a slow one, the working man was moving
towards a better status with the help of the Labour Party. The trade
union majority in the party was content to accept MacDonald's

approach which seemed to provide a 'scientific' basis for their natural caution. Those sections of the unions which were radically inclined, like the Welsh miners, were still syndicalist rather than Marxist, relying on their own strength to defend their own interests. The Fabians were enfeebled and ineffectual throughout the 1920s but subscribed generally to 'gradualism'.

The defection of the ILP and of MacDonald left an ideological vacuum in the labour movement. In the Labour Party as a whole there was an intellectual ferment which threatened for a time the deeply engrained 'gradualism' of most Labour politicians. Even the active members of the Fabian Society deserted its basic philosophy to consider the whole problem from a new perspective and through a new organization, the New Fabian Research Bureau. Those who formed the Bureau and the Socialist League were trying to find answers to new problems with little guidance from past experience. The Fabian and ILP traditions were discredited to the extent that they had been espoused by MacDonald. Emerging from sectarian isolation, the Marxist Left was able to capture the initiative and to win the widest British support for Marxism achieved in the fifty years following Marx's death. The collapse of 1931 and the passing of the old leaders meant that all the established attitudes of the Labour Party were challenged. For over two years even convinced 'gradualists' like Clynes spoke of socialism in tones which had not been heard since 1919. The Labour Party, moreover, not only had no coherent ideology but it had no developed system of political education. The Independent Labour Party had done most of the work in that area, aided by the Marxist Plebs League (later the National Council of Labour Colleges). Trade-union education officers, where they existed, were concerned with training negotiators and officials. Consequently those active members of the movement suddenly forced to search for a concise socialist ideology turned to the Left. In political education, as in propaganda, the Left forced the pace. In Socialist League meetings, in Left Book Club groups, in Communist Party and ILP schools, the active and particularly the younger members of the labour movement argued out their attitudes to politics on new lines. Marxism seemed to many of them to provide answers which had not been known to the MacDonald government. It also seemed to assist in understanding Fascism, a new phenomenon which few in Britain understood, including the leaders of the Labour Party and of the National Government.

British Marxism in the 1930s was a relatively unsophisticated ideology. The *1844 Manuscripts* and the *Grundrisse* were unknown and there was no discussion of alienation or indeed of the philosophical development of the 'young Marx'. European Marxists were untranslated and nothing was heard of Gramsci, Lukacs or the Frankfurt School. Rosa Luxemburg remained a name, praised by Trotskyists and by the Left of the ILP but otherwise ignored. Marx was seen as essentially an economist with a theory of capitalism which explained the Depression. Engels was the founder of 'scientific socialism' and his popularity in Stalinist Russia was reflected in the reprinting of his works in Britain. Lenin was regarded as the father of 'democratic centralism', an organizing genius and originator of the 'party of a new type'. But little was heard of his theory of imperialism except among the fringe of Indian and African students who were drawn into the orbit of the London Left. Stalin had little to say of a theoretical nature but the Stalinist system of economic organization, and particularly the Five Year Plans, were regarded as the quintessence of Marxism and probably attracted more people to Marxism than any of the classic theories. The Soviet Union was seen as a model society which embodied Marxism in concrete form and its ideological hegemony over Marxist thought was scarcely challenged except by minor and obscure sects like the Trotskyists, the SDF or the Socialist Party of Great Britain. Thus Marxism came to mean what the Soviet Communist Party said it meant and what T. A. Jackson, John Strachey, Emile Burns and Palme Dutt presented it as meaning to the English-speaking world. An ideology which urged the total rejection of parliamentary democracy in 1932 only to support it enthusiastically in 1936 had to be elastic; while to reach a wide audience totally unused to its terminology it had to be simplified and drained of much of its complexity. Marxism was not taught at the universities although a group of Marxist scholars began to emerge from intellectual supporters of the Communist Party in the late 1930s. Most of the Left saw Marxism as a set of fairly simple but internally consistent beliefs which could explain a confusing reality.[17]

This simplified ideology helped establish a basic uniformity to the political outlook of a Left which was divided organizationally into many groups and which had inherited several divergent intellectual traditions. It is more fruitful to stress the common outlook of the Left and to distinguish it from that of the established Labour leadership, than to pay too much attention to differences within the Left. Often these differences resulted from organizational conflict; differing ideas served to rationalize different interests. As J. Middleton Murry wrote on his resignation from the Independent Labour Party:

> To find an excuse for the existence of the ILP – that appears to have been the main preoccupation of its leaders ever since. They had to be different at all costs.[18]

Tactical considerations often determined the adoption of an ideological stance but the Left was less prepared to make major concessions than is common in pragmatic, constitutional parties. They were frequently faced with the contradiction between militancy and effectiveness. When the Communist Party and the ILP were most radical they were least popular. The Communists extricated themselves from this situation by reversing their policy and recruiting a new membership. They were able to manoeuvre in a way which was difficult for the more rigid (or honest) people on the Left. By 1938 they were leading the Left towards an electoral alliance with sections of the Liberal Party, an arrangement which the non-Marxist ILP had abandoned in 1893. All this was pure tactics which had nothing to do with Marxism but a great deal to do with the foreign policy of the Soviet Union.

Because of its oppositional nature, the tendency to stress the inevitable collapse of capitalism and a general pessimism about the possibilities of gradual change, Left ideology was of less value in formulating a new Labour programme than in rationalizing and focusing public indignation. Left socialism was instinctive rather than well defined, idealistic rather than practical. Probably most people on the Left had a broad idea of the form a socialist society might take. By its constitution the Labour Party aimed 'to secure for the workers by hand or by brain the full fruits of their industry and the most eqitable distribution thereof that may be possible, upon the basis of the common ownership of the means of production, distribution and exchange, and the best obtainable system of popular administration and control of each industry or service'.[19] This classic definition of socialism was accepted by those on the Left to a greater degree than by the bulk of the movement. Not until the Labour Party published *Labour's Immediate*

Programme in 1937 did it present any constructive idea of its long-term aims. The Left, which had always been highly critical of the 'ideological bankruptcy' of the official movement, accepted the new programme almost without criticism. 'The aims of *Labour's Immediate Programme* are common to us', wrote Harry Pollitt when he applied for Communist Party affiliation to Labour in mid-1939.[20] Sir Stafford Cripps, after the acceptance of the programme by the party, urged his followers to abandon the Unity Campaign. He was supported in this by the Communist Party. As far as the Left had plans for the future society they were largely expressed in *Labour's Immediate Programme*.[21]

Left ideas made some contribution to the programme of the Labour Party and the *Immediate Programme* reflected the debates of the preceding six years even though it had been endorsed by a National Executive and Conference in which the Left was only a small minority.[22] Despite these contributions the Left had little to offer on foreign policy in the early 1930s except for the united action of the international working class, an entity which was largely imaginary. In the realm of economic policy the Left prophesied the inevitable downfall of capitalism, seeing the solution in the advent of socialism rather than in piecemeal reform. The Left was disillusioned with gradual constitutional reform and gave little guidance to a party which had such reform as the central theme of its programme. Nor was it of much help in the development of political strategy. Any form of United Front with the Communists was quite unacceptable to the Labour Party which could still remember that the Conservatives had attributed 'Bolshevism' to Ramsay MacDonald only ten years before. The Left remained more interested in strengthening the Labour movement than in appealing to electors who would not even vote for the Labour Party. Much of the Left moved among the converted and believed that the Labour vote would increase if the party became more radical.

The Left often developed its ideas within a different frame of reference from that used by the offiical movement. When the ILP began talking of 'revolutionary Marxism', of Rosa Luxemburg or of the POUM it might have been talking of the Athanasian Creed for all such terms and names meant even to the politically conscious in Britain. When the Communists spoke of 'social-fascism' or the Socialist League of the 'National Fascism' of the government they were speaking in terms of an abstract theory. They could not persuade more than a tiny handful that Ramsay MacDonald was a Scottish Mussolini or that Neville Chamberlain and Stanley Baldwin were English Hitlers. Marxist analysis produced parallels between the British and European situations but this was of no interest to those who had little idea of who Marx was and less of what he had said. Inside the labour movement such elaborate ideological discussions appealed to a generation which had been starved of critical political analysis, only to be thrust into a world where ideologies and economic systems seemed of paramount importance. When expressed publicly such ideas often led to confusion. Just as Marxism had appealed to the previous gneration only when disguised in the simplistic terms of syndicalism, so it appealed in the 1930s when wrapped up in the slogans of the United Front against Fascism. Later generations of the Left had to work out their own analysis of British society without much reference to the ideas of the 1930s. What was bequeathed to the labour movement was a set of attitudes, a myth centred around action and organization and a vast collection of second-hand books.

CHAPTER 13

Revolution, Reform and Democracy

The Left had always been distinct from the rest of the labour movement in refusing to accept the limitations of Parliamentary democracy and gradual reform. The Communist Party, in its first application to affiliate to the Labour Party, had stated its belief in the Soviet system, that is for government through 'workers' committees' instead of parliaments, for the 'dictatorship of the proletariat' and for the use of Parliament only as a propaganda platform rather than as a legislature. The anti-parliamentary tendency in the CP led by Gallacher and Sylvia Pankhurst had been criticized by Lenin as 'Left Wing Communism' but, despite this criticism, there remained a suspicion of parliament inherited from the syndicalist movement.[1] The Communist Party Central Committee favoured 'the Soviet (or Workers Council) system as a means whereby the working class shall achieve power and take control of the forces of production'. It saw 'parliamentary and electoral action generally as providing a means of propaganda and agitation towards the revolution'.[2]

Though the early policies of the Communist Party reflect the revolutionary atmosphere of the immediate post-war period they were based on the Marxist-Leninist precept that the state was merely 'the executive committee of the bourgeoisie'. The transition to socialism would be brought about only by breaking out of the system of 'bourgeois democracy'. Only reforms acceptable to the established order were possible within the parliamentary framework. The extreme Left held that the attempt to create a new form of society by constitutional means distracted attention from the need for a complete break with the capitalist system. This attitude was particularly in favour during the period of office of the

MacDonald government and immediately after its collapse. At the time Palme Dutt, the foremost theoretician of British Communism, believed that 'parliamentary democracy remained as the most useful basis of the bourgeoisie for the deception of the masses and holding in of the class struggle, so long as this means of restraining the workers was adequate'.[3]

It was argued that the Labour Party would fail in its attempts to use existing institutions to bring about fundamental change. Sir Stafford Cripps wrote of the Labour Party's 'reformist' programme:

> The fundamental fallacy in this approach to the problem was in the belief that the capitalists will permit the change to be made within capitalism.[4]

Even if the Labour Party honestly intended to introduce Socialism it would be prevented from doing so. Fascism was seen as a violent attempt to protect capitalism against Socialism or Communism. The collapse of the Labour Government was attributed to a 'bankers' ramp' – to a concerted attempt of British and American bankers to undermine the Government's financial policy.

The more extreme critics of the Labour Party went so far as to accuse it of being 'the conscious agent of the class enemy'.[5] It had become nothing more than a Fascist organisation supporting 'peace in industry, rationalisation of industrial processes, and, eventually, the corporate state'.[6] John Strachey developed this argument in *The Coming Struggle for Power* published in 1932, holding that the capitalist system had entered its final crisis. The survival of the system was made possible only through Fascism. Social Democracy was continuing to operate within the degenerating capitalist system and had become infected by that degeneration. Strachey recognized, as did the entire Left, that the Labour Party was a working-class organization. Yet he saw its progressive role as being over. Labour had drawn the working class into politics, had helped in the provision of social services, but was incapable of coming to grips with the crisis of capitalism. In the revolutionary situation which had arisen, 'the secret of political social democracy is to use the appeal and dynamic of revolutionary socialism, but to use it in order to implement a programme of most mediocre liberalism'.[7] The Trade Unions, according to Strachey, were becoming merged with the management as a result of the Mond-Turner 'peace in industry' talks of 1928. In both the political

and the industrial sphere Social Democracy was intent on uphold-
ing capitalist democracy. As Strachey had already argued that
capitalism could only be maintained through some form of
Fascism, 'Social democracy becomes in fact "social fascism" '.[8]

This was an extreme view. Yet even Professor Laski held that the
Labour Party could not remain uninfluenced by the system within
which it worked. The crisis of 1931 had convinced him 'that disaster
is the inevitable consequence of a policy of half measures'.[9] As late
as 1936, when Parliamentary democracy was far more acceptable
to the Left, he described 'the subtle danger which confronts the
Party of the Left' as 'the sacrifice of the sharpness of its convictions
in order that it may attain and retain power'.[10] The Left believed
that, if the Labour Party remained committed to 'gradualism', it
would cease to be an effective instrument for the attainment of
Socialism. Even after the Communist Party returned to its previous
support for the election of a Labour government, it warned against
'reformist illusions in a Labour Government as an instrument of
the working-class struggle for socialism'. Its election would merely
be the first stage in removing capitalism. 'The revolutionary
struggle will have to be faced in Britain'.[11] Thus, whether supporting the Labour Party or regarding it as the main enemy, the Left
had little faith in the permanence of any gains made under a
Labour government.

The Labour Party on the other hand, made quite clear its
complete acceptance of the Parliamentary method. Its main
ideological objection to the Communist Party was that adherence
to the Comintern showed a lack of faith in democracy. For the
Communist International was dominated by the Soviet Union
which, until 1936, openly rejected liberal democracy, and after that
was democratic in name only. Under the Twenty One Conditions
for entry, adopted by the Comintern in 1920, Communists were
urged to form both legal and illegal organizations, and to regard
Parliament as a platform rather than as an effective method of
securing radical reform. Attlee stated the Labour attitude unequi-
vocally in *The Labour Party in Perspective.* 'The Labour Party has
deliberately adopted the method of constitutional action', he wrote,
'and has rejected the tactics of revolution'.[12] Although he accepted
the inevitability of violence in certain situations, he did not feel
that conditions in Britain were comparable with those in the
countries in which Fascism and Bolshevism had come to power.

The Communist Party, in his view, 'does not believe in the methods of the Labour Party.... Its whole philosophy is based on the seizure of power by an active minority'.[13] Attlee asserted the undesirability of totalitarianism in Britain, drawing some comparisons between Fascism and Communism, although he did not make the complete parallel drawn in the National Council of Labour statement, *Democracy versus Dictatorship,* published in 1933. Nor was his objection to the Communist Party confined to its long-term aims. Writing in *Tribune* in the same year Attlee explained why he had little sympathy with the short-term protest movements on the Left. 'The Labour Party has never taken up the role of a factious opposition', he writes, 'because its aim is to use parliamentary institutions and not to destroy them'.[14]

Left Wing critics of Parliamentary democracy assumed that freedom from economic hardship was as important as political freedom. The right to vote was unimportant unless it carried with it the ability to remove economic restrictions on leading a full life. In the 1930s the existence of areas of severe poverty greatly strengthened the old arguments against economic barriers to freedom. In capitalist society, according to Cripps, 'the essential of freedom – economic equality – is remarkable by its absence'.[15] While urging the defence of democracy against Fascism, Strachey believed that 'our existing civil liberties ... are, for the workers, poor, thin, and half illusory things'.[16] A contrast was drawn between the accepted right to free elections, and the absence of any right to full employment. In previous decades it had been possible to believe that economic conditions would be improved by the election of a Labour government. But the persistence of unemployment, and the collapse of democracy in most of Europe made it more difficult to accept the 'inevitability of gradualism'. The attacks of Marx and Lenin on 'bourgeois democracy' were revived and came to dominate the thinking of many who had previously accepted constitutional reform.

The analysis of democracy briefly touched upon above, was made mainly by intellectuals, dealing largely in abstractions. However, it reflected attitudes common to the extreme Left at the beginning of the decade. Disillusionment with Parliamentary Socialism was completed by the performance of the MacDonald Government. Democracy seemed as incapable of maintaining economic stability as of achieving Socialism. Moreover, the 1931

General Election result had grossly under-represented the Labour Party in the Commons. For the first time since 1918 the Labour movement felt itself unfairly treated by the Parliamentary system. In contrast to that earlier period, when agitation and unrest had been wide-spread, much of the heart had gone out of the Labour Party. The Depression seriously affected Trade Union strength, further diminishing the militancy already damaged in the General Strike. Thus, despite the apparent relevance of Left attacks on democracy, there was less concrete agitation than in previous years. There were sporadic disturbances throughout the 1930s, particularly among the unemployed.[17] However, few of the demonstrations of the period had revolutionary connotations. The most violent clashes which took place were those between the police and the unemployed. Later in the decade these were replaced by violent conflicts between rival political groups and the police, caused by attempts of the British Union of Fascists to march through Jewish, working-class districts.

Apart from the Invergordon naval mutiny of September 1931 and the activities of the National Unemployed Workers Movement, there was little to compare with the upsurge of activity immediately following the Armistice of 1918. The protests remained confined to a small section of the population, most of the Labour movement being concerned with protecting its livelihood. There was widespread disillusionment with the leadership of the Labour Party, but it was not replaced by any enthusiasm for the more extreme forms of Socialism. The Communist Party had isolated itself and it was that Party which supported revolutionary action most strongly. Of all the groups on the Left, they alone really believed in the possibility and desirability of violent revolution in Britain. Tom Wintringham developed the theme in 1932, that modern methods of air warfare had not lessened the potentialities of street fighting. Such enthusiasm for armed resistance to the modern State had lessened by 1934, when Dolfuss shelled the Socialist-held Karl Marx Hof in Vienna. Nevertheless it was widely believed in the Communist Party that a revolutionary situation was developing in which the techniques of 1917 could be used in Britain. In March 1933, two Communist speakers were bound over for urging armament workers and troops to 'keep your hands on the guns and use them here in Birmingham'.[18] Most of the revolutionary slogans of the Communist Party were oratorical bravado of this sort, coming from a group of less than 5,000, the majority of them only transitory members of the Party.

In effect the only section of the Left which challenged the State was the unemployed movement. Attempts were made, it is true, to obtain similar results to that at Invergordon by the distribution of a Communist newsheet *Soldier's Voice.* This caused the passing of the Incitement to Disaffection Act in 1934, which made it illegal to attempt the subversion of the armed forces. The National Unemployed Workers Movement, on the other hand, used methods which did not lead to illegality, though they led to considerable violence. There can be little doubt, from the decisions taken at international congresses of the Red International of Labour Unions and of the unemployed organizations, that the Communists hoped for a revolutionary crisis to grow as a result of unemployment and lowered standards of living. The Communist Party Election Manifesto for 1931 contained a section, censored by the printer, which outlined the Party's short-term aims:

> The fighting front of the workers organised in the factories, mines, trade unions and labour exchanges, being built up in thousands of meetings, in big demonstrations and leading to mass strikes, the general strike and mighty mass struggles – this is the only method whereby the workers can defend themselves and gain their victory over the capitalist offensive.[19]

The campaign for 'the immediate demands of the workers', though couched in terms of short-term objectives, was clearly revolutionary in its ultimate aims. In its appeal for support of the Workers Charter of 1931, the Communist Central Committee openly stated that 'only the revolutionary overthrow of capitalism and the conquest of power by the working class can solve the crisis'.[20]

It was largely as the result of such promptings that the unemployed demonstrations of 1932 became the occasion for serious rioting, although there was ample provocation from the police, particularly on Merseyside. The immediate result of the unemployed demonstrations was to strengthen the surveillance of the police over the leaders of the unemployed, and to create the impression, which the Communists at the time welcomed, that the Communist Party was a danger to the State. Several NUWM leaders had already been imprisoned, but always for definite civil offences, usually for obstruction. In 1934 Tom Mann and Harry

Pollitt were placed under 'preventive arrest' in order to preserve the peace during the Hunger March to the Bermondsey Unity Congress. Such arrests were unpalatable to liberal opinion.[21] Elaborate theories were developed to prove the 'Fascist' tendencies of the Government.

The Communists, with the Bolshevik tradition behind them, were the most consistent in their advocacy of revolution. The Independent Labour Party, which owed its existence to its founders' belief in Parliamentary action, adjusted to the revolutionary temper of the Left with more difficulty. For three years after its disaffiliation, it debated the extent to which it should become a revolutionary, Marxist party.

The ILP had disaffiliated from Labour because it believed that 'gradualism is bankrupt'.[22] Consequently some of its members were already favourably inclined to the revolutionary approach. At the Bradford Conference of 1932 the Revolutionary Policy Committee failed in its attempt to commit the Party to 'working up revolutionary militancy in the working class', as the RPC formula seemed to have little concrete meaning. There was a strong desire to 'take account of British traditions and psychology'.[23] The Party was determined to avoid the tactics and jargon of the Communists as far as possible. The ILP leaders believed their task to be 'the endeavour to secure a real militant revolutionary united Socialist Movement'.[24] They were nevertheless aware of the difficulties of explaining their programme to an electorate which had always resisted revolutionary slogans. In later years, when the ILP ceased to take account of these difficulties, its programme became more and more extreme and unrealistic.

The ILP finally arrived at an agreed statement of principles at the Derby Conference of April 1935. By this time it had lost almost all its moderate element and had become a fundamentally different party in outlook and composition. It now saw its main purpose as being:

> to prepare the workers and their organisations for the inevitable struggle for power and for the maintenance and use of power when it has been won. The instrument both of the struggle and of the administration of power should be all-inclusive organisations – Workers Councils, under the leadership of the Revolutionary Party, representing every section of the working class

movement as well as the workers at their places of employment and where they live.[25]

Much of the ILP's new policy was based on the syndicalist and revolutionary doctrines of previous decades. Nevertheless its representation in Parliament could no more be ignored than the fact that Britain was a Parliamentary democracy. 'The ILP aims at using the existing governmental institutions – Parliamentary and Municipal – to the utmost. They can be of value for agitational purposes and for winning concessions from the capitalist class.'[26] The ILP had become a forum for conflicting viewpoints, rather than a Party with a coherent policy. It was not organizationally or intellectually equipped to become revolutionary. By its democratic constitution it had to accept what point of view a well organized minority could enforce at any particular time. In its attitude to revolution, as in its other policies, the Party constantly vacillated.

Neither the Communists nor the ILP were likely to gain much support from the electorate, and could therefore afford to toy with the idea of revolution. The Left of the Labour Party, on the other hand, formed part of a constitutional political party. Nevertheless the Socialist League and its supporters favoured a radical programme which questioned the whole basis of British Parliamentary practice. In two pamphlets written for the Socialist League in 1932 and 1933 Laski attempted to answer the question; 'Has evolutionary socialism deceived itself in believing that it can establish itself by peaceful means within the ambit of the capitalist system?'[27] In *The Labour Party and the Constitution*, he developed the theme which was to provide the programme of Sir Stafford Cripps and the Socialist League for the next two years. Outlining the 'inadequacy of the constitutional system for the purposes a Socialist Party must propose to implement', he urged the adoption of an Emergency Powers Act to prevent interference with the operation of the Labour programme. Laski was careful to ensure that the proposed Act should be a defensive measure that would only be introduced when the normal constitutional devices had been exhausted. Cripps, on the other hand, wished for far more drastic reforms. The Emergency Powers Act, envisaged in his Socialist League pamphlet of 1934, 'will be wide enough in its terms to allow all that will be immediately necessary to be done by ministerial orders'.[28] Like Laski he favoured a revision of House of

Commons procedure but went further in suggesting that the Cabinet should be chosen by the Parliamentary Labour Party and not by the Prime Minister. The most far-reaching proposal for the constitutional attainment of Socialism was the suggested Finance and Planning Act under which the entire economy would be planned as in the USSR.

Laski believed that the British constitution had been designed for delay rather than progress. Nevertheless he did not go as far as Cripps in ignoring Parliamentary opinion. Cripps had borrowed ideas from the Soviet Union and from Nazi Germany, though he wished to retain some features of the British constitution. His proposals, which were officially adopted by the Socialist League, were consequently attacked as both Bolshevik and Fascist. Palme Dutt, too, noticed 'the weakening of the old, abstract democratic assumptions'[29] in the Socialist League propaganda. The League's proposals were undoubtedly dominated by a belief in the inadequacy of existing democracy, and by frustration at the failure to introduce Socialist legislation between 1929 and 1931. The Socialist League was intent on preserving as much of the existing State machinery as possible, in contrast to the Communists and the ILP who wished to replace it by Workers Councils. Yet in their enthusiasm the League supporters overlooked the incompatibility between many of their proposals and the democratic beliefs which they undoubtedly held.

Revolutionary slogans and criticisms of democracy became less popular after the victory of Fascism in Germany and Austria. Important changes in attitude followed on the decisions of the Seventh Comintern Congress which defined Fascism as 'the open, terrorist dictatorship of finance capital'.[30] In Fascist states the labour movement had been dissolved and had thus lost the advantages which it enjoyed under a democratic constitution. Measures like the Incitement to Disaffection Act were believed to threaten freedom of opinion in Britain and groups like the National Council for Civil Liberties became active in defence of the Left. Yet the Communists were not prepared to abandon their revolutionary programme in its entirety for some time. They still held to 'the necessity of the revolutionary overthrow of the rule of the bourgeoisie and the establishment of the dictatorship of the proletariat in the form of Soviets'.[31] It was to be another three years before Harry Pollitt would appeal to 'every British man and woman who treasures the prestige of Britain and the liberties of our people'.[32]

The new attitude to democracy could be justified with nearly as many references to the Marxist classics as the old. Lenin had emphasised in his *Left Wing Communism* that, despite its imperfections, Parliamentary democracy was an improvement on a system under which free political activity was impossible. It became less fashionable to speak of the British system as 'dictatorship over the working class'.[33] By 1939 the Communists were calling for 'support of all measures to secure the victory of democracy over Fascism'.[34] This formula had been in common use for over a year, though it was again withdrawn until the German invasion of the USSR turned the 'imperialist war' into 'the struggle against Fascism'. In Communist propaganda, and more noticeably in that of their subsidiaries like the British Youth Peace Assembly, Britain's democratic traditions had been constantly emphasized since the beginning of 1938.

One qualification should be made to this account of the changing attitude of the Left towards British democracy. It was never suggested that the British system was more than an approximation to the ideal. Although 'democracy, even under capitalist economy, offers the best field for the development of the class struggle',[35] the Communists and their supporters aimed at 'complete democracy, Soviet democracy'.[36] By 1938 this no longer meant the creation of Workers Councils. Soviet democracy was the system of pseudo-Parliamentary government developed under the Stalin Constitution of 1936. Its chief attraction to the Left was the provisions which it made to safeguard the economic rights of the citizen. The earlier support for the 'dictatorship of the proletariat' as an ideal form of government finally disappeared from Communist propaganda after 1936. The fundamental criticism of the inadequacies of capitalist democracy continued. The Unity Manifesto, which called for the return of a Labour Government, saw this only 'as the next stage in the advance to working class power'. To the Left the transition to Socialism could not be made without drastic revisions to the constitution of the country. The Labour Party, on the other hand, was fully prepared to accept virtually all the limitations of the British Parliamentary system, and to work entirely within its framework.[37]

The major parties in Britain were completely committed to the

Parliamentary method. Left criticisms found support, however, among those badly served by the existing system. In the Depression many of the unemployed were temporarily susceptible to revolutionary appeals and in areas with a radical tradition such as South Wales and Scotland, it was possible to arouse strong feelings against the Government's policies. The degree to which this anti-Government sentiment could inspire a movement against the State was, nevertheless, greatly exaggerated by Communists and Government alike. When Fascism presented a real threat to democracy, temporary discontents were forgotten. It would have been ill-advised to attack democracy when the advance of Fascism was the major concern of liberal opinion. Intellectual objections to capitalist democracy remained the distinguishing mark of the Left. However, those sections which allowed such objections to take the foremost place in their propaganda found themselves isolated. The Left could not escape from the political conventions of the mass labour movement any more than it could dispense with allies within the movement. The Left used revolutionary appeals and questioned established institutions. It was also necessary to retain the sympathy of others. This could only be done in the late 1930s by defending democracy against the militant Right.

CHAPTER 14

The Role of the Labour Party

The Left held that the existing labour movement was too susceptible to the conventions of British society and of Parliamentary
government, and was thus incapable of changing society. Yet even
the most sectarian groups recognized that the Labour Party, for all
its faults, could be a ready-made instrument for bringing about
Socialism. Left discussion of the role of the Labour Party was
constantly faced with a contradiction. If Socialism could only be
reached by the efforts of the mass working-class movement, then it
had to be assumed that the working-class movement could be
committed to a Socialist programme. Yet in the eyes of the Left the
British Labour Party was not Socialist. The dilemma was how to
convert the mass movement to Socialism, how to make it into an
effective instrument for changing society or, alternatively, how to
build a new working-class movement which would be more
Socialist than the Labour Party. At one time, the Left seemed to
favour complete withdrawal from the Party, at another to
attach itself to the Labour Party in an attempt to influence it in the
desired direction. The only continuing feature was the agreement
that the Labour Party was not pursuing a Socialist policy and was
not an effective organization, either electorally or politically, for
immediately advancing the aims of the Left.

The argument was no new one, either in Socialist theory or in the
peculiar circumstances in Britain. The Labour Party had not been
formed as a mass Socialist Party. Only a tiny minority described
themselves as Socialists in 1900, though it was this minority which
forced the pace. The great bulk of the Party's nominal membership
and voting strength wanted only to protect the interests of
organized labour. For many years the paradox remained that while

the new Party was led and inspired by Socialists, its membership was largely indifferent to Socialist ideology of any sort. The organized working class, the theoretical instrument for progress towards Socialism, was not Socialist in outlook. The purists of the Social Democratic Federation argued unrealistically that Socialists should remain outside a non-Socialist body like the Labour Party, even if it represented the only effective mass working-class Party in the country. The SDF did not acknowledge that a basically Liberal working class was still unprepared to allow itself to be led by Socialists, particularly where such Socialists threatened the deeply rooted prejudices and interests of the established leaders of the Trade Union movement. It was the strength of Keir Hardie's Independent Labour Party that it recognized the situation which existed, rather than waiting for a theoretically ideal situation in which a class-conscious working-class movement would demand a Socialist programme.[1]

The growth of syndicalism among the South Wales miners and the Clydeside engineers, the impact of the war and the Soviet revolution, created for the first time a strong body of working-class Socialists. The Labour Party adopted a Socialist aim in 1918 and the influence of the ILP became marked. Yet the Labour Party was by no means an ideal Socialist Movement. Most of the officials of the Trade Unions were not Socialists in any real sense of the word. The influx of wealthy Liberals into the ILP and the Parliamentary Labour Party created a further body of opinion hostile to the Socialism of the miners and engineers. Though the middle-class Left was strengthened by this new element, Fabian 'gradualism' was also reinforced both numerically and intellectually. For the first time something approaching the Parliamentary Social-Democrats so despised by Lenin came into being.[2] The Left in the 1920s had to determine its attitude to a Party which was not essentially Socialist in its sense of the word, which relied on non-Socialist Trade Union officials for much of its support, and which was fostering a 'gradualist' Parliamentary leadership under the undisputed control of Ramsay MacDonald.

The Communist Party, when it was founded, gave considerable thought to its future relations with the Labour Party. Its decision to work within the Labour Party was reached after much dissension and only on the assumption that such work was directed towards the creation of a mass Communist Party. For the Communists, who even in 1920 had close links with the Trade Unions, could not afford to take up the purist attitude of many Socialist intellectuals. They had to admit that the prospects of building up a new movement from scratch were remote, and that attempts to do so had only led to sectarian isolation.[3] Thus as late as four years after their foundation, despite disillusion with the first Labour Government and in the face of consistent attempts to expel Communists from the Labour Party, the official Party paper stated that:

> The Labour Party represents the proletarian mass organisation and consequently it is the absolute duty of the Communist Party to work inside the Labour Party.[4]

The resistance to the Comintern policy of 1928 and the disastrous effects of that policy on the British Party, clearly indicated the validity of supporting Labour, even when Labour Party regulations made it impossible for Communists to remain as individual members of the Labour Party. The ultimate aim of the Communists was to create a mass Communist Party. The strengthening of the Labour Party was contradictory to this aim, but this did not prevent Communists from working for a Labour Government after 1935 rather than face the extinction which would have resulted from rigid application of the 'Social Fascist' policy.

The Independent Labour Party had a much closer relationship with the Labour Party, and its subsequent contortions largely resulted from the attempt to establish a new relationship which combined independence with continuing contact with the Labour movement. It has been convincingly suggested that the Labour Party might not have come into being without the efforts of the ILP[5], and it is clear that in the first twenty years of the Party's history, the ILP took the initiative in forcing Socialism both on the Party and the electorate. Consequently, when unrest over the policy of the Labour Government started to grow within the ILP, there was considerable discussion about the future relationship of the two organizations. The debate on the new Standing Orders of the Parliamentary Labour Party has been fully covered above. Behind this discussion was the more fundamental problem of the part which the ILP could play in a mass Party which was moving away from the federal and Socialist ideas which the ILP championed. The problem facing the ILP was more complex than that confronting the Communists. It had to decide whether its Parliamentary representatives were to be bound by the decisions of the ILP Annual Conference or by those of the Parliamentary Labour Party. It had to face up to the fact that the ILP was no longer the dominant force in the political wing of the Labour Party. What was most important, at least for the average member of the ILP, was that the Labour Party appeared to have abandoned the policies which the ILP had been attempting to force upon the Party for thirty years.

The eventual decision to sever all official connections with the Labour Party was not reached without a maximum of debate and dissension. The doubly unfortunate resolution passed at Bradford, excluding ILP members from any positive role within the Trade Unions, the Co-operatives and the Labour Party, hastened the inevitable decline of the Party into an obscure faction. The Bradford decision to sever all contact was admitted to have been disastrous by the Reorganisation Commission set up by the ILP in 1934 to examine the causes of the drastic decline in membership. The Commission regarded 'as a fundamental principle, the necessity of directing our activities towards making contact with the mass of the workers in the ordinary conditions of their daily life, namely the workplace and the home'.[6] The Party was realizing, as were the Communists, that there were very great advantages to be gained from participating in the official Labour movement, however 'reformist'. The subsequent attempts to return to the Labour Party, and the belated decision to work in the Co-operative Party, underline the ineffectiveness experienced by the ILP in isolation.

The two minorities outside the Labour Party placed more reliance on orthodoxy than on influence, though they desired the eventual conversion of the Labour movement to their point of view. Inside the Labour Party there remained a Left, growing in influence towards the end of the decade, which for various reasons was not prepared to break with the Party. Its attitude to the Labour Party was in some ways similar to that of the Left minorities. The Left wished the Party to adopt a Socialist programme, and used every method available to force such a programme on the Party. The fundamental difference was that the Left within the Party considered the Labour Party to be a potential instrument for the attainment of Socialism, while both the Communist Party and the ILP wished to supersede the Labour Party by a radically differen form of organisation. That is not to say that the Left accepted the Labour Party machine or constitution. Indeed, the Left within the Labour Party was distinguished by the vigour with which it urged new forms of organization on the Party, particularly where such new forms would increase the influence of the active individual member at the expense of the Union officials or Members of Parliament.

The Left aimed both at more effective organization and at greater democracy within the Labour movement, goals which might seem contradictory. The Communist Party carried militancy and discipline to the point where democracy became more nominal than real. The ILP, on the other hand, was so democratic that it had no internal discipline and fell apart. The Labour Left was trying to reach a situation where the Labour Party would be streamlined and yet democratic, effective as a political force and yet responsible to its active individual members. There is much to be said for their approach. The Labour Party structure was not really suited to unified action, nor had it the advantage of giving the militant some sense of active participation in the work of the party on the national level. There is ample evidence that the Labour Party made little use of its great resources between elections. It was this lethargy on the part of Labour which attracted many to the Communists and provided the impetus behind the Unity Campaign. While it might seem reckless to endanger the cohesion of the Labour Party by bringing into it a small and fractious group like the Communists, the Left could argue with some reason that the Communists did more work with greater effect than the Labour Party, taking relative size into account. Much of this work was mere showmanship with no electoral significance, but it was still invaluable in terms of recruiting and propaganda.

The fullest statement of the Left attitude to the Labour Party is given by John Strachey in his *What are we to do?* published in 1938. To a large extent he summarized the attitudes of the Left, though they would perhaps have resisted his emphasis on discipline. Strachey reiterated the usual argument that the Labour Party was unaware of its ultimate aims and had little or no ideology. He accused the Labour Party of failing to build up any resistance to Fascism or capitalism, and of collaborating with the National Government. He suggested that the Labour Party was ideologically and organizationally unsuited to effective campaigning for Socialism and he prescribed a 'New Model' for a mass Socialist Party. This would closely resemble the Communist Party in so far as it was tightly knit, disciplined and united behind an ideology. Strachey did not wish this ideology to be too sectarian; nor did he wish the reformed Labour Party to remain aloof from non-Socialist Parties. He saw the 'New Model' as closely allied with the 'progressive and democratic forces', only playing a dominating role through its discipline and adherence to Socialist principles.

There is little difference between Strachey's 'New Model' and the Leninist conception of the Party applied with varying degrees of success by the British Communists. Strachey envisaged a disciplined, mass party, rather than a disciplined minority working inside a mass movement. The small Communist Party exerted continuous pressure on its individual members, something which a mass party, based on strong local branches, could not do. Indeed, the attempt of the Labour Party to impose discipline on its local sections was already proving difficult.

There is no reason to suppose that the Labour movement, with its democratic traditions and strong local machinery, would submit to the kind of discipline which the Communist Party could exert over its small membership. The cohesion and efficiency of the Communist Party was rather illusory in any case, as members who disagreed with Party decisions and were given no effective outlet for their criticisms merely left the Party or were expelled for 'factionalism'. Moreover, the Communist Party, for much of the decade, had a very tenuous branch life, and was constantly trying to spread its influence through its individual membership.

The Labour Party worked within the Parliamentary system, and formed part of a movement which claimed that internal democracy was central to its philosophy. The same was true of the ILP, despite attempts of its Left Wing to transform the party into a disciplined unit. The Communists, on the other hand, saw themselves as the 'vanguard of the proletariat', ready for action of any sort, whether constitutional or not. The Party worked under the threat of illegality, for although it was never banned, its leaders were liable to imprisonment on several charges, and most of them had been arrested at some stage of the Party's history. Whether or not there was any real danger of illegality, the Party acted in a self-consciously conspiratorial manner. Even during the days of the

Popular Front, the old habits continued, and every effort was made to integrate new recruits into the Party's 'democratic centralist' structure.

The Left in general wanted the Labour Party to copy the apparent efficiency and enthusiasm of the Communists without sacrificing its internal democracy. The Labour Left held, with considerable justification, that the Communists were attracting youth, the 'intellectuals' and militant Trade Unionists, because there was no scope for such people inside the Labour Party. On the other hand, the non-Communist Left knew only too well that most Communists eventually found the atmosphere inside the Communist Party distasteful. The leadership of the Left included a significant number of former Communists who had been through this experience and had strong personal objections against excessive discipline.

While the Left regretted the incoherence and ineffectiveness of the Labour Party's political activities, it was unwilling to sacrifice the conditions which enabled it to flourish and spread its influence. This attitude prompted the widespread and partly successful campaigns of the Constituency Parties Association to gain an improved position for the local Labour Parties. Although the Left was in full agreement with this aim, the Association also represented a quite genuine feeling of discontent with the structure of the Party.[7] Local Labour Parties at their most active, were forums for discussion of policy, did all the work of campaigning, often in hopeless Conservative seats, and contained capable and talented members. Yet they had a negligible effect on the voting at Party Conference. Although the Trade-Union delegations at national and regional conferences consisted of officials with little real experience in local political work, their block votes decided all issues. Much of the frustration and bitterness of the Left can be traced to the subordinate position of the militants. Indeed, it is quite possible that the Unity Campaign would not have attracted much enthusiasm, had the Labour Party's individual members been fully mobilized in an effective Party based on local membership. This would have continued to be Left Wing, but its more erratic tendencies might have been modified in genuine discussion in a democratic organization. As it was, there was a constant clash, in which much energy was wasted with little result.

The eventual compromise at Bournemouth in 1937, which gave

the local Parties a direct voice on the National Executive, satisfied many of them and was one of the factors which weakened the United Peace Alliance campaign in the following year. The problem remained the same, however. The active militant saw the Labour Party as a democratic movement, in which policy, leadership and tactics should be determined by the ordinary members, and not by an imposed leadership. All the official statements of the Party and its Constitution encouraged this belief. Militants held that only the half-million individual members could be regarded as active Labour supporters with a right to a direct voice in the running of the Party. It was widely believed on the Left that the 'rank and file' were sympathetic to a more radical approach than the leaders of the Party and the Unions. In 1939 Cripps suggested, on this basis, that a plebiscite of the Party membership be held to discover its attitude to his National Petition for a Peace Alliance.

Most of the frustration at the Party's slow progress was canalized into complaints against its undemocratic nature; it was believed that the active militant should be free to organize a more forthright attack on the Government. It is clear from the history of the Labour League of Youth that the bureaucratic structure and atmosphere of the Party did, in fact, inhibit enthusiasm and distort it into opposition to the Party leaders. There was a certain amount of antagonism against the slowly growing number of professional officials in the Party who were responsible to the National Executive Committee rather than to the Party membership. The Constituency Parties Association asked that all Party officials should be elected, a Trade-Union practice quite unacceptable to the Party bureaucracy though not impracticable.

Because the Labour Party gave little real power to its militants, and was hesitant to adopt a sweeping Socialist programme, the Left had often to consider its own position inside the Party. The place of the Socialist inside the Labour Party was a constant theme of the debates on the Left. The ILP had originally seen the Labour Party as 'not merely a political machine, but a vital Movement representing the Socialist aspirations and ideas of the working class'. It had believed that 'close association with the Labour Party is essential for the fulfilment of its Socialist purpose'. However, after experience with the second Labour government, the ILP felt it could only maintain this relationship 'as long as the Labour Party maintains the principles and pursues the purposes for which it was founded, and so long as the right of the ILP to express its distinctive point of view in word and deed is recognised'.[8] Once it had decided to leave the Party, the ILP soon swung over to the opinion that the 'so-called "Left" opposition within the Labour Party serves one purpose, and one purpose only. It creates the illusion among masses of working people that by working within the machine, a Revolutionary Socialist line might perhaps be adopted by that machine.'[9] The Left constantly vacillated between attempts to convert the Labour Party into a militant Socialist Party, and despair at the possibility of the Labour Party ever really abandoning 'gradualism'. The argument was not new. It was essentially the argument which had separated the ILP and the SDF forty years before. The arguments and results were basically the same. Those who remained within the Labour Party moved slowly, if at all, towards their goal. Those who stayed outside maintained their militant stance in isolation.[10]

The Left was more constructive and realistic in its attempts to transform the Labour Party into a socialist party of active militants than in many of its other policies. The official Labour Party view that 'we already have so much "policy" that we can't get through it',[11] was only too easily accepted. In fact, it was not until 1937 that the Party really acquired a convincing programme, and many of the measures adopted after 1945 were developed in the wartime Coalition rather than by the Party alone.

As for conscious ideology, there was little or none in the Party as a whole beyond a few vague ethical beliefs. In the 1930s, political ideologies were under constant discussion, particularly among young people, in the Universities and the professions. The Socialist League and other Left minorities, however unrealistic their conclusions may now seem, attempted to develop some kind of basic attitude towards Socialism, and to attract those who were looking for fresh ideas. The Left's conception of the 'New Model', its attempts to evolve an ideology and its campaigns for a more effective Party machine, may have showed no immediate results, but they helped to educate many new Party members into thinking out the implications of democratic Socialism.

CHAPTER 15

The Future Society

Every militant on the Left believed himself to be a Socialist, working towards a certain form of social organization. He was part of a movement of protest against capitalism, unemployment, Fascism and war. He stood for the aims of peace and Socialism. The great majority of Labour politicians and officials were also prepared to accept a radical definition of Socialism but were not prepared to reshape their programme accordingly. The Left, on the other hand, took the egalitarian and democratic goals of Socialism seriously. It is worth examining the Left's ideas for the future society because they form the main body of British Socialist ideology in the 1930s.[1]

The Communist Party, so dominant in other spheres, offered little in the way of visions of the future. The model society already existed in the Soviet Union. Communists were more intent on explaining how Russian methods could be applied in Britain than in elaborating a 'Utopia'. The example of the USSR was constantly held up to Communist sympathizers. Even during the collectivization famine in 1932, the Friends of the Soviet Union had remarkable success in persuading the Left that the USSR was a desirable model for the future. Until 1936 the Communist Party had no hesitation in using the Soviet Union as a model society. As Harry Pollitt said in 1932, 'The Moscow road is the only road to working class victory'.[2] After 1936, however, the 'Moscow road' was no longer presented as the only road to Socialism.

But the Left still did not view Parliamentary democracy as an end in itself. Nor were they prepared to stop at the amelioration of social conditions. The most important pressure exerted by the Left on the rest of the Labour movement was directed towards the adoption of a long-term Socialist objective. This had been the function of Keir Hardie's ILP between 1900 and the outbreak of war and led to the writing of a socialist aim into the Labour programme in 1918. In the 1920s the ILP had worked for the implementation of this aim and against the 'gradualism' of the official leadership. The ILP 'Living Income' or *Socialism in our Time* report was the major constructive programme presented to the Labour movement between Sidney Webb's *Labour and the New Social Order* in 1918, and *Labour's Immediate Programme* in 1937. None of these, of course, embodied the aims of the Socialist Left in full. Yet each in its way attempted to commit the Party to a carefully planned programme whose aim was a society organized along fundamentally different lines.

In the years following the collapse of the Labour government, the Socialist League attempted to fulfil the functions of the ILP and the Fabian Society in developing a new platform.[3] The policies adopted by the Communist Party or the ILP in 1935 were agitational in intent rather than concerned with practical lines of action. *For Soviet Britain* and the Derby programme of the ILP were expressions of complete frustration with all aspects of existing society rather than attempts to develop a constructive alternative. The Socialist League, on the other hand, consisted of those who had followed the Fabian and ILP traditions, and who made concessions to Marxism rather than letting it dominate their entire approach.

The Socialist League advocated various reforms of the machinery of government. But when the Left spoke of the future society it had something more in mind than constitutional reform. All Socialists regarded drastic economic restructuring as a basic necessity. The relative importance of constitutional and economic aims can be seen in the only 'Utopia' produced by the Left, *The First Workers' Government* by G. R. Mitchison. Although written as a Utopia in the sense of an imaginary future society, this work incorporated all the measures advocated by the Socialist League; indeed it was recommended as doing so in a foreword by Sir Stafford Cripps. Once elected, the 'First Workers' Government' was to protect itself against possible 'sabotage' by the passage of an Emergency Powers Act. After that its most immediate task would be the nationalization of the credit system and of the land. Mitchison's advocacy of higher unemployment benefit and a compulsory forty-hour week, reflected the desire to meet the 'immediate demands of the workers'. Anticipating *Labour's Immediate Programme* of two years later, Mitchison supported the formation of a National Investment Board to control new investment. He differed from the Party programme in suggesting the election of regional councils to plan the industry of particular areas under an elected National Planning Commission. Here, as in his proposals for the management of nationalized industries, Mitchison shows more sympathy with the syndicalist and democratic traditions of the Labour movement than with the Fabians' emphasis on efficiency and centralization. The Socialist aim of the Party, embodied in its constitution, was taken over from the ILP and stressed that nationalization was a means for increasing the participation of the worker in the control of industry. The Labour Party had adopted the concept of the public corporation and the control of nationalized industries through a national board of experienced administrators, not necessarily representative of the workers or professional staff of the industry. The Left remained committed to some form of employee participation in management.

Mitchison developed his argument along the lines laid down by syndicalists and Guild Socialists in previous decades, including in his plan a highly developed form of 'regionalism'. The coal industry (apart from the land the only asset the entire Labour movement was committed to nationalize) was to be controlled through a system of election from local pit councils to a National Mining Council. Mining, like the other proposed nationalized industries, was to be organized on a regional basis. For 'regionalism' was, in part, an attempt to solve the problem of the Distressed Areas by the planned location of industry, and to reverse the trend towards concentration around London at the expense of the industrial areas. As well as regionalism and workers control, the Left favoured the encouragement of industrial unionism, the organizing of unions by industry rather than on craft lines[4] Workers' control would be simplified if each industry was organized by one union. For the Left saw Trade Unions as having a positive function in the transition to Socialism. They would train a new management which would eventually replace the private control of industry.

The programme of the 'First Workers' Government' differed

from that developed by the Labour Party in the next three years. Yet there are sufficient resemblances to suggest the existence of a common approach. *Labour's Immediate Programme* resembled the Socialist League plans in many respects. The advocacy, for example, of locating industry in the Distressed Areas through State action; of controlling hours of work in all industries; of forming a National Investment Board; and of nationalizing the land, coal, transport and power. This was a great advance on the programmes of the 1920s and was accepted as such by the Left. The Labour Party went far towards acknowledging the possibility of 'obstruction from vested interests or unrepresentative bodies'.[5] It declared its goal to be the 'Socialist Commonwealth'. In all this the new programme showed concessions to the thinking of the moderate Left. Nor was this surprising, as most of the Party's intellectuals, whether in the Socialist League or the New Fabian Research Bureau, were thinking in terms of a fundamental shift towards Socialism. The Party Leader, C. R. Attlee, while deputy leader, had agreed with many basic assumptions of the Socialist League. He gave his support to the formation of 'a central planning body' and to the setting up of regional councils.[6] So although *Labour's Immediate Programme* was not directly inspired by the Socialist League, it owes a certain amount to the discussions of the previous four years, discussions in which the Socialist League took the leading part.

The official programme of the Labour Party went a long way towards meeting the wishes of the moderate Left; the Labour Party was still, however, without a long-term aim. The *Immediate Programme* called for a 'national plan under the guidance of the State' which would 'use the resources of our country so as to create a real prosperity in which all share'. However this was not quite what the Left meant by Socialism. There was a strong current of resistance to what was termed 'State capitalism' or even 'Fascism'. The continuing desire of many Union leaders for some form of workers' control was reflected in an article by Harold Clay in 1933. 'The Labour movement', he wrote, 'demands the substitution of a planned economic and industrial system on a definite Socialist basis, for the anarchy of capitalism.' In the same book G. D. H. Cole elaborated a long-term view of Socialism which was quite distinct from that accepted by the Party's leaders, though compatible with the Party's official aims. 'Socialism', in his view, involved 'the complete transference of all major industries and industrial operations to public ownership and Socialist control.'[7]

There was no mention of 'workers' control' in *Labour's Immediate Programme* nor was there any suggestion that nationalization would extend outside certain basic industries. Even the land, nationalization of which had been included in every Labour programme since 1918, was to be acquired, where necessary, by compulsory purchase and would not be placed entirely under the control of the State. The Left, however, wanted to look beyond the first term of office of a Labour government. A few on the extreme Left did not accept that Socialism could come about democratically. But the entire Left, and many others agreed that there must be a transition from one form of society to another. Attlee made a clear-cut distinction between the Labour Party and 'those parties which believe fundamentally in the retention of a class system of society and in a Capitalist system as the economic foundation of society'. 'The former', he wrote, 'must have a definite plan, and must from the start work to make that plan a reality.'[8]

The extreme Left had a rather naive conception of the 'transition'. During the 'Social-Fascist' phase, for instance, the Communist Party called for the creation of a Socialist society based on Workers' Councils. As Emile Burns argued in *The Only Way Out*, these councils would be the organs for taking over control of industry: 'All the large-scale means of production would immediately be nationalised (of course without compensation) and taken over by the workers.' Burns was expressing the official Party policy of the time and he argued that Workers' Councils should assume the management of distribution and production under a 'general plan of production to meet social needs'.[9] Burns was writing at the worst point of the depression, and he justified such an extreme policy in terms of the collapse of capitalism: 'A few years ago such conceptions as these might have been dismissed as utopian. But now there is the positive example of the Soviet Union.'[10] John Strachey, writing four years later, used the Soviet Union, or his own image of it, as the model for a Socialist society. He saw the abolition of social classes through the expropriation of private capitalists as the main aim of socialism. Rather than emphasiziang Workers Councils, which had long ceased to have any real power in the USSR, Strachey saw the 'transition' as coming about under the 'dictatorship of the proletariat'. He argued that because the State was an instrument of class domination: 'what the workers have to do then, is to set up their State, to set up an apparatus of coercion by means of which they may exercise their rule over the other classes of society'.[11]

The Independent Labour Party, after its break with Labour, began to think up elaborate schemes for reorganizing society. Like the Communists, the ILP had little experience of national administration and was quite unrealistic in its sweeping programmes. The Workers Council was to become as important to them as it had been to the Communists. The more practically minded leaders of the ILP had little part in the discussion of the new policies being put forward, except to criticize them as unrealistic. John Paton's detailed criticism of Workers Councils was based on the argument that to desert practical politics for such abstract themes would totally isolate the ILP. The London Divisional Council which provided the main support for the theory, wished to set up Councils 'in which every member is primarily representative of his group, rather than of a Political Party'. Like so many of the more sweeping ideas of the ILP Left, Workers Councils were meant to be an alternative, not only to the existing Unions, but to the central and local government and to industrial management. The ILP was often guilty of taking on the whole world in this way.

The Left wanted radical and immediate change while the official Party, though no longer thinking in terms of gradual evolution over the centuries, was content to wait for longer. Moreover, the main consideration in shaping Labour Party policy was not a long-term view of a new society so much as the need to solve the immediate problems of unemployment, bad housing and inadequate living conditions. But it was also necessary for a Party which claimed to be Socialist to be able to offer a long-term view. Much of the controversy between the Left and the established leaders of the Party centred on tactical questions, the most important of which was the pace of development towards Socialism. Virtually the whole of the Labour and Socialist movement in Britain believed that Socialism involved a considerable degree of public ownership, the lessening and eventual abolition of class differences and the 'active participation of the greatest possible number in the making of decisions'.[12] The role of the Left in the discussions of the 1930s was to pose a radical, often syndicalist alternative to the ideas of efficiency and planning which had been inherited from the Fabians. Hence the Socialist ideal was constantly modified by reference to practical problems, while the purely administrative approach was infused with a certain amount of idealism, without which it would have had little appeal.

CHAPTER 16

Attitudes to War and Foreign Policy

It is important to understand some of the basic attitudes which determined the Left approach to foreign affairs during the 1930s.[1] To a great extent the Left based its policy, or rather its propaganda, on attitudes formed during the First World War and made little concrete contribution to the hesitant and confused development of Labour's foreign policy. On the other hand, it did as much as the Labour Party to arouse public indignation against the policy of the National Government. The way in which that policy was presented to the public aroused the opposition of the Left and of the entire Labour movement, the Liberal Party and a section of the Conservative Party itself. In the denunciation of this policy its opponents were necessarily negative. Yet on the Left there were common attitudes to war and foreign policy.

The pre-1914 Second International had accepted the Marxist view that war was the result of rival imperialists clashing in their search for colonies and new markets for capitalist industry. In Britain the ILP was more influenced by pacifist convictions; by objection on religious or humanitarian grounds to the taking of life. In the late 1930s the Left found itself in open opposition to the pacifist element in the Labour Party, led by George Lansbury and Dr Alfred Salter. In the previous decade, owing to the predominance of the ILP over the Left, pacifism had been widely accepted throughout the radical wing of the Party. Only after 1935 did the gulf open up between individual pacifism, the belief in 'collective security' of the official Labour Party, and the 'war resistance' outlook of the extreme Left.

From the end of the First World War until the rise of Fascism in Europe, the Labour Party was fully committed to supporting the

League of Nations as the agent for 'collective security', and to supporting general disarmament in keeping with the aims of the League. In 1935 Clement Attlee described the official policy of the Party, (of which he was to become leader after the defeat of its pacifist leader, George Lansbury) as follows:

> We stand for collective security through the League of Nations. We reject the use of force as an instrument of policy. We stand for the reduction of armaments and pooled security.... Our policy is not one of seeking security through rearmament but through disarmament. Our aim is the reduction of armaments, and then the complete abolition of all national armaments and the creation of an international police force under the League.[2]

Until 1935, there was considerable agreement within the Labour movement on foreign policy. There were some differences, of course, which had in them the seeds of later violent controversies. Until the entry of the USSR into the League of Nations, the Communists continued to characterize it in Lenin's words as a 'thieves' kitchen'. The Communist International, particularly in 1932, was concerned with what it believed to be an imminent 'war of intervention' against the Soviet Union. These attitudes lingered in the Socialist League and the ILP for some years, and were used to justify the Hitler-Stalin pact in 1939.

The main controversy within the Labour movement in the early 1930s grew round the question of 'war resistance' – to some extent an abstract discussion which became irrelevant after the rise of Nazi Germany. Yet it illustrates the differing approaches of the Left and the rest of the movement. In 1924, the International Federation of Trade Unions, the Social-Democratic organization, had declared that 'there is one power which can end war, and only one. That power is organised labour'.[3] This meant that industrial action should be used if political action failed to prevent the entry of a national government into war, a view modified by the widespread belief in the potential effectiveness of the League of Nations as an agency for solving international problems. In August 1933, the Brussels Congress of the International Federation of Trade Unions recognized 'that the general strike is the ultimate weapon of the working class against war' but modified this position by stressing that the 'general strike against war' should be used only when an immediate danger of war presented itself.[4] The

British Trade Unions were also committed to strike action. Yet most Trade Union officials were prepared to leave the decision on ways to prevent war to the political leaders of the movement. Bjarne Braatoy, in his exhaustive survey of the theory of labour action to prevent war, concluded that until 1934, 'the main objective of Labour pressure has been to bring the disarmament negotiations into being and to make them a going concern'.[5]

The Left remained committed to direct action. The new Constitution of the ILP, drafted in 1932, stated that 'if war is declared in spite of all opposition, the ILP will demand and work for an immediate general strike and seek to use the war situation for the downfall of Capitalism'.[6] Three years later, when the Party had become far more extreme and lost its pacifist group, it had developed a detailed policy for 'action against war', which was adopted by the Paris International Bureau. This contained most of the attitudes common to the extreme Left at the beginning of the decade, but largely abandoned by 1935. Before the outbreak of a war the ILP suggested the 'exposure of the League of Nations'; opposition to war preparations; united working class action against war; withdrawal from the Colonies; the penetration of the Forces with anti-militarist propaganda; international working-class co-ordination; and, if necessary the declaration of the General Strike. Should war break out, the Party would work for mass-resistance and the overthrow of the capitalist class; revolutionary propaganda; the encouragement of unrest in the armed forces, the encouragement of 'fraternization'; and the formation of Workers Councils for the seizure of power.[7] The ILP was not an organization which could conceivably achieve any of these aims. But they were shared by the entire radical Left at the beginning of the decade. By the actual outbreak of war the policy of the ILP was only acceptable to a tiny minority.

The widespread pacifism and support for 'war resistance' in the Labour movement at the beginning of the decade reflected a natural and justifiable desire to prevent a repetition of the events leading to the First World War. The Marxist interpretation of war was subconsciously accepted by many in the leadership of the Labour Party who were not themselves on the Left. Most of the Party leaders would have agreed with Laski that 'while the roots of war cannot be traced to any single habit, its main causes lie in the economic field'.[8] The Party officially lent its support to the abolition of the manufacture of arms for private profit, and was prepared to consider the revision of those parts of the Versailles Treaty which were held to impose undue burdens on Germany. There was, thus, a very sympathetic audience in the Labour movement for the arguments of the extreme Left. In 1933, for instance, the Miners' Federation of Great Britain decided to urge the TUC to call a general strike in the event of war. This policy had also been adopted without resistance by the Labour Party Conference of 1932.

Conflict between the Left and the rest of the Labour movement only became apparent on this issue after the rise of Hitler. The question of 'direct action' provided the most obvious bone of contention. It had been adopted by all those sections of the Left which were most unpopular with the Union leadership, including groups like the Socialist League which had hardly any contact with industrial organizations. In 1935, the Socialist League at its Bristol Conference, decided that 'the Movement must declare that under no circumstances will it assist in a war waged under capitalist rule'.[9] It adopted the familiar argument that mass resistance to war must be organized, with local Trades Councils as the centres of action and it organized area conferences to discuss 'mass resistance' to war.

At the time of the Socialist League Conference the Abyssinian War was in progress, and a crisis on foreign policy was coming to a head within the Labour Party. Christian and humanitarian pacifists like Lansbury were unable to accept the use of coercive League of Nations sanctions against Italy. From another point of view, Cripps, Maxton and their followers were opposed to the League of Nations and unsympathetic to Abyssinia. 'The struggle over Abyssinia, whatever the composition of the conflicting forces, will be waged for the economic aggrandisement of national capitalist interests', stated the official journal of the Socialist League.[10] The ILP, too, opposed League sanctions; it urged instead a 'working class boycott' directed against the sending of war material to Italy.

The Communists, on the other hand, agreed with Bevin, Citrine and the vast majority of the Labour Party, that support for the League of Nations meant support for the use of sanctions. The Labour Party Annual Conference of 1935 adopted this view overwhelmingly. Herbert Morrison, summing up for the National Executive, specifically rejected the approach of Cripps. 'Do not let us delude ourselves', he said, 'that what some people call Trade Union working-class sanctions are likely to be fully effective.'[11] The decisions of the 1935 Brighton Conference embodied a complete rejection of 'war resistance' within the Labour Party and also a complete rejection of the Christian pacifist viewpoint. What had previously been widely accepted became the policy only of such small minorities as the ILP, the No More War Movement or the Trotskyists. The bulk of the Left adopted a totally different approach.

In September 1935, Harry Pollitt wrote that 'we are for working class action on a national and international scale and we are for the League of Nations imposing all forms of sanctions on Italy in defence of Abyssinia'.[12] The objections of Cripps to the League of Nations were dismissed as 'negative pseudo-socialist'.[13] The earlier British Anti-War Council was replaced by the British Youth Peace Assembly, formed in 1936, to broaden the appeal of the movement. This accorded with the Comintern decision that 'the drawing of pacifist organisations and their adherents into the united front of struggle for peace acquires great importance in mobilising the petty bourgeois masses, progressive intellectuals, women and youth against war'.[14] Despite this aim, the analysis of war common to all Marxists was not abandoned. Communists did not accept 'that war can be eliminated while the capitalist system still exists'. They still called for 'the struggle for the transformation of the imperialist war into civil war'.[15] Though this attitude was to be submerged for three years, it was to be revived in a modified form on the outbreak of war.

The Left could not remain aloof from world affairs any more than the Labour Party. The discussions of the early 1930s assumed that war would be the result of rivalry between capitalist powers or of intervention against the Soviet Union. However, the introduction of conscription in Germany, the invasion of Abyssinia and, most important, the Spanish Civil War, made this approach outdated. It became necessary to face the fact that the Fascist states had aggressive intentions and that Fascism had to be checked. The pacifists still refused to accept any violent resistance, whatever the consequences. George Lansbury undertook a European tour in which he discussed the danger of war with Hitler and Mussolini. The Left, in contrast, wished for the violent overthrow of the Nazi regime, for armed resistance to Fascism in Spain and, with an important reservation, for rearmament. The reservation was that rearmament should be carried out by a 'Peoples Government' and not by the National Government, which the Left held to be favourable to the Fascist powers. Considerable discussion and doubts preceded the decision to support rearmament. It was not until July 1937 that the Parliamentary Labour Party abandoned its opposition to the Government's belated rearmament programme. Even then it did so by a majority of only six, after continual pressure from the TUC and in opposition to its leaders, Attlee, Morrison and Greenwood. In the same year, the Annual Conference of the Miners' Federation unanimously attacked rearmament.

Not until the end of the Unity Campaign of 1937 was the dilemma on the Left over rearmament settled, if the compromise to support armed force only when used by a Peoples Government can be called a settlement. The Unity Manifesto expressed opposition to rearmament, though G. D. H. Cole suggests that 'the words in question got into the document because the ILP would not come in without it'.[16] The ILP still adhered rigidly to the analysis of war as an imperialist struggle. At the end of 1936 it had warned that 'once the Labour Party tells the National Government that its support can be counted upon in a policy of rearmament, its effectiveness as an Opposition will be destroyed'.[17] With the winding up of the Socialist League and the disappearance of the ILP from the Unity Campaign, this opposition to rearmament gradually lessened. Even in the middle of 1937, however, the Communist Party Congress adopted a resolution on 'The Fight for Peace' calling for opposition to any war in which the Soviet Union was not involved. In the following year, with the annexation of Austria and the growing threat to Czechoslovakia, the Party changed its attitude. A pamphlet published in the middle of 1938 argued that the policy of a Peoples Government should include the adoption of: 'any rearmament and defence measures necessary in the interests of peace and based on the principle of collective security'.[18]

Left propaganda was couched in terms of preserving peace, as was that of the Labour Party. The United Peace Alliance posited a strong alliance between Britain, France and the USSR as the basis for peace. From 'mass resistance' the Left had moved to advocating an alliance system. The Left was in a serious dilemma, one it shared to some extent with all opponents of the National Government. It was illogical to attack the Government for 'appeasement', while at the same time opposing rearmament on the grounds that to support the British Government would not strengthen resistance to Fascism. The confusion and fear in the public mind at the time of the Munich crisis was fully reflected in the policies of the Left and in those of the Labour Party. James Maxton, in common with all Party leaders in the Commons except the one-man Communist Party of William Gallacher, welcomed the agreement brought back from Munich. He 'believed that what we have got in the world is the possibility of laying the foundations of peace', though he went on to assert the impossibility of peace 'on the basis of the capitalist order of society'.[19]

Relief at the Munich settlement vanished almost immediately. Attlee called for a new peace conference which would include the United States and the USSR. The Left became even more vocal in its attack on the Government, which it coupled with criticism of the Labour Party for its increasing co-operation in the rearmament programme. The only measure of defence to which the Left lent support was the provision of deep shelters against air attack. A group of Cambridge scientists, led by Professor J. B. S. Haldane, pressed for such protection, which the Government resisted. Over all other issues the dilemma remained. It is expressed in the statement on conscription made by the Communist Party on 24 May 1939 which argued that under the Chamberlain Government conscription was 'a weapon on the side of Fascism'. Under a Peoples Government, on the other hand, the Party would be prepared to 'support the compulsory military training of the population on the basis of the democratic army system'.[20] The Communist Party and the Left were still unprepared to accept rearmament under the National Government, though they had come a long way from 'war resistance'.

It is one thing to develop a theory of war in the abstract, and another to be faced with war itself. In September 1939, the only section of the Left with an unequivocal attitude to war was the ILP and associated and equally unrepresentative groups. These groups held the war to be an 'imperialist struggle' and kept to that attitude throughout. 'The ILP, which opposed the war from the first, urges the workers to demand that it be stopped', ran a statement in support of the Stop the War Candidate in East Stirling.[21] The Communist Party, in contrast, was in a difficult position. Its propaganda for the past two years had stressed the need to oppose

Fascism by every means. The draft report to the Party's Sixteenth Congress, published shortly before the war, had called for 'continuous efforts ... to counter the widespread pacifist propaganda in the Labour and Co-operative Movements, which is undermining the resistance to Fascist aggression and opening the way to war'.[22]

The statement *How to Win the War* published by the Party on 2 September was partly the work of the entire Central Committee, and not simply a personal statement by Harry Pollitt. It put forward the theory of the 'struggle on two fronts', a continuation of the ambivalent attitude to rearmament. The statement called for 'the military defeat of Hitler and the political defeat of Chamberlain'. However, the Pact of Non-Aggression signed between Germany and the Soviet Union rather altered the situation. It had been central to the 'United Peace Alliance' that it should include the USSR. Once the USSR was allied to Nazi Germany the Party had to reconsider its hastily made decision to support the war. A Central Committee Manifesto, issued on 7 October, made it clear that 'the responsibility for the present imperialist war lies equally on all the warring powers'. One month later the Communist International described the war as 'an out and out imperialist war and not in the interest of the working class'.[23]

This change of attitude was rationalized on two grounds. To those outside the closed circle of the Left it was explained that Western attempts to encourage a Nazi attack on the USSR had failed and that, consequently, the Western powers were forced into war with Germany to preserve the balance of power and their own imperialist interests. Within the Left the Communists used the Marxist analysis applied to the First World War, though they did not go so far as to adopt the 'revolutionary defeatism' of Lenin. The only group to do so were the Trotskyists, following the plea of the International Communist League made in 1934 for 'the transformation of imperialist war into civil war'.[24] The ILP called for 'a workers' Socialist Government in Britain with the will to establish social equality and to liberate the peoples of the empire'.[25] This was close to the Communist wish for 'a Peoples Government, truly representative of the working people and able to command the confidence of working people throughout the world'.[26]

The great bulk of the Left within the Labour Party accepted the 'struggle on two fronts' against Germany and the Chamberlain Government. Those who completely opposed the war were an ill-assorted and mutually suspicious minority. An amendment to the Speech from the Throne, calling for an immediate peace conference, which was moved by John McGovern of the ILP in December 1940, was supported by the three ILP Members, by Gallacher for the Communists, by David Kirkwood, representing the anti-war sentiment of the 1916 Clyde, and by Dr Alfred Salter, the most rigid pacifist in the Labour Party after the death of Lansbury.[27] In by-elections, too, the opposition to the war was divided, the ILP and its Stop the War allies usually doing better than the Communist Party. As usual, however, the Communist Party found more support in the Labour movement than in the electorate. The calling of the Peoples Convention in January 1941, was the culmination of the Party's campaign for the 'victory of the Peoples Government'. It embraced the usual impressive variety of Labour organizations, and had some marginal influence on the Labour movement. The Peoples Convention was, however, short-lived. No sooner had its campaign for 'the building of wide, popular and powerful opposition'[28] got under way, than the Soviet Union was invaded by Germany. The Communists now called for 'the united front of all sections of the people (not only of the Left anti-imperialist or pro-Soviet elements, but of all opposed to Hitler, and supporting the Pact) to drive forward the maximum effort in the joint war with the Soviet Union for the defeat of Hitler'.[29] By the end of the year, J. R. Campbell was explaining 'How Leftism Helps Hitler'. 'Many people are driven to fury and demand a "Peoples Government etc." ', he wrote. 'We welcome their eagerness for a new front to aid the Soviet Union. But can we get it by clamour for a peoples government which would exclude the parties in the existing coalition, or can we get it best by mobilising the people and forcing the existing Government to act? The latter is surely the only way to get Britain in the shortest possible time to play the part of a full ally of the Soviet Union.'[30]

The difficulties of the Communist Party at the beginning of the war illustrate the problem facing the Left in elaborating a theory of war and foreign policy. The Left had maintained its traditional opposition to war and armaments, while trying to act as the spearhead of the protest movement against 'appeasement'. Similarly the Labour Party remained devoted to collective security, while grudgingly supporting the rearmament which it realized to be inevitable in the face of German expansion. The attitude of the

Left to these concrete problems demonstrates the difficulty of adapting ideology to a rapidly changing situation. The Left, through their basically unrealistic attitude to rearmament, placed themselves in an impossible position. Similarly, the dogmatic advocacy of 'war resistance' earlier in the period was, when coupled with hostility to the League of Nations, no more practical a contribution to foreign policy than the pacifism of Lansbury. The Left, together with most of the Labour Party, experienced the difficulties of trying to develop a principled rather than pragmatic foreign policy. What was common to the Left was the belief that the main object of foreign policy was to preserve peace and to advance the interests of the international Socialist movement. The Left had a vaguely defined common attitude but it was unable to develop a coherent policy.

CHAPTER 17

The Anatomy of the Left

The Labour Party had grown out of the combination of three minor political groups with the trade unions. Although in a permanent minority, the ILP, the Fabian Society and, more erratically, the British Socialist Party, continued to infuse new ideas into the growing party. The Left in the 1930s consisted of groups tracing their descent from these three pioneering socialist societies and of individuals who accepted policies largely emanating from such groups. The Labour movement was very conscious of its past. Ideas were transmitted in political propaganda and discussion from one generation to the next, shaped by the peculiar circumstances of the times but remaining fundamentally unchanged. The internal life of the Left was intellectually self-contained. Arguments were based on unstated assumptions and actions were often governed by organizational loyalties rather than by externally dictated realities. The Left had a history and tradition which was as consistent and coherent as that of the Labour movement as a whole.

The Communists and the ILP provided the two major streams of opinion within the Left. At the beginning of the 1930s the former were revolutionary and the latter constitutional though eventually these positions were to be almost reversed. An essential difference between the two streams appeared to be the Communist belief in Marxist-Leninist 'science' as contrasted with ILP 'sentiment'. In fact the Left tradition represented an intermingling of the traditions of the syndicalists, the Marxists and the Liberal reformers, and its adherents accepted sufficient basic common principles for there to be some ground for agreement. Factional disputes reflected attempts of one minority to dominate over others rather than fundamental cleavages. Organizations, despite their differences, recognized the existence of shared ties. Common links, though stretched to breaking-point, were sufficiently important for common action on the Left to be possible. Even the Marxists had an ideology which was becoming increasingly flexible, while others on the Left had such loose ideological moorings that they swung in whichever breeze was the strongest.

There was every reason for the Left to try to act in harmony. Its base in the Labour movement was fairly small and its impact on the working class at large even smaller. The more factionalized and hostile the component elements of the Left, the less effective its modest influence was likely to be. After initial difficulties a form of United Front was built up. A form of 'working class unity' had been developed by the Communist International as early as 1921 to provide channels for Communist infiltration into the Labour movement. The initial expansion of the Communist Parties had been checked partly by attempts to impose uniformity on what were essentially nonconformist groups. Communist Parties, by adopting the popular slogan of 'Unity', hoped to reverse these setbacks by influencing the mass social-democratic movements.[1] The origin of the United Front as a Communist tactic made it unacceptable to the leadership of the British Labour movement. Yet after 1935 there were strong incentives towards united action which drew increasing numbers of people into the orbit of Left activity. It became an insufficient argument against the Unity Campaigns to say that they were merely a continuation of long-established Communist tactics. The rapid expansion of the United Front in the 1930s from a tenuous alliance between small groupings into something resembling a nationwide movement, was spectacular, giving the Left a unity of outlook and activity which it had tended to lose in the dissensions of previous years.

The strength of the Left

As the Left was a 'tendency' rather than a strictly defined organization the dimensions of its support are difficult to measure. The only reliable figures for Left strength are to be found in the membership figures of the Left minorities, and there was much overlapping and fluctuation even in these. The total enrolled in the two groups outside the Labour Party, the Communists and the ILP,[2] declined as members left the disaffiliated ILP, and rose as new members joined the Communists during the United Front campaign. In 1931 there were 24,000 in the two parties, including some in the ILP who were only nominal members. By 1933 this had dropped to 16,000 and, two years later, to 13,000. In 1937, first year of the Unity Campaign, there were 19,000 in the two groups, increasing to 24,000 by the outbreak of war. In 1931 the great majority of these were in the ILP. By 1939 the great majority were in the Communist Party. The only way to estimate the Left following within the Labour Party is to subtract the above figures from the membership of the Left Book Club, a rough but not unreliable approximation. In 1937, on this calculation, the Left in the Labour Party had a strength of about 30,000, while two years later this total had risen to perhaps 35,000. These figures correspond closely to the total number of signatories to the Unity pledge of 1937 and to the circulation of *Tribune* during 1939. The circulation of the *Daily Worker*, another indication of minimal sympathy with the Left, reached 80,000 a day immediately before the war, or some 20,000 more than the combined total of Left militants inside and outside the Labour Party as estimated above. The regular circulations of the five leading Left periodicals per issue ranged between 12,000 and 80,000 copies.[3] As a final indication of the strength of the Left, the membership claimed by the Friends of the Soviet Union fluctuated around the 60,000 mark.

The Left, then, had at the most some 60,000 followers in the Labour movement, one third of them outside the Labour Party but working in affiliated organizations.[4] The Labour movement as a whole included about 450,000 activists either working regularly within their unions, enrolled in the Labour Party or members of Left minorities outside the Party. However, the number of those who could be termed militant in the sense of being regular participants in propaganda, election and agitational work was relatively small. Those who worked for the party regularly were almost as exceptional as the trade unionist who attended branch meetings. In many industrial areas the Labour Party had no real need to maintain constant political propaganda and the membership in predominantly Labour areas rarely took part in the controversies being discussed in the South and in the larger cities. In some places the Labour Party scarcely existed, claiming the minimum allowable figure of 120 members in order to remain affiliated.[5]

From the welter of dubious and overlapping figures which make up the membership totals for the Labour Party it is just possible to gain some impression of the proportion of regularly active members. If a quarter of the enrolled membership were active, and this is probably overgenerous, then about 100,000 people would have taken part in Labour politics regularly and would presumably have been interested in the political controversies of the day. This was the constituency to which the Left could appeal. Assuming that the Labour Party was subject to democratic control, and leaving aside the problem of winning influence in the trade unions, the Left could transform Labour into a socialist party through these 100,000 militants. The most influential were the voluntary officials of ward and constituency parties and the members of their respective committees. At the most an active constituency Labour Party might include over two hundred regularly participating members who could be described as militants. The six hundred constituencies with some form of Labour Party would include a total, once again, of over 100,000 militants.

If the balance of conference voting power rested with the inactive two million affiliated unionists, the responsibility for conducting the Labour Party's political compaigns belonged to these 100,000 militants. It was from this group that the increasing number of parliamentary and local government candidates was drawn as the party's electoral following began to expand away from its strongholds around the coalfields and into the new industrial areas of the Midlands and the South-East. If it is accepted that the Left numbered about one-third of the active members of the local parties, or 30,000 out of 100,000 militants, a clear idea of their importance and likely influence emerges. This estimate is possibly borne out by the fact that one-third of the constituency parties called for a Labour Party conference in 1938, or sent representatives to Constituency Party Association conferences. Both these activities were supported by *Tribune* and official support from a local party suggested some sympathy with the Left. The degree of activity of Left-wingers is difficult to determine but it seems probable that the great majority of them were militants rather than otherwise. Only 6,000 were actually enrolled in the two Left minorities within the party, the Socialist League and the Scottish Socialist Party, but these had a limited appeal. Several thousand members of the Labour League of Youth must be included among the Left at the peak period of that organization. The activities of the Left within the Labour Party were supplemented by the Left minorities outside and particularly by the Communist Party. All members of that party were obliged to manifest a degree of commitment not found in other groups. Anyone who remained in the ILP after the first few years of disaffiliation can only be regarded as a militant. Both minor parties worked in the same areas, organizations and campaigns as Labour Party militants, especially during the Unity Campaigns which were specifically designed to encourage such collective effort.

The balance of political forces within the Labour Party was thus more favourable to the Left than might be supposed. One-third of the active militants of the Labour Party were probably favourable to radical policies. Much of the electoral and propagandist activity of the Labour Party was in the hands of radical militants. Ultimately, as local Labour Parties became more favourable to the Left, it became common for them to choose their officials and candidates from among the radicals. The danger of this tendency from the official viewpoint is obvious. Moreover, many young people were being recruited into the party on the strength of unofficial policies, thus creating a further reserve of militants in the future.[6] It seems highly probable that many of the 100,000 new members gained by the party in the late 1930s were recruited by the Left, especially in the areas of new Labour strength outside the traditional industrial and mining areas.

The geography of the Left

The Left within the Labour Party was restricted in its electoral activities by its relationship with the party. Yet the Left minorities were able to use electoral contests to spread their influence; for example, the Oxford and Bridgwater by-elections in 1938 drew attention to the aims of the United Peace Alliance. The electoral strategy of small groups is likely to differ from that of the national parties. The Communists knew from past experience that chances of election were remote in all except half-a-dozen constituencies, as indicated by their withdrawal from all but two contests in 1935. Communists saw their contests as a means of drawing attention to their Party's existence and to its programme, and as an opportunity for strengthening the Party in a particular area.

The ILP was in a much stronger electoral position than the Communists throughout the decade. In the first place they had a number of sitting MPs and could not so easily be accused of 'splitting the Labour vote'. Indeed, where the Labour Party intervened against established ILP leaders it suffered the most humiliating defeats in its history. The ILP did not specialize, as did the Communists, in opposing leading Labour candidates, preferring to concentrate on those seats where the ILP was well established. The contrasting electoral strategy of the two Left minorities illustrates the differences between a parliamentary and a revolutionary party. Unlike the ILP the Communists were pledged to using parliament only as a platform and saw electoral contests mainly as a way of spreading Communist ideas. The Communist Party never achieved the popular following accorded to the ILP in some areas.[7]

In the inter-war years the two-party system had not assumed the rigidity of subsequent decades. The Parliament of 1935 contained five representatives of Left minorities to whom was added a sixth, elected as a supporter of the United Peace Alliance. In the General Election of 1931, the ILP and the Communists polled 335,168 votes and, with rather fewer than half the candidates, gained 166,694 votes in the more prosperous conditions of 1935. Neither of these totals is startling, but they do suggest the existence of some sympathy among the electors, particularly as every Left vote had to be gained at the expense of the Labour Party.

The political geography of the British Labour movement helps us to understand the support for the Left. In the 1930s the Labour Party was not a national party in the sense that its following was not evenly spread over the country. Until 1945 the Labour Party represented the poorest areas of London, Glasgow, Manchester, Leeds and Sheffield and the miners of South Wales, Yorkshire, the North-East and Scotland. Laski went so far as to suggest that in both 1931 and 1935 the unemployed, away from the coalfields, mostly voted for the National Government.[8] Consequently the Left, which was essentially the radical wing of the Labour movement, secured electoral support in the same limited areas. In some mining and industrial areas, particularly in the North of England, Methodism and the trade unions and co-operatives had built up Labour support on previously Liberal foundations. Here the Left could not gain an electoral foothold. Only in those areas where socialist minorities had already established followings did the Left find sympathy for its radical socialist message. In Scotland, in South Wales and in the poorest parts of London, the Left was often able to meet the Labour Party on its own terms. Elsewhere it had no choice but to support Labour candidates or to face ignominious defeat.

Regional variation in political sympathy was still well marked in the 1930s. Scotland was the main area of support for the Left minorities.[9] All five Left MPs came from Scotland and both the ILP and the Communists got the bulk of their votes from Scots.[10] The ILP had started life as the Scottish Labour Party and still retained the sympathy of many voters in Glasgow, Renfrewshire, Lanark and Ayr. Both past traditions and the harsh realities of the present strengthened the appeal of the ILP. For central Scotland was not only the worst-housed urban area in Britain, if not in Europe, it was also a Distressed Area. The Parliamentary politics of the Labour Party had little appeal to many of the worst-hit voters of Scotland. In Glasgow the classic conditions of early industrialism were still present and the ILP, with its slogans drawn from that era, could command a large following.[11]

Because of the dominance of the ILP in the poorer districts of Glasgow, the Communist Party was never of much electoral significance, polling as little as a tenth the ILP vote in municipal elections. On the other hand, in parts of the Clyde Valley, in Clydebank, in the Vale of Leven and in Greenock, the Party had continuing success which has not totally disappeared even today. Its main stronghold was in Fife owing to its control over the United Mineworkers of Scotland. This 'Red Union' was led by Abe Moffat and claimed over 3,000 members.[12] It was larger than the official Fife, Kinross and Clackmannan Miners' Association and was thus able to secure the defeat of the Labour MP, William Adamson, who was associated with the latter body. In South Wales, too, the strength of the Communists was in their hold over the miners' union. Arthur Horner, a well known Rhondda Communist, was elected as chairman of the South Wales Miners' Federation in 1936.[13] Harry Pollitt, reporting to the CP's Thirteenth Congress in 1935, emphasized the importance of influencing that union:

The thing that has to be stressed is that the South Wales experience has revealed that where we have a foothold in the miners lodge, in that place we can use this as a lever for drawing in the ward committees of the Labour Party, for getting the trades councils and shopkeepers.[14]

In 1935 the CP had sixteen councillors in South Wales, six of them on the Rhondda Urban District. Their twenty-five candidates secured nearly 1,000 votes each in the April local elections, approaching very nearly the Labour vote in the seats contested.[15] While this was not spectacular, it compared very well with the English results.

Two South Wales MPs, Aneurin Bevan and S. O. Davies, worked regularly with the Left. The strong 'Lib-Lab' tradition of miners' MPs was weakened in South Wales which was one of the worst Distressed Areas in Britain. There was a long tradition of syndicalist and socialist activity and a large following for the National Unemployed Workers Movement. Industrial relations on the coalfield had been bad for many years and in the 1930s places like Nantyglo and Maesteg came close to complete unemployment. The whole Labour movement, official and Left-wing, was forced into radicalism. Until it was dissolved by the Labour National Executive in 1936, a South Wales Council of Action united all sections, the Labour Party, the Miners' Federation, the ILP, Communists and the NUWM. To a lesser extent even areas like Durham, much more conservative than Wales, were forced into radical action by unemployment. There were very few Communists in the North-East, yet the Durham district of the MFGB joined with South Wales in supporting Communist affiliation to Labour and the Unity Campaign.[16] In 1932 the Labour-controlled Durham County Public Assistance Committee was suspended for refusing to operate the Means Test. Although Left minorities never had much electoral following on the English coalfields, economic conditions encouraged radicalism. To an important degree the leadership of this slowly growing working-class radicalism fell to the Left and particularly to the Communist Party.

In the rest of the country, outside London, there was sporadic support for Left minorities and more consistent support for the Left in the Labour Party. Isolated ILP branches flourished in Bradford, in the Manchester area, in Norwich and in such distant places as Cornwall. The Communist Party too had a rather scattered following. It was strong numerically around Manchester but its

Lancashire District was often under fire from the Party leaders for its 'sectarianism'. Its membership in the North-East was very small. Individual Communists were scattered around the country often giving a false impression of a nationwide following. Neither the Communist Party nor the ILP, let alone groups like the Socialist League or the Scottish Socialist Party, could hope to create a national party. They had to be content with their influence in one or two key industrial areas which were dominated by mining and engineering. In Wales and Scotland trade union influence and radical traditions favoured the Left. This was only true in very limited parts of England, and only among the working classes. But as the emphasis of Left campaigns shifted from unemployment to fascism, the Left was able to reach out to the growing middle classes of the South-East who were still largely untouched by trade unionism or even by the Labour Party.

London was both the centre for these middle classes and also the focus for most national political controversy. There was no single dominant union and those unions which were most important in traditional Labour areas were the strongly anti-Communist Transport and General, General and Municipal, and National Union of Railwaymen. Political factions flourished in London. Both the pro-Communist and the Trotskyist groups in the ILP were centred on London and the Labour League of Youth was dominated by London branches. Nearly half of the Communist Party membership lived in London.[17] The Socialist League and the Left Book Club found most support in the middle-class suburbs, and the backbone of the radical Constituency Parties Association was formed by the London and Home Counties Labour Association. All this was in marked contrast to the Labour Party's reliance on the provinces for its electoral support. Yet the London Labour Party was already the best organized in the country and constituency parties around London were stronger than elsewhere. The Parliamentary Labour Party, the National Executive Committee and the Party Conference reflected Labour's power in the provincial industrial areas. Nevertheless Party headquarters and publishing houses were all in London while all activity involving political pressure on Parliament had necessarily to concentrate on London as the centre of government.

The electoral strength of the Left in London was weak. Except in Stepney with its long radical tradition and a concentration of immigrants from Europe, the Communists made little impression on Labour voters. In Battersea and Bethnal Green, centres of Communist support in the 1920s, the disbanding of pro-Communist Labour Parties in 1926 limited Communist influence. In Bermondsey,[18] Lambeth, Poplar and Southwark, strong Labour Parties with good records prevented the Communists from making any impression. Thus in the poorest districts of London the Communist Party had little alternative but to co-operate with Labour as far as possible. London provided the best opportunities for such co-operation and for the various Unity campaigns. For not only were there nearly 10,000 members of Left minorities in Greater London to about 90,000 individual Labour Party members but at the height of the Unity Campaign something like one-fifth of these Labour Party members were associating with the Left through the Socialist League, the Left Book Club and the Labour League of Youth. The activities of the British Union of Fascists also contributed to the growth of Left-wing sentiments. For while there was a division of opinion on the methods to be used in opposing the BUF, the London Labour movement was agreed on the need to stop fascist violence in the East End.[19]

Where there was no Labour movement there was no Left. With the strengthening of Left sympathies in local Labour parties and the spread of Left ideas through the Unity Campaign, the Left slowly tended to become as nationwide as the Labour movement itself. This spread of support could not have been achieved by the independent Left minorities on their own. In the 1930s the Communists and the ILP were still confined to those areas in which the ILP, the syndicalists or the Marxists had flourished at the beginning of the century. While sectarian minorities remained the main agency for the spread of Left propaganda this situation was bound to continue. The resources of the small groups were limited and their access to the mass media depended on their newsworthiness in the eyes of editors and proprietors who were unsympathetic to them.

With the growth of local Labour parties this situation changed. Contacts were easily established through county, regional and national conferences. The speaking campaigns of Cripps, Maxton, Pollitt, Bevan and others were assured an audience from local Labour parties. While the influence of radio and the press was becoming more important in shaping the opinions of the electorate, the Labour movement still relied on its wealth of good speakers to spread propaganda. Increasingly these were to be found on the Left. Through the network of meetings, conferences and rallies which characterized a Labour movement steadily nationalizing its organization, the Left was finally able to break out of the industrial ghettoes in which most of its work had been concentrated for the previous four decades.

The Left and the Labour movement

The Left became strongly established in the Labour movement during the 1930s, yet it seldom came near winning a Labour conference in its favour let alone transforming the policy of the party. Despite its elaborate pretensions to the contrary, the Labour Party gave little real opportunity to its active members either to change its policies or to control its Parliamentary leadership. The Left, in demanding inner-party democracy, was adhering to the convention of the Labour movement which accepted the principle of control of the higher by the lower ranks. But this was only a convention and not a reality. Essentially the entire control of party policy remained in the hands of the Parliamentary leadership, which in turn relied on an increasingly professional party organization to elaborate and propagate the policy and to build an electoral machine capable of returning a government. The Parliamentary leadership and the professional organization could not function without the approval of the trade union leaders. It was they who ensured solid support for the party in the country and provided most of the funds to maintain the central organization. The triumvirate of Parliamentary leadership, professional organization and union officials exercised a control over the policy and activity of the party as complete as was possible in a mass movement based on federal association and varied traditions. This control was maintained by the device of the block vote at annual conference and the increasing tendency to stress the unity rather than the diversity of the Labour Party.

While the union, Parliamentary and professional elements in control of the party remained united there was only a slight possibility of the Left achieving their objectives. Nevertheless, a tiny number of people managed to constitute a national political movement of some note. On the wider issues which dominated politics after 1935 the Left often took the initiative away from the Labour Party in terms of agitation and propaganda. The success of the Labour movement in the 1930s rested on protest and agitation and in this respect the Left was indispensable. It legitimized itself within the movement not by its ability to win decisions but by its functions as conscience and propagandist.

The Left had its own policies, machinery and leadership. Although there were often bitter dissensions within it, there was also, particularly during the Unity Campaigns, a common feeling and identification on the Left, to the exclusion on occasions of an identification with the rest of the Labour movement. The controversy between the Communists and the ILP or the Trotskyists was a controversy within narrow limits. Had there been no acceptance of a common fund of ideas and a common field of action there could have been neither discussion nor co-operation. Most Left activity was confined within the Labour movement. In reality it was often confined to an even narrower sphere, to the militants. Only at the height of the United Peace Alliance was there any real desire or attempt to influence the 'class enemy'. Left propaganda dealt largely with the internal politics of the Labour movement. Such sectarian activity had a limited appeal. It bore little resemblance to the deliberate broadening of appeal to which all mass constitutional parties must resort. The 'movement' was the framework within which the Left operated, its militants the constituency being sought.

The Labour Party formed only a section, if the major one, of the political universe within which Left-wing activity took place. The ultimate aim was the capture of the official machinery and its utilization to carry out a Left Socialist programme. But there were other ways of influencing the Party than by confining activity to the political section alone. Parallel to the Labour Party and numerically larger than it were the trade unions and the Co-operatives. Anyone working in or supporting either of these could rightly regard himself as part of the Labour movement. Communists and other minorities could be active in the movement without being committed to the Labour Party. The Co-operative societies guarded their independence, refusing in 1936 to enter into any joint agreement with the Labour Party which would bind Co-op Party representatives to Labour policies. Similarly the individual unions resented any attempts by the TUC to force decisions on them in the political interests of the Labour Party.

The Left, then, could work in the Labour movement without being tied to the Labour Party. As that party was the political expression of the movement, however, it inevitably became necessary for political minorities to consider ways of influencing it. They could do so by moving the adoption of certain policies in affiliated bodies, which could then transmit them to the Labour Party through the rights inherent in affiliation. The activity of the Left in the Labour Party was thus supplemented by work in the affiliates. The bulk of affiliated members represented through the block vote at Labour conferences was in the unions and not in the local parties. In the 1930s, it is true, the ratio between the union and individual membership was the highest in Labour's history. This was what gave Left agitation such wide significance. Many believed that the party was becoming transformed into a genuine partnership between political and industrial wings, and that parity would eventually be achieved. However, the highest ratio reached was in 1937 when there were still nearly five affiliated unionists to every individual member. Moreover, the individual members of the party were subject to a centralized control in political matters which did not apply to the individual unionist.

An essential feature of overlapping organizations within the Labour movement was that most Labour Party militants were also in a trade union or the Co-operative Party, as well as in other groups such as the Fabian Society and the Labour League of Youth. While Communists were excluded from individual membership by the Liverpool decision of 1925, they remained eligible to record their votes through a number of organizations affiliated to the Labour Party nationally or locally. Every constituency Labour party mirrored the national federal structure. Leftism in local Labour Parties often reflected a similar sentiment in local unions. The Miners' Federation or the Amalgamated Engineering Union were as subject to Left pressure from local branches as was the Labour Party, and sometimes with more success for the Left. In several important party conference debates, notably in 1936, it was their vote, rather than that of the local parties, which provided most of the total for Left resolutions.

One militant was literally worth more than two or three inactive members of the Labour movement and his influence could be more extensive than seems possible for one individual in an organization numbering millions. Any Left minority which failed to take advantage of this fact was bound to be ineffective. The attempt of the ILP to sever all its connections with the official Labour movement led to its complete isolation. Repeatedly the Left had to work within the Labour movement however unpalatable the official policies of the Labour leadership. For despite its variety, the movement was a unified whole and influence in one section implied influence in another. Each section overlapped or, in some instances, was identical in personnel with another. The numerous organizations under Left control often prove on inspection to be but different aspects of the same group of people. The rather illusory nature of the diversity of the Labour movement is reflected in the equally illusory nature of the membership figures and of the votes recorded at Labour Party conferences. These figures do not indicate the actual strength of conflicting groups within the Labour Party. Under the block vote system every affiliated member was recorded as favouring all the decisions reached by the body in which he was enrolled. It was quite usual for one individual to have his vote registered for two opposite decisions should he belong to two organizations with differing views.

This system is the easiest way to record decisions in a mass federal party. Unfortunately at times of crisis it gave rise to antagonism. The dominant feature of all Left-wing calls for constitutional reform within the Labour Party was a desire to end the block vote system. As this involved infringing the rights of the unions it exacerbated existing tensions. The Left aimed to gain a conference majority instructing the National Executive to adopt a Left programme. This was impossible as long as the control of the great majority of votes at the conference remained in the hands of union officials who were unsympathetic to radical policies. Union delegations were largely composed of such officials, who were in constant consultation with the leaders of the Labour Party as to which policy to pursue.[20] The Left was trapped within a system which it could not abandon or change.

The Left and the Labour Party

The Left worked under the shadow of the largest democratic socialist party in the world, attempting to influence it and, if possible, to transform it into a radical socialist party committed to changing society. For despite its adoption of a socialist programme the Labour Party had an imperfectly developed corporate life. Many of its activities were mundane and routine. The average Labour Party resembled a union branch, dealing largely with business and leaving the political militant to find his political education elsewhere. Anyone who wanted more from the party than dreary business meetings, turned to the Left for education and recreation in a political setting. Some of the unions, the Co-operative Union and the National Council of Labour Colleges tried to fill this gap. The British Workers' Sports Association attempted to provide recreation for party members similar to that organized by the European Social Democrats. But if a militant wanted serious discussion he had to turn away from the official Labour movement to Left-wing groups.

The contrast between the mundane considerations dominating the official movement and the flourishing intellectual and recreational activities on the Left had two sources. The Labour Party in those areas where it had most support arose from the trade union branch, the Co-operative management committee and other businesslike and essentially non-political bodies. Apart from election months its political functions were limited to occasional canvassing and the distribution of propaganda. Its most active members were occupied in the countless party and union committees which flourished in a federal and democratic organization. Only the influx of a body of younger enthusiastic militants could alter this situation. The Independent Labour Party had originally provided such a core of enthusiasts, essential if Labour was ever to be anything more than a labour representation committee confined to a few union-dominated districts. But this enthusiasm was not always welcomed. The antagonism which built up against the ILP as a result of its attempts to force socialism on the newly formed Labour Party contributed to the smaller party's secession as much as did the sectarianism of its leaders and its supersession by the local Labour Parties in the 1920s. This antagonism was inherited by the Left, which took over the functions of the old ILP and replaced it as the driving force for socialism in the Labour movement.

The preoccupation of the Labour Party with constitutional reform through Parliament and the local authorities also contributed to its failure to hold the complete loyalty of its militants. The refusal to support what might be construed as irresponsible or unconstitutional action was epitomized by the attitude of many Labour leaders to the unemployed demonstrations. Not only did the TUC condemn the activities of the National Unemployed Workers Movement but it also frowned on any section of the unemployed adopting similar tactics; for example, both the TUC and the Labour National Executive refused to support the Jarrow Crusade. Trades Councils along the route were advised by circular not to help the marchers. Ellen Wilkinson commented that 'the comradeship of the trade unions and the Labour Movement was circular-proof on such an occasion'[21] but noted that in Chesterfield it was the Conservative Party which fed and accommodated the marchers after the local Labour movement had obeyed the instructions of the TUC.[22] The practical value of the march in arousing public opinion was considerable. Yet the official leadership of the Labour movement was so concerned with using constitutional methods that it failed to see the value of the protest.

The conservatism of the Labour movement reflected its roots in long-established working-class institutions and its acceptance of the constitutional conventions established by even older Parliamentary parties. The Left was united in rejecting such conventional methods and attitudes. This rejection, the distinguishing mark of radicalism, was genuinely disturbing to many leaders of the Labour movement, and no less disturbing to the bulk of the working-class electorate many of whom still supported the Conservative Party or were recent converts from Liberalism. Yet without some criticism of existing society the Labour Party could never have developed into a mass movement. Without its critical stance it would have lost its appeal for the thousands of talented and capable militants who supplied its local leaders, who kept its machinery functioning and who brought in support from areas and social groups where the traditions of the trade union and Co-operative movements were of little significance. The Left acted as a source of inspiration within the party, sustaining those local Labour Parties which might never succeed in returning a Labour MP but which might increase their local government representation or recruit future leaders for the Labour movement. The Labour Party wanted to convert millions of people to its cause and to build up a machine to continue this work among the younger generation. Labour could not strengthen its hold without a nationwide movement, managed in many cases by enthusiasts. Even had the Left had nothing constructive to say at all, it would still have performed a useful function in inspiring such activists.

In the 1930s Labour was a mass movement rather than a political party. The Left believed that only through a mass movement could a new society be created based on democratic and egalitarian principles. The Labour Party had not consciously committed itself to the need for such a movement, but the democratic constitution of the party, its faith in the good sense of the membership, the constant emphasis on building the party, were conducive to this end. The Left placed greater emphasis on the control of policy and leadership by the 'rank and file' than was acceptable to the movement's leaders. The ILP saw itself in 1930 as carrying out conference decisions of the Labour Party against the refusal of the Labour government to implement them. The Unity Campaigners, allied with the Constituency Parties Association, saw themselves as champions of the active local labour Parties against the trade union bureaucracy which dominated conference decisions.[23] The same populist spirit lay behind the antagonism of many union officials towards the 'intellectuals', including Cripps. The officials believed, often correctly, that they were voicing the opinions of the organized workers against the attempt of a few wealthy individuals to force their views onto the mass movement. This faith in the mass movement, common to Left and Right alike, comes out clearly in reactions to the defection of Ramsay MacDonald.

The Left, whatever it might have urged to the contrary, functioned as an ancillary to the Labour Party throughout the 1930s. The Party was eliminating organized minorities, broadening its outlook and integrating Left-wing individuals into the local Labour Parties. By 1940, the political wing of Labour was no longer federal in the sense of containing organized minorities with their own machinery, leaders and policy. The Labour Party had been almost unique in encouraging the existence of organized factions within its framework; and by the end of the 1930s that experiment in democracy had been abandoned as unworkable. The whole disagreement with the Labour League of Youth centred around the refusal of the Party to give its youth section the rights formerly enjoyed by affiliated organizations. The affiliated minorities were replaced by the constituency parties, which perpetuated the federal principle and received the affiliation of local union branches. They were nominally affiliated to the Labour Party as autonomous units, but in effect they were simply branches of a national organization. The National Executive, which had no right to limit the activities of affiliated unions, had complete control over the local parties, though it rarely exercised it. Should a candidate unacceptable to the National Executive be adopted, he could be refused endorsement.[24] Should a local Labour Party defy conference or Executive decisions, it could be disbanded or reorganized.[25] By the end of the 1930s the Left was faced with the alternatives of merging into an increasingly disciplined Labour Party or of remaining outside an increasingly effective mass organization. Those who stayed within the party lost much of their identity but this did not mean that the ideas inherited from the Left minorities were lost or that the Left became less effective in acting as a radical pressure group. It merely lost its character as an alliance of separately organized, sectarian and obscure minorities.

Influencing the movement

The Left had, inevitably, to associate itself closely with the Labour Party. Even the Communists, who aimed at ultimately creating a mass party of their own, could not do so without winning recruits and support from within the existing movement. The only untapped source of voters and supporters other than those who followed Labour was the young, middle-class radicals, and they were largely undiscovered until after 1936.

The Left continued to have the attributes of a coherent political tendency yet it was prevented from developing into a major autonomous force by the circumstances in which it found itself. It was forced to act as a pressure group rather than as a party. All attempts at independent electoral action were either a complete failure, or as in parts of Scotland and Wales, a very limited and localized success. Within the Labour movement its influence was hardly measurable in terms of immediate results. Yet the incorporation of a strong radical socialist tendency within the major opposition party had important consequences. Public opinion was shaped to an important extent by the well-publicized Left-wing attacks on the National government. Despite attempts to dissociate Labour from the more violent demonstrations, the party had inevitably to adopt many of the arguments of the Left if it were to continue to lead opposition to the government's economic and foreign policies. The pressure of the Left, though unrepresented in official Labour Party decisions, was reflected in its political outlook and actions.

The methods of pressure used by the Left collectively or by Left minorities separately, varied considerably in effectiveness. The Labour Party was originally a federation of pressure groups for political and industrial objectives and from the beginning small socialist groups had attempted to get a socialist programme adopted. When such pressure became intolerable to the 'gradualist' element in the leadership, the federal basis of the organization was replaced by a centrally controlled political wing. But this political wing became, in time, a pressure group as vocal as its predecessors. The basic assumption of the Left remained that the Labour Party could eventually be committed to a radical socialist programme through the many channels for registering decisions. The constitution of the party encouraged this belief despite all the limitations on participatory democracy. After 1931 serious attempts were made to develop new ideas from discussions among the membership in which the Socialist League took a major part. Party rules were taken to mean that policy could be altered by the passage of conference resolutions.[26] But it was left to the National Executive to draw up the party's electoral statement and in any case the party programme could only be adopted by the annual conference if passed by a two-thirds majority, an impossibility without the support of the major unions. It was not, therefore, entirely correct to say that 'there can be only one authority in this Movement, if ever it is going to be effective, for coming to decisions on Party policy, and that is this Conference'.[27] What remained true was that public attention was focused on the annual conference debates, and the Left was able, by presenting a large number of resolutions and putting up an effective argument, to maximize its audience.

The barriers to the adoption of Left resolutions did not seem to discourage the Left. There was no constitutional reason why the major unions should not adopt a Left attitude although it took another thirty years before many of them were to do so regularly. In the 1930s many unions were not greatly interested in the issues which agitated the Left and this reflected attitudes common to the working class in general. The key to the failure of the Left to build a mass following in the unions was the unacceptability of its views to the average working class elector, trade unionist or Labour Party member. The Left exercised its influence over the active and politically minded, a type rarer among unionists than in the local Labour Parties. Despite Left sentiments in the Miners' Federation, the Amalgamated Engineering Union, the Railwaymen, Shop Assistants and Furniture Workers, the control of the unions remained under the 'Bevin-Citrine dictatorship'.[28] Even in the favourably inclined unions the Left only maintained its position by continual pressure on officials and militants, a kind of activity for which the Communists were organizationally the best equipped.

The methods of pressure adopted to maintain and strengthen Left influence were varied. Fraction work, often thought to be the preserve of the Communists, was common to most Left minorities. It was largely the abandoning of this technique which led to the isolation of the ILP after 1932. The Communists took full advantage of the ILP withdrawal to increase their own influence. Any small and closely knit group can use a mass movement in this way, if for no other reason than the difficulty of generating enough enthusiasm to keep voluntary machinery working. The organized fraction, by preparing resolutions and by combining to elect suitable officials, can often succeed in 'capturing' a mass movement. The Red International of Labour Unions, in collaboration with the Executive Committee of the Comintern, laid down elaborate regulations for fraction work within unions in 1926. The General Council of the TUC tried in 1928, and again in 1934, to limit Communist rights within affiliates. This was largely ineffective because of the federalist traditions of the unions although regulations against Communists holding office were adopted by the General and Municipal Workers Union and by Trades Councils. The greatest limitation on Communist fraction work in the unions was simply that there were very few employed Communist Party members until 1935 and most unions had no Communist members at all.

Fraction work was not confined to Communists although only they had their activities controlled from a national and, ultimately, an international centre. The Socialist League stated that its aim was: 'to ensure within the wider movement a core of convinced Socialists'.[29] Though no group, except perhaps the Trotskyists, had such a highly developed theory of fraction work as the Communists, Left sympathizers found it essential to work together in an organized way to gain control of larger organizations. The growing local Labour Parties were a fruitful field, particularly after the reform of the party constitution at the Bournemouth conference of 1937. 'It is this new channel of agitation and pressure', said Cripps after the conference, 'that we ask all those who desire to see a more militant fighting policy to use to the utmost'.[30] The aim of the Constituency Parties Association was 'to give the five hundred independent units of the political section of the Party some method of expressing its corporate views on such matters as policy, propaganda and selection of candidates'.[31]

Fraction work, however successful, did not bring lasting results unless accompanied by recruitment to the fraction and the winning of wider support through effective propaganda. The failure of the Left to maintain its hold on Labour opinion after the end of 1937 underlines this difficulty. The Moscow trials, the adoption of *Labour's Immediate Programme* and the constitutional amendments at Bournemouth, antagonism to Liberals and intellectuals, all contributed to this falling off in support. The Left, however well organized among Labour Party militants, could not continue to control any major sections of the movement in which it did not enjoy wide sympathy, however passive. Mechanical fraction work, characteristic of the Communists in the early 1930s, often narrowed rather than increased support for the Left because of the resentment which it generated. Unless there was a continuous campaign of Left propaganda, fraction work and infiltration often defeated the objectives of its practitioners.

The distinction between agitations within the Labour movement and attempts to influence the general public became increasingly blurred in the late 1930s. For example, the Unity Campaign's call for 'unity of all sections of the Labour movement' had only a limited appeal within the movement. The campaign was also directed towards the voter as well as the active militant. The speaking tours of the Unity campaigns filled a gap in official Labour propaganda, and on many occasions attracted larger audiences than officially sponsored meetings.[32] The Labour Party was able on its own to attract public attention but the Left often played a more energetic and charismatic role in expressing opposition to government policies and in drawing attention to the implications of Fascism. Cripps summed up Left attitudes when he wrote that: 'the Labour Party will never inspire the necessary enthusiasm to win a majority at a general election if it comes to be regarded as a rather inefficient alternative capitalist party'.[33] For Labour was still discredited by its performance in 1931, when it lost its hold not merely on middle-class voters, who had always been predominantly hostile, but on many of the unemployed and on the industrial workers outside a few traditionally Labour areas. The Left forced the pace in regaining the sympathies and support of many former Labour voters and of the younger generation to whom the traditions of the Labour Party meant very little. By vigorous campaigning and by association with the Labour Party, the Left helped to create an atmosphere sympathetic to the Opposition which Labour, with its excessive caution, seemed incapable of creating for itself.

Left campaigns, though limited by funds and numbers, were conducted on as large a scale as those of the Labour Party itself. In 1937, for instance, the Unity Campaign Committee established contacts from Cornwall to the Hebrides and its principal speakers visited all the main industrial areas of the country including the Midlands where Labour support was weakest. Only the official Labour Party Crusade in September 1937 compared with the campaigns of the Left for scope and initiative. When the Left tried to exert mass pressure on parliament and local councils, it was adopting methods common to all excluded groups. For the Left, as long as it was barred from effective control over the Labour movement, felt itself to be a genuine political tendency deprived of the opportunities for expression granted to the major parties. The Left tended to reject the methods used by constitutional parties, turning back to the tactics of nineteenth-century agitation. It was more than symbolic that the first campaign of the decade should take the name of the Charter Campaign and that the last should be the holding of a Peoples Convention, with its suggestion that Parliament was unrepresentative. Such devices, common where a body of opinion cannot secure a constitutional outlet, were typical of Left activity. Nor was it out of keeping with Labour traditions to organize pressure on the government from outside Parliament. Many of the most vehement opponents of the Left had themselves taken part in the General Strike only a few years before, believing that it was a justifiable attempt to preserve the living standards of those unfairly treated by government and employers. Both George Lansbury and Clement Attlee, as mayors of Poplar and Stepney, had led protest demonstrations to Downing Street in the early 1920s to protest about unemployment and the poor rate. There were hardly any national or local Labour leaders who had not taken part in marches, demonstrations, even riots in the past. Several had been to prison as a consequence. With all this behind it, the Left turned naturally and without much questioning to 'mass action'.[34]

During the Unity campaigns a number of prominent people became associated with the Left, and through them it became far simpler to gain attention than in the past. For the Left, with its limited resources, had to rely on the press to provide information about its activities to the great bulk of the population who remained outside active politics. As long as the restricted news-value of the Left prevented it from occupying the headlines it had little chance of spreading its influence. This situation naturally changed when prominent individuals became involved with the Left and they attracted attention to those groups and ideas with which they were associated. The Communists knew only too well the value of 'fellow travellers' as such 'non-Party Bolsheviks' were known in the early days of the Soviet Republic.[35] The elaborate network of 'front organizations' was designed to institutionalise the participation of such people. It was characteristic of all Communist-inspired campaigns that they were supported by well-known non-Communists, some of whom joined the Party though seldom for long. Among them were those like Stephen Spender or J. B. S. Haldane who found the Communist Party expressing views which they themselves held, but which were not acceptable to the major parties or to established opinion. Others, like D. N. Pritt, were utilized to the full because of their position within the Labour Party and the respectability they gave to pro-Soviet positions. The association of such people with the Left often had an important impact on public opinion, though after some time known sympathizers came to be discredited as no longer independent.

The limitations on Left influence

The Left, in its attempts to exert pressure or to gain control, revealed its character as a protest movement grounded in the local Labour Party, the union branch or the small minority group.

Except for the Communists, who were powerless in isolation, none of the Left had any elaborate plan for the capture of the real centres of power in the Labour movement. The Left set out to convert, and through conversion and the democratic process, to change the amorphous Labour movement into a coherent socialist party. Left tactics, even those of elitist Communists, were based on the assumption that the mass movement was capable of conversion. Naturally this led to considerable frustration at many of the devices which were used, quite consciously, to bar the progress of radical ideas and individuals. It also led to frustration at the apparent indifference of the bulk of the movement to what the Left saw as 'the crisis of capitalism'. The Labour Left reacted by looking for outside affiliation and by united action with small like-minded radical groups. Yet hardly ever did any important Left group despair of the eventual support of the 'masses', even when scepticism about democracy was a commonplace. This support did not materialize but the Left nevertheless played an invaluable role in educating and enlivening a professedly radical but basically conservative movement. This was the function of most Left pressure, a by-product of its conscious aim of capturing and converting the movement.

The fragmentation of the Left into minorities seriously limited its effectiveness in many ways. Organizational loyalties arose which separated the member of one Left group from members of other groups or from unattached sympathizers. Nowhere is this more evident than with the Communist Party, the only Left minority of importance which was permanently outside the Labour Party. The funding of the Party, its contacts with the Comintern, its tight control over its members, its general exclusiveness, fraction work and subservience to Soviet policy cast continual doubt on its integrity and its right to be considered as a legitimate part of the Labour movement within which it had undoubtedly originated. So long as Communists were prepared to work with the rest of the Left much of this was overlooked. But Communists and members of other independent groups had consistently to assert their common aims in order to win influence. Whenever a clash of loyalties developed between a minority and the Labour Party, there was always a loss of members from the minority, accompanied by severe friction and ill feeling. In the 1920s the Communist Party lost many of its leading members because they were forced to choose between the Communists and the Labour Party. The disaffiliation of the ILP led directly to a loss of membership, isolation and collapse. In every case where the Left was organized into a minority it came into conflict not only with the leadership of Labour, which was inevitable, but also with many of its own followers.

Where minority work was useful in spreading Left ideas was in the ability of an independent group to discuss and publish its policies free from the discipline of the official movement. The Left was still able to put forward views inside the Labour Party with a certain degree of freedom because of the federal traditions of the past and the vagueness of the party's ideology. This was a limited right, as the drastic action by the National Executive against the Cripps Petition Campaign of 1939 showed. Yet there was little attempt to impose uniformity of views on members of the party so long as their behaviour conformed with party rules. Such uniformity would have involved the elaboration of a democratic socialist philosophy, which only a handful of party members were prepared to undertake. It would have meant building a system of political education, the improvement of party literature and, above all, the adoption not only of a fairly radical programme but of constant agitation on that programme and against the National government. This the Labour Party seemed reluctant to undertake except for a short period in 1937, by which time much of the initiative had already been lost to the Left. Most political debate within the mass movement remained strongly influenced by the Left and was consequently shaped by those minority groups with the best presented and most plausible propaganda. The Communist Party, the ILP, the Socialist League and other small groups appeared almost to monopolize political action on unemployment, 'appeasement', 'non-intervention' and most major topics. Though manifestly unrepresentative of majority opinion within the Labour movement, the Left provided an alternative leadership. As Cripps argued after the 1936 Edinburgh Conference of the Labour Party, 'we see the results of the Conference not only in the doubt and hesitation that is apparent, but in the vague searching for outside affiliation and leadership that is going on today'.[36]

The Left minority, whatever its weakness and however extreme its policies, could always attract sympathy and attention when it seemed to be genuinely concerned with the issues which were agitating many Labour Party members. For this reason many of the campaigns of the 1930s seem oddly conceived. The Unity Campaigns were campaigns for a new foreign and domestic policy but they also put great emphasis on the need to bring small organizations into the Labour Party and to form alliances which would not necessarily increase the Labour vote. The Labour leadership concentrated its criticism on these tactical aspects, which soon overshadowed the substantive policy objectives. Those who were quite sympathetic to the broad aims of the campaigns could see little point in the call for organizational unity.[37]

As long as the Left was dominated by small competing groups it was possible for their opponents to ignore many of the deeper implications of the Left critique such as the need for effective Opposition and for the development of a strong political Labour movement with a coherent ideology. There was a tension in the Left between the desire to remain organized in small groups and the need to associate with the broad Labour Party. This tension gave rise to much of the wrangling, dissension and ineffectiveness which characterized the Left. The historical development of the Labour movement had given to small groups the function of carrying on the political work of the party, despite the growth of local Labour Parties. The perpetuation of these small groups meant that they were able to appeal as legitimate entities. By doing so, however, many fundamental issues were obscured in a welter of minor frictions and disagreements. The constant clash of organizational loyalties is the background against which the more positive achievements of the Left must be set.

The Left was under Communist control to a large extent but it was basically democratic and it was sympathetic to the Soviet Union as an ideal and as an opponent of Fascism. Such belief in an 'abstract' USSR was a source of strength in the late 1930s and was counterposed to an equally 'abstract' belief in Fascism on the Conservative Right. The Left may have been misguided in seeing the National government as little better than Fascist. However it was not misguided, as were so many in the government, when it treated Fascism in Germany, Italy or Austria as having the same menacing characteristics. It was not misguided in the slogan 'the defence of Madrid is the defence of London'. It was not misguided in keeping the problems of the Distressed Areas before the public eye. Certainly the Left was correct when it urged vigorous opposition to the National government; correct, that is, in terms of the political future of the Labour Party.

The Left, then, had a right to be regarded as a fairly coherent and important political tendency with some positive achievements to its credit. It was not a party yet it had many party characteristics, from the acceptance of common principles to an internal struggle for power. It expressed the dissatisfaction of the politically aware; a dissatisfaction which arose from an unprecedented situation with which the established parties were incapable of dealing. The Left became the voice of the militant against the gradualist. As in every progressive party, the disagreements within the Labour Party often centred around the pace rather than the direction of reform. Any political organization which desires radical change is necessarily faced with the same situation for the same basic reasons. The party leaders, with greater practical experience, knew the difficulties facing them in changing a complicated society. Often they were so conscious of these difficulties that they lost the urge for change which keeps a radical party in being. On the other hand, the active member with nothing to gain from caution and often inadequately informed about the difficulties, could only maintain his enthusiasm by protest and agitation.

Most of the evidence of the 1930s points to the failure of the official Labour movement to ensure the loyal co-operation of many of its active members. Many of the national leaders were caught in the dilemma of trying to influence a government over which they had no control and for which they had considerable and justified contempt. The failure was that of the collective leadership, political and industrial, national and local. For the Labour movement, whatever the aims of its socialist minority, was fundamentally unsuited to the type of protest campaign so ably conducted by the Left. It was battered and disillusioned by the General Strike, the MacDonald defection and the Depression. Apart from its Left-wing militants it was a movement of local councillors, of union branch officials, of working-class women with no clearly defined outlook beyond an instinctive pacifism. It accepted the conventions of constitutional government more completely than most other political parties in the world of the 1930s. From that perspective the Left often seemed like yet another threat to what little stability and decency still remained.

The achievement of the Left was to enliven a cautious and

conservative mass movement. In its self-appointed task of creating a unified radical socialist party the Left failed: the ILP failed to maintain its existence as an important force; the Communists failed to get into the Labour Party; the Socialist League collapsed, though its contribution to Labour thinking was more important than might appear.[38] The Unity Campaign and the Hunger Marches failed in their immediate objects, for the government did not adopt a new foreign policy until too late and it did little to solve the problem of the Distressed Areas. Despite this the Left had a function. Had it not been able to express widely held sentiments, had it not appealed to many in the Labour movement, it could not have attracted a fraction of the support which it was obviously able to mobilize. The Labour Party was groping towards a new foreign and domestic policy and training a new leadership which would rule Britain after 1945. But much of the history of the Labour movement in the 1930s, the history of radical thought and propaganda, recruiting and conversion for socialism, is the history of the Left.

CHAPTER 18

Forty Years On

The 1930s have been remembered as a time when the arguments for socialism, for opposing fascism, for supporting the Soviet Union, in short for being 'on the Left', were almost self-evident.[1] This was not how matters always appeared to those potentially most receptive, the working-class electorate, the trade unions and the Labour Party. Those who search for a 'heroic age' in working-class politics, are more likely to find it located somewhere between 1900 and 1926 than in the quiescent unions, factional squabbling and disappointed hopes of the 1930s. The one major, radical and unmistakably proletarian movement of the decade, the National Unemployed Workers Movement, was abandoned by its creator the Communist Party when Soviet foreign policy required the sympathy of the liberal middle classes. Apart from the street battles against Mosley, most of the concern with European Fascism was to be found in those middle classes, whose loyalty to the Labour movement was questionable until 1945. An approach to them from the Left often meant raking over the dying embers of the Liberal Party in search of a viable electoral alliance, an activity guaranteed to disillusion those who had fought for independent Labour since 1900.

The Communist Party, with its various acts of 'betrayal' and its subservience to the whims of its dictatorial paymasters in Moscow, has frequently been blamed for the unrevolutionary and reformist behaviour of British workers.[2] Certainly it is impossible to write about the successes and failures of the Left in the 1930s without putting the Communists at the centre of the story. If the Left failed, as in most formal senses it did, then that failure must be blamed to some extent on the Communist Party. They had devotedly tried to create a rift between themselves and the rest of the Labour movement between 1928 and 1934 by abuse, violence, lack of co-operation and distinctly uncomradely behaviour. They made no recognizable distinction between MacDonald, Henderson, Lansbury or Maxton, between Bevin or Cook, between the Labour Party and the ILP, between their potential allies and their dedicated enemies. For the next five years they swung to the opposite extreme, embracing Attlee and Lloyd George, the Duchess of Atholl and Duncan Sandys, everyone and everything that could be used to campaign against fascism and for the Soviet Union. In less than five years they made it fashionable to be pro-Soviet, to study Marxism, to visit the USSR, to rally for Spain. But just when the anti-fascist movement needed them most they were out on the platforms of the past, denouncing the imperialist war, attacking the political truce behind Churchill, attempting to woo sections of the Labour movement to the Peoples Convention. The Communist Party switched its political position quite drastically three times in the 1930s. It was hardly surprising that large sections of the Labour movement viewed it with suspicion and refused to associate with any of its causes, however noble.

Having said that, it must be acknowledged that the Communist Party was no more successful in the previous or subsequent decades, when its political line was more consistent. Against the 'Stalinist betrayal' thesis currently fashionable among some analysts of British labour history, it should be remarked that no Marxist organization has ever had much measurable, long-term effect on the trade-union movement, the working-class electorate or their parliamentary representatives. The only electoral successes recorded for independently sponsored Marxist candidates were in the elections of 1935 and 1945 and the only constituencies ever substantially influenced by Marxism were the Rhondda, West Fife and Stepney during those years. Even this was overshadowed in electoral terms by the support for ILP candidates in Glasgow between 1931 and 1945. Never, before or since, has there been such support, however limited, for radical socialist candidates. The Communists and the ILP, for all their vacillating and periodic absurdity, achieved something which eluded the founding Marxists of the SDF, the British Socialist Party or the neo-Marxists of today. They won votes at the local and national levels in competition with all other parties and built local bases in which they were respected and followed.

When the Marxist Left aimed at creating a mass, socialist alternative to the Labour Party, they had very little to work upon. Marxism was not a part of the British intellectual tradition at any level of society and organized Marxism had never established any major base on which to build. Union officials were either former Liberals, or vague populists or, at the most, radical syndicalists. Only the latter could be reached by Marxist appeals and the line of descent from South Wales syndicalism to Rhondda Communism is quite easily traced. The predominance of a mass, union-based and ideologically amorphous Labour Party always defeated those who had either to snipe from the outside or conspire on the inside. No amount of effort, whether guided by the scientific method of Marx, the organizational principles of Lenin, or the long-distance charisma of Stalin, could make much difference to the inescapable fact of Labour Party hegemony among the working classes at all levels, in all regions, and in all organizations. To 'blame' the Communist Party for failing to deal with the situation is quite unreasonable in the light of the miniscule membership, peripheral influence and tenuous cohesion of the Party throughout the period. The oscillations of the Comintern certainly did not ease the task of local Communists. But had Communists pursued the most enlightened and consistent path imaginable, it is still extremely unlikely that they would have done much better than they did, at least in the short term between the Depression and the outbreak of war. Marxism-Leninism had nothing to say to the British working class that they could be expected to understand or respond to. Communism had its appeal when it was couched in simple syndicalist analyses of the class struggle or in liberal-democratic denunciations of Fascism. In both cases the reasonable conclusion was to support the Labour Party as the most effective instrument for achieving the widest range of objectives.

Just as there was nothing in the then current British intellectual tradition which meshed with Marxist-Leninist ideology, so there was nothing in the century-old conventions of working-class organization which could be called into play behind the strategy of building a Leninist alternative to Labour. From the Chartists onwards all the political effort of the working-class (as of liberal reformers) had been directed towards extending the franchise and using it to put suitable representatives into parliament. Britain did not achieve universal suffrage until 1928; nor did more than a quarter of MPs ever have working-class backgrounds. Despite the disappointment with MacDonald it was wholly reasonable to believe that a majority Labour government would do better, as indeed it did after 1945. Labour activists and voters could never be persuaded that the function of their party was over, particularly during a period of Conservative parliamentary dominance. Both the Communists and the ILP erred fatally in the early 1930s by announcing the impending collapse of Labour and its replacement by themselves. Not only did this seem inherently unlikely to anyone who looked at the voting figures, the membership and the degree of union support for the three 'rivals', but it urged treachery towards a mass organization which was still close to its original organizers and members. When millions of voters and hundreds of thousands of activists refused to move away from Labour the Left sank without a trace as an independent political force in British politics.

In the short run, the Left failed in the 1930s. Normal politics were interrupted by the war and after 1945 the issues were quite different. The Labour Party proved itself in government between 1940 and 1945, was overwhelmingly returned to office with its first absolute majority in 1945, and in 1951 secured the highest total vote for a British party either before or since. The trade-union movement was able to take advantage of full employment to double its enrolment and by the 1970s had recruited a larger proportion of the workforce than ever before. The electoral support for Communists and independent socialists was relatively high in 1945 but could not survive the Cold War and the polarization of politics between Labour and Conservative. For the past twenty years the Communists have been a negligible element electorally, even in Rhondda and West Fife. The ILP had become an obscure sect by 1950, sustained only by its considerable holdings of property acquired during its dominance over the political wing of the Labour movement. Marxism made no appreciable electoral headway even with the rapid increase in student Trotskyism in the 1960s. It was almost invariably the case that Marxist candidates came bottom of the poll, whatever their label and whatever the social composition of the constituency. Amongst intellectuals Marxism went into retreat between 1950 and the mid-1960s: it was revived in a form critical of the Soviet Union, of the British Communists and of the Labour Party.

All this suggests superficially that the work put in by the Left in the 1930s was a waste of time in terms of influencing the formal political processes. The revival of Marxism in the 1960s was largely based on a different generation and on ideas, like Trotskyism, which had very little currency in the 1930s. It also involved a rejection of the Labour Party and of parliamentary socialism reminiscent of the ultra-Leftism of the Communists between 1928 and 1933. The Communist Party itself continued to decline in membership and influence, especially after the Hungarian revolution of 1956. Labour in Britain and Communism in Eastern Europe had become established forces to which the Left often found itself in opposition. The disappearance of mass unemployment, of widespread basic poverty and of European Fascism, also removed old targets for Left-wing emotion. Concern with events in Asia or Africa was much more likely to arouse cosmopolitan students than the British working class, which went through two decades of apparent satisfaction with the political and economic situation. The difficult task of meshing the campaigns against unemployment and Fascism, which the Communists undertook with modest success in the 1930s, was replaced by the even more daunting task of gaining mass support for attacks on the Labour Party, on the British economy, on the Soviet Union and on the imperialists, all from a miniscule base among the voters and from a socially remote base in the universities.

However, that is only one part of a story which became increasingly confused in the 1970s. After 1970 the British economy, like that of other industrial nations, began to show symptoms of crisis reminiscent in some ways of the 1930s. Unemployment climbed beyond two million, although its social effects were less disastrous than in the 1930s and its concentration among the young, immigrants and women, all politically ineffectual, reduced the possibility of a mass mobilization around the issue. While unemployment returned to the old Distressed Areas, it did not destroy whole communities and industries. Massive post-war investment and the state-sponsored rundown of previously depressed industries meant that there was a wider variety of employment on offer. Coal-mining communities did not relive the experience of the 1930s and for much of the postwar period miners were amongst the most highly paid of all British manual workers, the best unionized and the least likely to be unemployed. Mining itself ceased to dominate areas where it had been the sole industry in the 1930s, in particular some of the previous Communist districts in South Wales. Thus the miners, whose militancy brought down the Conservative government in 1974, were no longer at the heart of agitation against unemployment, nor were their communities susceptible to radical attacks on the existing social system. This was also true for the ILP strongholds in Glasgow and central Scotland, which, by the 1970s were being heavily influenced by Scottish nationalism.

The social conditions upon which local bases could be built for the Left had changed remarkably since the 1930s, and not even the return of large-scale unemployment could revive what had always been a very small and highly localized following for the Left outside the Labour Party. Inside that party it remained true, as in the 1930s, that when the Left accepted Labour hegemony over the working-class movement it was able to make substantial advances. Within the party and the trade unions, the legacy of the 1930s remained and was built upon when the political climate became more favourable. *Tribune* became the voice of the Bevanites in the 1950s, of Michael Foot in the 1960s and of the trade union and Labour Left in the 1970s, using arguments and terminology which seem to have changed little since the 1930s. Its appeal was always confined to the organized Labour movement, its circulation was no higher than during the Unity Campaign, and yet it remained a focal point not merely for constituency activists but for a large and growing Tribune Group of Members of Parliament who constituted a much larger parliamentary Left than existed at any time in the 1930s. The Labour Party to which *Tribune* appealed in the 1970s was no larger than that towards which it aimed its articles in 1937. Its enrolled membership was certainly no more than 400,000 by 1977, the number of its full-time agent-organizers was lower than in the 1930s, its proportion of the vote in 1979 was lower than 1935, and the number of activists was certainly no greater than during the Unity Campaign and may well have been less.[3] The fundamental difference was that by the 1970s Labour was thinking of itself as the 'natural party of government' and its parliamentary strength was almost twice that of 1935. Its active organization was no stronger than forty years before, but its access to power was immeasurably greater and it was associated with a trade union movement at the height of its numerical strength and national importance.

To be effective in a permanently established movement it is necessary to devote a lifetime to it and to use structures and ideas inherited from previous generations. Even a superficial examination of the Left suggests a basic continuity throughout the history of the organized Labour movement. Issues, personalities and organizations change over the years but the essential concerns, objectives and tactics remain remarkably similar. In the 1970s, as in the 1930s, the Left was divided between those within or attached to the Labour Party and those outside and opposed to it. In the 1970s attitudes towards Marxism and the Soviet Union were still considered relevant to the politics of Britain. Some still believed that Labour should be converted from within, through the constituency parties, the annual conference, influence in the unions, the passing of resolutions and the distribution of literature. Others saw the difficulties of such an endeavour, without acknowledging the even greater futility of attempting to build a 'party of a new type' outside the existing working-class institutions and in opposition to a century of parliamentary traditions among working-class voters.

The Left became relatively more important within the Labour Party, where a number of former Communists and Trotskyists sat in parliament and on the National Executive. The parliamentary Labour Party remained less susceptible to Left appeals than the constituency activists. The professional union leadership became much more receptive than in the 1930s while still reserving their right to deal with governments as they thought fit. The relative importance of the Communist Party declined but its role as an adjunct of the Labour Party became even more marked and such successes as it could still mark up resulted almost exclusively from the exercise of that role.

Outside the party, a massive Left literature developed, oriented towards the greatly increased number of those with tertiary education. Links with, and echoes of, the 1930s and even the 1920s remained clear. What has already been said about the Labour movement as a partially insulated sub-culture still holds for the 1970s, despite the far greater intensity of the mass media barrage to which the British electorate has been exposed.

The common features of the 1930s and the present are more remarkable when it is remembered that most of those active in adult politics in the pre-war period were dead by the end of the 1960s.[4] Different people are acting in similar ways, largely learnt within the Labour movement either from personal contact with an older generation or, in the case of many student socialists, by reading the greatly increased polemical literature in which the issues of the past were kept alive or even revived from obscurity.

The youth movement of the Labour Party remained under Left control. The Trotskyists of the Militant tendency (whose very name recalls the similar group of forty years ago) successfully took over a Young Socialist organization which was much weaker than the pre-war Labour League of Youth, though capable of gaining many more concessions from the party. In student politics there was no organizational continuity between the pre-war University Labour Federation (which as the Student Labour Federation disappeared in the 1960s) and any groups active in National Union of Students politics. But still in 1977 a Communist Party member was elected president of a vastly enlarged NUS, with an executive overwhelmingly dominated by various factional Marxist groups.

In adult politics, the great bulk of constituency Labour parties continued to elect politicians regarded as on the Left to the National Executive, a trend which dates from the party reforms of 1937 and which, during the bleak years of the 1950s, preserved the only niche in the party leadership open to the Left. By the 1970s relatively detached reports give the Left control over almost half the National Executive, a situation undreamed of in the 1930s and contributing to a breakdown of the close working relationship which had existed between the party bureaucracy and the Parliamentary leadership. This close relationship had been one of the most serious obstacles to Left-wing influence in the 1930s. Another serious obstacle, the unrelenting opposition of the trade union officials, had also become much less serious by the 1970s. Here the influence of the 1930s can be directly traced in the career patterns of many national full-time officials. A high proportion of the most politically important officials came from the coalfields and particularly from South Wales and Scotland. In the migration of workers during the 1930s they had gained early organizing experience outside the traditional Left areas and industries but had taken the traditions of those sectors with them. Many had been in the

Communist Party at the height of its membership expansion between 1935 and 1950. While virtually all had resigned, the legacy of CP membership often remained. Even those who had stayed in the Party rose up the union hierarchy with the passage of time to the extent that there were three Communists on the TUC General Council by the late 1970s, something which had never been allowed under the 'Bevin-Citrine axis' of the pre-war period. The steady work of the Communist Party in South Wales, Scotland and London, while it paid no electoral dividends, was returning some small interest, years after the vision of a mass, independent Communist Party had faded away.

By the end of the 1930s about one-third of constituency Labour parties, three members of the National Executive, a dozen Members of Parliament and a handful of full-time union officials were consistently associated with the Left. At the same time the Labour Party officially expelled the most prominent supporters of the Unity Campaign, with the overwhelming support of a Labour Party conference, and wound up the party's youth and student organizations because they were under Communist control. Whatever might have been true among intellectuals, the score for the Left in the Labour movement was no higher on the outbreak of war than it had been before the Depression.

By the 1970s the impact of the Left was apparently far greater than in the 1920s and 1930s. Over half the National Executive, one-third of the Parliamentary Labour Party (and some Cabinet Ministers), perhaps one-third of the TUC General Council, the Labour Party Young Socialists and the National Union of Students were all loosely associated with the Left, although certainly not with a Left led by the Communists. Within three months in 1977 a former Labour Cabinet Minister, a former Left-wing Labour MP and a former editor of the *New Statesman* all publicly declared for a Conservative election victory to save the country from the 'Marxist Labour Party'. A professor of sociology published a documented claim of serious 'Marxist infiltration' of British universities. Trotskyist-led groups battled with the National Front, which also had tenuous links with the Mosleyite 1930s; their slogans recalled the 1936 'battle of Cable Street'. Travelling even further down memory lane, the 1977 Labour Party conference voted for the abolition of the House of Lords, just as its predecessors had done in 1934. Eventually, at the end of 1980, the

Parliamentary Labour Party elected as Leader Michael Foot, who had joined the Labour Party in 1934 and been consistently associated with *Tribune* and the Left for over forty years.

All this suggests that the inheritance from the past has not merely been remembered but has been drawn upon to maximum profit in circumstances more favourable than the 1930s. These circumstances include the breaking of the nexus between the parliamentary leaders, the organizational leaders and the union officials which presented such an impenetrable barrier to Left advance within the Labour Party. Once Labour government became normal, and unionization became characteristic of public employees, union officials naturally found themselves in positions of conflict with Ministers drawn from their own party. This did not lead to the kind of formal rupture between the party and the unions which many academic theorists of the 1960s predicted. Nor did it create the base for a significant Marxist industrial movement, if only because Marxists were so much more fragmented and sectarian than in the 1930s. But it did make the Labour National Executive Committee, where union votes determine a majority of the positions and union money pays the salaries of officials, much less of a pawn for parliamentarians than McKenzie had suggested in 1955.[5] Union officials, partly because of their experience with Labour governments, no longer saw party unity as a prime consideration. Nor, with their memories of the Depression and the work of the Communists among the unemployed, did they echo the hostility of the 1930s. The earlier hostility was engendered by recriminations over the General Strike and the sectarianism of the Minority Movement. In the 1970s union officials were no longer antagonistic to the Left or the Communists, and the internal politics of the Labour conference and Executive changed accordingly.

But once Labour was seen as normally the government, Left activists began to turn their attention away from party or union officials and towards the parliamentarians, who had remained remarkably free of criticism during the 1930s. *Tribune* began to campaign for greater local control over the selection of candidates and, eventually, for conference election of parliamentary leaders, objectives largely achieved by the Blackpool conference of 1980. In the new mood neither the National Executive nor conference was as ready to protect parliamentarians as in the past, nor to exercise the detailed control over the Left which had marked the regimes of Herbert Morrison in the 1930s or of Morgan Phillips as party secretary in the 1950s.

Solidarity at the top thus dissolved and frustration lower down redirected itself against Members of Parliament. All this took place in an atmosphere of critical questioning of British institutions and of the British economy. While there was no equivalent of the Left Book Club, this was hardly necessary given the explosion of critical writing on politics and society which took place in the 1960s. As in the 1930s, it was possible to gain a complete self-education in socialist ideas simply by visiting the local bookshop. The accompanying explosion in tertiary education expanded a base for radicalism which had been very narrow in the 1930s and confined to the socially isolated 'gentleman socialists' of Oxford and Cambridge. Much of this tended to pass the Labour Party by, partly because as a governing party it could rarely identify itself officially with radicalism, partly because its rank and file was just as elderly and working-class as in the 1930s and just as difficult to win over to complex ideologies couched in alien terminology.[6] The great strength of the Communists and the Left Book Club in the 1930s had been precisely that they were able to move from the incomprehensible rubbish of the 'social fascist' spasm to the well-produced and immediately appealing literature of the late 1930s. The post-war New Left, with its high university component, found this more difficult and wallowed in a sea of jargon and sectarianism which isolated it from the Labour movement, and reinforced its tendency to reject the Labour Party for other reasons. In contrast to the 1930s there existed a large reservoir of educated young people who were fascinated by sectarian polemics, rejected Labour as a governing party and attempted to reach out to the working-class on the basis of age, rather than through existing institutions. Not only did they reject Labour, but Labour, including the Labour Left, rejected them. The party at all levels remained elderly and the arguments used by the Labour Left were much more reminiscent of the 1930s than arguments used outside the party in the younger New Left. It was one of the features of the New Left that not only did it not seek a 'United Front', but it spent a great deal of energy denouncing compromises of that sort. After the decline of the Campaign for Nuclear Disarmament in the early 1960s the search for 'Unity' was almost completely abandoned on the New Left, although CND revived in 1980 and tentative negotiations were begun between various Trotskyists in the late 1970s. Not only was there no Fascism against which to be united but there could be no agreement on who was to lead such a united force and in what direction.

The organizational legacy of the 1930s consisted of a permanent base for the Left in constituency Labour Parties, a set of tactics in internal Labour Party politics aimed at influencing conferences and the National Executive, a substantial number of politically rising individuals who had been influenced by the Left and the Communists and particularly through the Labour League of Youth, the Young Communist League and the National Unemployed Workers Movement, a set of periodicals, most importantly *Tribune* and the *Morning Star* (formerly *Daily Worker*), and a network of connections built up mainly through the Unity Campaigns and the Left Book Club. All of this is still relevant forty years later. The intellectual legacy is more diffuse although many ideas and even phrases in use today are almost identical with those used in the 1930s. The argument as to whether the Labour Party is a suitable instrument for achieving socialism continues, as since the party's foundation. Although a much higher proportion of contemporary Marxists deny Labour's potential than in the 1930s, the question is one not susceptible to final empirical proof and must always remain open as long as Labour calls itself 'socialist' and allows Marxists and other socialists to operate freely within its ranks.[7]

The debate between Marxism and radical populism, which was essentially the debate between Communist and ILP traditions on the Left, is now highly confused, not least by the polemical debate between different Marxist positions which scarcely existed in the 'monolithic' days of 1930s Stalinism. A leader of the Labour Left like Tony Benn is certainly closer to the ILP than to the British Marxist tradition, but has no fundamental disagreements with many on the Labour Left who would call themselves Marxist. The campaign for bringing MPs under local party control is strongly in the ILP tradition and quite contrary to Leninist ideas of the disciplined centralist party. But it is backed by Leninists within the Labour Party who believe that it will enhance their effectiveness and influence. The simultaneous adherence to centralization and decentralization which characterizes the British Left today was being argued out in the policy conferences of the Left in the early

1930s. Essentially the Left still believes, as in the 1930s, in a predominantly state-owned, centrally planned economy. It still believes that this should not threaten democratic and trade-union rights built up over the past century or more. It still believes that socialism is primarily for the benefit of industrial workers. It is, on the other hand, less influenced by *dirigiste* ideas than in the 1930s and more seriously concerned with notions of workers control.

In international relations the Left still believes in the importance of maintaining peace but also gives its support to those fighting physically against repressive conservative forces. Just as the Left took sides with the Soviet Union against the Axis powers in the 1930s, so it tends to sympathize with the Soviet Union in any conflict with the United States. But it is generally much less naive about the internal policies of the Soviet government. This is perhaps the one area in which a Leftist miraculously transferred from the 1930s would find it hard to fit into the current world of the Left.

The Left in the 1970s established a fairly strong position within the Labour Party organization. The alternative Left, which rejects any compromise with Labour, has become well represented in institutions of higher education. Yet there is little evidence of a comparable degree of support among the general population, nor even among Labour voters. As in the 1930s, the Left has found its following among the militants of the Labour movement and among liberal intellectuals. The Left still see themselves as potentially leading the masses; the masses themselves are not following in any greater numbers than in the 1930s. A great deal more is known about public opinion than forty years ago and all such public opinion research has revealed is the cautious conservatism of most of the British electorate. The Parliamentary leadership of the Labour Party, whether under Wilson or Callaghan, has been fully aware of this situation and has tailored its appeal accordingly. It is less anxious to repress the Left within the movement than were Morrison or Bevin in the 1930s. But it is equally aware that the marginal support which kept Labour in power came from those whose views were closer to the Conservative and Liberal Parties than to the mainstream of thought within the Labour Party, let alone within the Left.

The function of the Left in the 1930s was to enliven a cautious working-class movement, many of whose leaders had been brought up as Liberals. In the 1970s the Left saw itself as the conscience of a movement which had gained office without yet moving towards socialism. The grievances of Labour activists, of young radicals and of trade unionists are seized upon and given expression by the various factions on the Left. Yet none of these factions, separately or together, has been able to move large sections of the people away from their adherence to the Parliamentary system, to the Labour Party or to the cautious reformism of Labour governments. The Left remains, as in the 1930s, a movement of protest and criticism. It still seems unlikely to coalesce into an effective leadership for any large section of the British people.

Despite the reappearance of unemployment under a Conservative government and the growing disaffection of the Labour conference and National Executive with the Parliamentary party, the Left remains a faction within a broader movement rather than the expression of mass discontent on a scale likely to transform that movement into the government of the Socialist Commonwealth.

Notes

CHAPTER 1

1. See especially G. Peele and C. Cook (eds.), *The Politics of Reappraisal 1918–1939*, London, 1975 and M. Kinnear, *The British Voter: an Atlas and Survey since 1885*, London, 1968.
2. See W. Kendall, *The Revolutionary Movement in Britain 1900–21*, London, 1969.
3. See K. Middlemass, *The Clydesiders*, London, 1965.
4. See e.g. Kendall, *op. cit.;* R. Challinor, *The Origins of British Bolshevism*, London, 1977; J. Hinton and R. Hyman, *Trade Unions and Revolution*, London, 1975; and B. Pribecevic, *The Shop Steward Movement and Workers Control*, London, 1959.
5. For a recent assessment see Margaret Morris, *The General Strike*, Harmondsworth, 1976.
6. See G. Peele and C. Cook, *op. cit.*
7. For the fullest account of the MacDonald government see R. Skidelsky, *Politicians and the Slump*, London, 1967. See also D. Marquand, *Ramsay MacDonald,* London, 1977.
8. In 1931 a New Party was formed which attracted some Labour Party support but developed into the British Union of Fascists under the leadership of Sir Oswald Mosley, Chancellor of the Duchy of Lancaster in the MacDonald government. See W. F. Mandle, 'The New Party', *Historical Studies*, October 1966.
9. George Lansbury and Alfred Salter were the two most prominent pacifists in the Parliamentary Labour Party. The most important pacifist organization was the Peace Pledge Union, formed in 1934.
10. For the official history and results of the ballot see Lady Livingstone, *The Peace Ballot*, London, 1935. Over eleven million voted.
11. For a fuller, if unsympathetic analysis of this dilemma see R. Miliband, *Parliamentary Socialism*, London, 1961.
12. See Ben Pimlott, *Labour and the Left in the 1930s*, Cambridge, 1977.

CHAPTER 2

1. This was exacerbated by the treatment of Ernest Bevin by the Society for Socialist Inquiry and Propaganda in 1932. See Margaret Cole, 'The Society for Socialist Inquiry and Propaganda' in A. Briggs and J. Saville (eds.), *Essays in Labour History 1918–39*, London, 1977.
2. For the definitive account of MacDonald's relations with the Labour Party see David Marquand, *op. cit.*
3. 'As a result of this drastic lesson much of the Christianity and brotherhood and optimistic utopianism of the Labour Party hardened into a more militant socialism.' (Kingsley Martin, *Harold Laski*, London, 1953, p. 82).
4. See R. Skidelsky *op. cit.*, pp. 318–21 for ILP opposition to this measure.

215

5. Described by its supporters as 'an ingenious and workable compromise between insurance benefit and poor law relief'. (R. C. Davison, *British Unemployment Policy*, London, 1938, p. 16.)
6. *Labour Party Annual Report for 1935,* p. 153 (speech by Susan Lawrence).
7. See J. Stevenson and C. Cook, *The Slump*, London, 1977 (chapters 4, 5, 9 & 10); W. Hannington, *Never on our Knees*, London, 1967 and H. McShane, *No Mean Fighter*, London, 1978.
8. *Labour Party Annual Report for 1932.*
9. In practice the safeguards adopted here and in the following year were ignored in 1945. See C. R. Attlee, *As it Happened*, London, 1954, p. 156.
10. Quoted in G. D. H. Cole, *A History of the Labour Party from 1914*, London, 1948, p. 287.
11. The Communist leader Thaelmann adopted the phrase 'after Hitler, us'. He died in a Nazi concentration camp.
12. Arthur Koestler, a member of the German Communist Party in 1933, wrote that 'we lost the battle against Hitler before it was joined' (*The Invisible Writing*, London, 1954, p. 24).
13. For an account of the Olympia rally see R. Benewick, *The Fascist Movement in Britain*, London, 1972, chapter 8.

CHAPTER 3

1. In 1911 well over 70 per cent of all employed males in the Rhondda were in mining. Sixty years later only 10 per cent were employed in the industry.
2. For Hyndman's views and political development see C. Tsuzuki, *H. M. Hyndman and British Socialism*, London, 1961.
3. As Jennie Lee, a young radical from the West Fife coalfields, wrote: 'I was impatient with the cheap quackery of infallibility that all Communist Party spokesmen laid claim to. I found nothing warming or sustaining in this diet of hate and mechanical Marxist clichés. This was at best a barren caricature of what I believed a revolutionary socialist party should be.' (J. Lee, *This Great Journey*, New York, 1942, p. 93.)
4. For a history of the Minority Movement see R. Martin, *Communism and the British Trade Union Movement*, Oxford, 1969.
5. For the Comintern discussions see CPGB, *Communist Policy in Great Britain*, London, 1928.
6. See John Mahon, *Harry Pollitt*, London, 1976.
7. *New Leader*, 25 March 1932. This prediction was much truer for Scotland than for the United Kingdom.
8. C. R. Attlee, *The Labour Party in Perspective*, London, 1937, p. 90.
9. See John McNair, *James Maxton, the Beloved Rebel*, London, 1955.
10. The National Administrative Council of the ILP only endorsed Maxton's action by seven votes to six (NAC Minutes, 30 June 1928).
11. *Labour Party Annual Report for 1931,* Appendix VIII.
12. *Ibid.*
13. ILP NAC Minutes, 12 June 1931.
14. Labour Party Constitution, clause IX, section 7(d).
15. ILP NAC Minutes, 7 November 1931.
16. *New Leader*, 13 November 1931.

17. See J. Stevenson and C. Cook, *op. cit.* chs. 9 and 10.
18. Tom Bell, *The British Communist Party,* London, 1937, p. 146.
19. See Stevenson and Cook, *loc. cit.*
20. Tom Bell, *op. cit.,* p. 145.
21. *Inprecorr,* 30 October 1931.
22. See R. Martin, *Communism and the British Trade Union Movement,* Oxford, 1969.
23. *Communist International,* no 4/5, 15 March 1932.
24. Harry Pollitt, *The Road to Victory (Battersea Congress Report),* London, 1932.
25. *Inprecorr,* 15 August 1935.
26. Lozovsky subsequently died in prison during the Soviet purges of 1949–52.
27. 'The idea of the SSIP is to carry on the work of research within the Labour Party. It aims at examining the various aspects of socialisation, laying the conclusions reached before ordinary people (*Clarion,* July 1931). See Ben Pimlott, *op. cit.* ch. 5.
28. At the end of 1926, the first year of its existence, the League of Youth had over 200 branches, the Guild of Youth 182. A national conference of the LLOY was held in January 1929 which elected a Youth Advisory Committee to co-ordinate the League in consultation with the Labour Party National Executive Committee.

CHAPTER 4

1. In the English towns with the highest level of unemployment in 1931 (Sunderland, South Shields, West Hartlepool, Tynemouth, Middlesbrough, Gateshead and Newcastle-on-Tyne) the Labour Party held only two seats out of twelve in 1935. In 1931 they won no seats at all.
2. See H. Pelling, *The British Communist Party,* London, 1958.
3. See CPGB, *Communist Policy in Great Britain,* London, 1928.
4. Tom Bell, *op. cit.,* p. 126.
5. Tom Bell, *op. cit.,* p. 127.
6. A. J. Cook had consistently supported the Left until his death in 1931 and signed the Mosley manifesto along with Left Labour MPs in 1930.
7. *Communist International,* 15 May 1931.
8. *Inprecorr,* 27 April 1931.
9. *Inprecorr,* 15 January 1931.
10. *Inprecorr,* 16 April 1931.
11. *Communist International,* 15 March 1932.
12. *Communist International,* 1 October 1932.
13. For the Communist attitude to these negotiations with the ILP see *Communist International,* 15 May 1931.
14. Otto Kuusinen, writing on 'Lessons of the English Election', revealed that the Comintern had expected the Party to win over 100,000 votes. (*Communist International,* 15 March 1932.)
15. *New Leader,* 29 January 1932.
16. ILP NAC Minutes, 20 & 21 February 1932.
17. Report of the Fortieth ILP Conference of 25–29 March 1932.
18. ILP NAC Minutes, 30 March 1932.
19. *New Leader,* 8 June 1932.

20. *New Leader*, 12 February 1932.
21. *New Leader*, 14 October 1932.
22. ILP NAC Documents – Party Accounts. See also R. Dowse, *Left in the Centre*, London, 1966.
23. John Paton, *Left Turn*, London, 1937, p. 398.
24. *Labour Monthly*, December 1931.
25. *Inprecorr*, 5 November 1931.
26. *Labour Monthly*, October 1931.
27. *Labour Monthly*, January 1932.
28. *Labour Monthly*, July 1932.
29. *Pravda*, 9 October 1931 (quoted in *Inprecorr*, 15 October 1931).
30. *Labour Monthly*, November 1931.
31. *Labour Monthly*, December 1931.
32. ILP NAC Minutes, Policy Discussion June–August 1933.
33. *Labour Monthly*, April 1933.
34. ILP NAC Minutes, 8 October 1932.
35. *Labour Monthly*, January 1933.
36. *Labour Monthly*, November 1931.
37. ILP NAC Minutes, 7–8 November 1931.
38. 'Months of organising finished like a damp squib' (Fred Copeman, *Reason in Revolt*, London, 1948, p. 65). For John McGovern's version see his *Neither Fear nor Favour*, London, 1960.
39. *New Leader*, 10 February 1933.
40. For the founding of the Socialist League and its subsequent history see Ben Pimlott, *op. cit.*, especially chapters 5, 6, 9 and 13.
41. *New Leader*, 28 September 1932.
42. *New Clarion*, 15 April 1933.
43. *New Clarion*, 30 September 1933.

CHAPTER 5

1. *New Leader*, 18 February 1933.
2. Labour Party Annual Report for 1933, p. 16.
3. *Inprecorr*, 9 March 1933.
4. *Ibid.*
5. Labour Party Annual Report for 1933, pp. 8–9.
6. ILP NAC Minutes, 4–5 March 1933.
7. *Inprecorr*, 7 April 1933.
8. Labour Party Annual Report for 1933, pp. 8–9.
9. Labour Party Annual Report for 1934, p. 241.
10. Socialist League Annual Report for 1933.
11. *Labour Monthly*, April 1933.
12. *New Leader*, 21 April 1933.
13. *New Leader*, 25 August 1933.
14. Comintern letter of 17 August 1933 (reprinted in *New Leader*, 29 September 1933 and *Inprecorr*, 29 September 1933).
15. *New Leader*, 29 September 1933.
16. *Inprecorr*, 5 January 1934.
17. *New Leader*, 16 February 1934.

18. ILP NAC Documents – letter of 15 February 1934.
19. *New Leader,* 9 March 1934.
20. *New Leader,* 16 February 1934.
21. ILP NAC Minutes, 21 December 1933.
22. Quoted in *Communist International,* 5 March 1934.
23. *New Leader,* 2 March 1934.
24. *Inprecorr,* 5 March 1934.
25. According to *Inprecorr,* 22 March 1934.
26. *Inprecorr,* 3 November 1934.
27. ILP NAC Documents, report of meeting of 12 December 1934.
28. ILP NAC Documents, report of meeting of 21 October 1934.
29. *New Leader,* 25 November 1934.
30. See Reg Groves, *The Balham Group,* London, 1974.
31. Harry Pollitt, *op. cit.* p. 56.
32. *New Leader,* 23 March 1934.
33. *Forward,* November 1932.
34. *Daily Herald,* 20 February 1933.

CHAPTER 6

1. For a critical view of Labour Party and TUC attitudes towards the 'hunger marches' see E. Wilkinson, *The Town that was Murdered,* London, 1939, chapter 12.
2. See R. Benewick, *The Fascist Movement in Britain,* London, 1972, and W. F. Mandle, *Anti-Semitism and the British Union of Fascists,* London, 1968.
3. For descriptions of the 'battle' of 4 October 1936, see Benewick, *op. cit.,* pp. 225–36.
4. The BUF did not run parliamentary candidates until the war but they polled well in Shoreditch, Bethnal Green and Limehouse (all in East London) in local elections in 1937.
5. See National Council of Civil Liberties, *The Thurloe Square Baton Charge,* London, 1936.
6. See Lady Livingstone, *The Peace Ballot, op. cit.*
7. Viscount Cecil, of the League of Nations Union, emphasized on the completion of the Ballot that, as a result, 'a great change had come over the tone of public statements about the League'. He advocated 'a programme of immediate action' to 'tell the world, including the Government, Parliament and public opinion, what the Ballot had revealed to be the opinion of the British people' (Lady Livingstone, *op. cit.,* pp. 61 and 64).
8. See J. C. Robertson, 'The British General Election of 1935', *Journal of Contemporary History,* 9 (1), January 1974.
9. See C. T. Stannage, 'The East Fulham By-election 25 October 1933', *Historical Journal,* 14, 1971 and R. Heller, 'East Fulham Revisited', *Journal of Contemporary History,* 6 (3), 1971.
10. See H. Thomas, *The Spanish Civil War,* Harmondsworth, 1965.
11. G. D. H. Cole, *A History of the Labour Party from 1914,* London, 1948, p. 328.
12. André Gide, *Return from the USSR,* London, 1937, p. 15.
13. S. & B. Webb, *Soviet Communism – a New Civilisation?,* London, 1935.
14. See especially D. N. Pritt, *The Moscow Trials,* London, 1936.

15. Cripps had referred during 1934 to the probability of opposition 'from Buckingham Palace' to the programme of a future Labour government, and this had been widely publicized.
16. F. Williams, *Ernest Bevin*, London, 1952, p. 185.
17. Labour Party, *Labour's Immediate Programme*, London, 1937.
18. See H. Dalton, *The Fateful Years*, London, 1957.
19. Municipal and by-election results are surveyed in J. Stevenson and C. Cook, *The Slump*, London, 1977, chapters 7 and 13.
20. See Ben Pimlott, *Labour and the Left, op. cit.*, chapters 11–14, for the history of the agitation leading to these changes.

CHAPTER 7

1. *New Leader*, 23 November 1934.
2. *Communist International*, 20 December 1934.
3. ILP NAC Documents, report of meeting of 12 December 1934.
4. *Communist International*, 20 June 1935.
5. *New Leader*, 26 April 1935.
6. ILP NAC Documents, circular of 5 December 1936.
7. Labour Party Annual Report for 1934.
8. *Socialist Leaguer*, December 1934.
9. *Socialist Leaguer*, May 1935.
10. Report of the Socialist League Conference, London, 1933.
11. *New Clarion*, 10 June 1933.
12. *New Leader*, 14 June 1935.
13. Wilhelm Pieck summed up the new Comintern structure thus: 'We need not conceal from our enemies the fact that the ECCI gives instructions to its separate Sections. Nevertheless we desire that the separate Sections settle their own organisational questions more independently than hitherto' (*Inprecorr*, 10 August 1935).
14. *Communist International*, 20 March, 1935.
15. *Communist International*, 20 June 1935.
16. Ibid.
17. *New Leader*, 14 June 1935.
18. Wilhelm Pieck posed the question of creating a single Left Party during the Comintern debates on the United Front: 'The united front is the first step towards overcoming the split in the working class movement, towards the creation of a strong joint revolutionary party of the proletariat' (*Inprecorr*, 15 August 1935).
19. *New Leader*, 4 August 1935.
20. *Inprecorr*, 17 August 1935.
21. *New Leader*, 14 December 1934.
22. *Communist International*, 5 November 1935.

CHAPTER 8

1. *Inprecorr*, 12 October 1935.
2. Tom Bell, *The British Communist Party, op. cit.,* p. 83.
3. See Labour Party Annual Report for 1936, p. 50.
4. Labour Party, *op. cit.,* p. 51.
5. *Inprecorr*, 9 November 1935.
6. *Inprecorr*, 11 January 1936.
7. *Advance*, July 1936.
8. Economic League, 1936 series no. 6: Communism and British Youth.
9. For Willis's own account of his role in the League of Youth see his *Whatever Happened to Tom Mix?,* London, 1970.
10. *Communist International*, November 1936.
11. *Inprecorr*, 30 May 1936.
12. J. T. Murphy, *New Horizons*, London, 1941, p. 325.
13. G. D. H. Cole, *The Peoples Front*, London, 1937, pp. 288–90.
14. Liberal Party, *The Liberal Party and the Popular Front*, London, 1937.
15. 'In the view and experience of the ILP, affiliation to the Labour Party is not the effective way to secure working class unity' (ILP NAC circular, *New Leader*, 24 July 1936).
16. A. F. Brockway, *Inside the Left*, London, 1942, p. 273.
17. In a circular of July, 1936, the NAC of the ILP suggested the formation of a Permanent Federal Committee of Left-wing parties (NAC circular – 'Workers Front', July 1936).
18. *Left Book Club News,* September 1936.
19. G. D. H. Cole, *The Peoples Front*, p. 268.
20. See Labour Party Annual Report for 1936, esp. Appendix IX, pp. 207–11.
21. Against 1,728,000.
22. Labour Party Annual Report for 1936, pp. 71–5.
23. Labour Party, *op. cit.,* pp. 238–47.
24. See Ben Pimlott, *Labour and the Left, op. cit.*
25. Labour Party, *op. cit.*

CHAPTER 9

1. The Kings Norton (Birmingham) and Glasgow Pollok Constituency Labour Parties were suspended by the National Executive for breaking the truce.
2. The strike was particularly controversial as it threatened to affect public transport in London during the Coronation.
3. As George Orwell wrote: 'However much one may hate to admit it, it is almost certain that between 1931 and 1940 the National Government represented the will of the mass of the people. It tolerated slums, unemployment and a cowardly foreign policy. Yes, but so did public opinion.' (G. Orwell, *England, Your England*, London, 1953, p. 207.)
4. See Hywel Francis, 'Welsh Miners and the Spanish Civil War', *Journal of Contemporary History*, 5 (3), 1970.
5. John McGovern, among others, got himself involved in several controversies

both with co-religionists and with the Left. See his *Why Bishops Back Franco*, London, 1936.

6. See H. Thomas, *op. cit.*, pp 544–50 and 713–14.
7. See H. Thomas, *op. cit.*, pp. 665–6.
8. Fred Copeman, *Reason in Revolt*, London, 1948, p. 150.
9. See especially R. Conquest, *The Great Terror*, Harmondsworth, 1971.
10. D. N. Pritt, *The Moscow Trials, op. cit.* Pritt, writing after Khrushchev's denunciation of some aspects of the trials, avoided repudiating his previous position (see his *Autobiography*, London, 1966).
11. There was far less support for Cripps at the 1939 Labour Party Conference than there had been for Communist affiliation in 1936, although 'intellectual' and 'fellow-travelling' support for the Left did not seem to be seriously affected by the trials.
12. D. N. Pritt. *Light on Moscow*, Harmondsworth, 1939, p. 156.
13. See e.g. Labour Party, *Finland*, London, 1940.
14. Sir R. S. Cripps, *'National Fascism' in Britain*, London, 1935.
15. K. Zilliacus (Vigilante), *Between Two Wars?*, Harmondsworth, 1939, p.210.
16. Quoted in Sir E. Wrench, *Geoffrey Dawson and our Times*, London, 1955, pp. 362–3.
17. Claud Cockburn, editor of *The Week*, claimed to have 'invented' the Cliveden Set (see his *In Time of Trouble*, London, 1956). However the Set was still being referred to ten years later (see Margaret George, *The Hollow Men*, London, 1965).
18. These included the University Labour Federation, D. N. Pritt MP, and supporters of the Peoples' Convention, including the Newbury and Maidenhead Constituency Labour Parties. See the Labour Party Annual Reports for 1940 and 1941.

CHAPTER 10

1. Report of the 14th Congress of the CPGB, London, 1937.
2. *Inprecorr,* 13 March 1937.
3. *Inprecorr,* 23 October 1937.
4. Economic League, *The Present Trend of Communism in Britain*, London, 1938.
5. 'An analysis of the new membership shows that an appreciable percentage of it is of non-industrial character, being made up of black-coated workers, young intellectuals and middle class elements' (Economic League, *op. cit.*).
6. Report of the 14th Congress of the CPGB.
7. *New Leader*, 22 April 1938.
8. *The Times*, 14 February 1937.
9. *Daily Herald*, 25 July 1938.
10. The ILP and the Labour Party negotiated re-affiliation during 1939 and a conference was to have been held by the ILP on 17 September at which the NAC was to recommend acceptance of the Labour Party's terms. However the outbreak of war changed the situation and the ILP began to contest by-elections on 'Stop the War' platforms. See A. F. Brockway, *Inside the Left*, London, 1942 and R. Dowse, *Left in the Centre*, London, 1966.

11. See Charlotte Haldane, *Truth will Out,* London, 1949 and Douglas Hyde, *I Believed,* London, 1951 for accounts by two ex-Communists of their infiltration of local Labour Parties in 1939. Mrs Haldane was even elected as a Labour councillor.
12. See G. Almond, *The Appeals of Communism,* Princeton, 1954, p. 224.
13. Left Book Club leaflet, June 1937.
16. For a full list of Left Book Club publications see John Lewis, *op. cit.,* Appendix.
17. *Daily Worker,* 28 January 1938.
18. *Daily Herald,* 31 December 1938.
19. *Manchester Guardian,* 20 March 1939.
20. *Forward,* 20 April 1941.
21. Report of the 15th Congress of the CPGB, London, 1938, Credentials Report.
22. The ULF president, John Cornford, was killed in Spain.
23. See Advance Publications, *Youth Triumphant,* London, 1938 and a report submitted to the Labour Party National Executive by *Advance* in March 1938.
24. ILP Annual Report for 1940, p. 16.
25. *Communist International,* September 1938.
26. A. Bernstein in *Advance,* June 1937.
27. *Advance,* June 1937.
28. Labour Party League of Youth Conference Report for 1938.
29. See L. Trotsky, *In Defence of Marxism,* New York, 1942 and J. P. Cannon, *Struggle for the Proletarian Party,* New York, 1943.
30. For the relationship between these groups and the Trotskyist movement in modern Britain see Peter Shipley, *Revolutionaries in Modern Britain,* London, 1976, Appendix B.

CHAPTER 11

1. *The Socialist,* February 1937. See also Ben Pimlott, *Labour and the Left, op. cit.,* p. 97.
2. *Controversy,* February 1937.
3. J. R. Campbell in *Tribune,* 15 January 1937.
4. For the text of the Unity Manifesto see the Appendix.
5. *Left News,* March 1937.
6. *Tribune,* 26 February 1937.
7. Labour Party Annual Report for 1937, Appendix VII.
8. *New Leader,* 12 February 1937.
9. *Tribune,* 9 July 1937.
10. Labour Party, *op. cit.,* p. 25.
11. Labour Party, *loc. cit.*
12. *Tribune,* 15 October 1937.
13. *Tribune,* 29 October 1937.
14. *Ibid.*
15. R. Palme Dutt in *Advance,* October 1937.
16. *Left Review,* October 1936.
17. *Manchester Guardian,* 8 February 1937.
18. *Daily Worker,* 8 May 1937.
19. *Inprecorr,* 29 May 1937.

20.   According to the ILP 'it was on the advice of the CP that the Socialist League was dissolved. It was on the advice of the CP that the joint meetings between Labour Unity supporters, the ILP and the CP were stopped' (*New Leader*, 12 November 1937). However, W. Gallacher in *The Chosen Few*, London, 1940 (written during the Communist anti-war campaign) puts the blame for suspending joint activities on Cripps.
21.   *Tribune*, 7 January 1938.
22.   *Daily Worker*, 17 January 1938.
23.   *Tribune*, 14 April 1938.
24.   *Tribune*, 6 May 1938.
25.   *Tribune*, 13 May 1938.
26.   Quoted in *New Leader*, 20 May 1938. The Labour vote rose from 11 per cent at the general election to 19.1 per cent at the by-election, with the Liberals running second to the Conservatives. However, the combined Liberal and Labour vote was only 45.9 per cent.
27.   Labour Party, *Labour and the Popular Front*, London, 1938.
28.   *Controversy*, August 1938.
29.   *Tribune*, 20 May 1938.
30.   See Iain McLean, 'Oxford and Bridgwater' in C. Cook and J. Ramsden (eds.), *By-elections in British Politics*, London, 1973, pp. 140–64 and R. Eatwell, 'Munich, Public Opinion and the Popular Front', *Journal of Contemporary History*, 6 (4), 1971. Lindsay's vote at Oxford was 43.9 per cent and Bartlett's at Bridgwater 53.2 per cent, both against Conservatives only.
31.   *Tribune*, 6 January 1939.
32.   Also known as the '100,000 Group'.
33.   *Daily Worker*, 4 January 1939.
34.   *Daily Worker*, 6 January 1939.
35.   Full details are in the Labour Party Annual Report for 1939, pp. 43–53.
36.   *Ibid.*
37.   *Tribune*, 27 January 1939.
38.   *Tribune*, 10 February 1939.
39.   *Railway Review*, February 1939.
40.   Labour Party, *loc. cit.*
41.   See Ben Pimlott, *Labour and the Left, op. cit.*, chs 17 and 18.
42.   'He disappointed the delegates and gave his supporters in the Conference a poor lead for their attempt to get the Executive Report on its actions referred back' (G. D. H. Cole, *A History of the Labour Party*, London, 1948, p. 360.)
43.   Open Letter to the Labour League of Youth from the National Youth Officer, May 1939.
44.   See the discussion on Pollitt's role in this episode in the *Bulletin of the Society for the Study of Labour History*, nos. 33 and 35, 1977.
45.   V. Gollancz and others, *The Betrayal of the Left*, London, 1941.
46.   See Hugh Thomas, *John Strachey*, London, 1973.
47.   *Labour Monthly*, June 1941.
48.   Labour Party Annual Report for 1941.

CHAPTER 12

1.   W. Hannington, *The Problem of the Distressed Areas*, London, 1937, p. 282.

2. J. T. Murphy, *New Horizons,* London, 1941, pp. 300–2.
3. *Forward,* 20 April 1941.
4. In November 1938 the Left Book Club distributed two million leaflets on the Munich crisis and followed this up in December with ten million leaflets on the Spanish Civil War.
5. Half the shares in the *Daily Herald* passed from the TUC to Odhams Press in 1929 and its circulation was increased to over two million in the newspaper circulation race of the 1930s.
6. For a discussion of the *New Statesman and Nation* in the 1930s see C. H. Rolph, *Kingsley,* London, 1973 and K. Martin, *Editor,* London, 1968.
7. ILP NAC Documents – Accounts and Circulation Reports on *New Leader.*
8. Between 1928 and 1934 the Comintern spent US $4 million on the Party press throughout the world. See *Inprecorr,* 15 August 1934.
9. The *Daily Worker* foreign news coverage was often bizarre in its early days. See e.g. its reports on the election of Hitler in 1933 (*Daily Worker,* March 1933). The paper was also banned by the major newspaper distributors.
10. The weekly *Rhondda Vanguard* had a circulation of 4,000. In 1937 the Communist Party was publishing 28 factory and industrial papers with an aggregate circulation of about 50,000, the most influential being *Busmen's Punch.*
11. Apart from *Tribune* the most influential papers expressing non-Communist Left opinions were regionally located in Lancashire (*Northern Voice*) and Scotland (*Forward*).
12. *Communist International,* September 1937.
13. For the early attempts at Marxist organization in Britain see Y. Kapp, *Eleanor Marx,* London, 1976, vol. 2, and C. Tsuzuki, *H. M. Hyndman and British Socialism, op. cit.*
14. See W. Kendall, *The Revolutionary Movement in Britain,* London, 1969 for a critique of the SLP and R. Challinor, *The Origins of British Bolshevism,* London, 1977 for a defence.
15. See E. Archbold and F. Lee, *Social Democracy in Britain,* London, 1935,
16. See B. Barker, *Ramsay MacDonald's Political Writings,* London, 1972.
17. Perhaps the most influential non-Communist analysis of Marxism was G. D. H Cole, *What Marx Really Meant,* published in 1934.
18. *Adelphi,* January 1934.
19. Labour Party Constitution, clause 4, subsection 4.
20. CPGB letter of application, 12 July 1939.
21. For a much more critical, later, approach see R. Miliband, *Parliamentary Socialism, op. cit.*
22. For an analysis of the influence of the Socialist League on Labour Party thinking see Ben Pimlott, *op. cit.*

CHAPTER 13

1. In 1920 Gallacher 'had little regard for parties and still less regard for parliament and parliamentarians' (W. Gallacher, *Revolt on the Clyde,* London, 1941, p. 251).
2. Tom Bell, *The British Communist Party, op. cit.,* p. 64.
3. R. P. Dutt, *Fascism and Social Revolution,* London, 1934, p. 58.

4. *New Nation*, September 1934.
5. See *Communist International*, 15 May 1931, Report of the XI Plenum of ECCI.
6. See R. P. Dutt, *op. cit.*
7. E. J. Strachey, *The Coming Struggle for Power*, London, 1932, p. 301.
8. Strachey, *op. cit.*, p. 338.
9. H. J. Laski, *The Labour Party and the Constitution*, London, 1933, p. 1.
10. *Left Book Club News*, September 1936.
11. *Labour Monthly*, November 1935.
12. C. R. Attlee, *The Labour Party in Perspective*, London, 1937, p. 113.
13. Attlee, *op. cit.*, p. 135.
14. *Tribune*, 31 December 1937.
15. R. S. Cripps, *Why this Socialism?*, London, 1934.
16. E. J. Strachey, *The Theory and Practice of Socialism*, London, 1936, p. 198.
17. See J. Stevenson and C. Cook, *The Slump, op. cit.*, chs 4, 5, 9 and 10.
18. *Daily Telegraph*, 8 March 1933. There was no Left support for individual terrorism. For the Communist attitude to the IRA bombing campaign of 1939 see W. Gallacher, *The Ruling Few*, London, 1940.
19. *Inprecorr*, 22 October 1931.
20. *Inprecorr*, 15 January 1931.
21. Other major disturbances involving the trial of Communists surrounded the Harworth miners' strike of 1937 and opposition to evictions in Blaina in 1938.
22. *New Leader*, 2 October 1931.
23. *New Leader*, 11 November 1932.
24. *Ibid.*
25. *What the ILP Stands For*, London, 1935, section 27.
26. *Op. cit.*, section 43.
27. H. J. Laski, *The Crisis and the Constitution*, London, 1932, p. 9.
28. R. S. Cripps, *Can Socialism come by Constitutional Means?* London, 1932.
29. R. P. Dutt, *Fascism and Social Revolution, op. cit.*, p. 61.
30. Resolutions of the Seventh World Congress, London, 1935, p. 4.
31. *Op. cit.*, p. 18.
32. Report of the 15th Congress of the CPGB, London, 1938, p. 27.
33. E. J. Strachey, *Theory and Practice of Socialism*, London, 1936, p. 154.
34' H. Pollitt, *How to Win the War*, London, 1939, p. 3.
35. Report of the 15th CPGB Congress, p. 60.
36. *Op. cit.* p. 63.
37. See e.g. the Labour Party's Election Manifesto for 1935 where it states that 'Labour seeks a mandate to carry out this programme by constitutional and democratic means and with this end in view, it seeks power to abolish the House of Lords and improve the procedure of the House of Commons' (in F. W. Craig, *British General Election Manifestos 1900-1974*, London, 1975).

CHAPTER 14

1. See especially H. Pelling, *The Origins of the Labour Party 1880-1900*, London, 1954 for the role of the ILP and other socialist groups in founding the Labour Party.
2. See C. A. Cline, *Recruits to Labour*, Syracuse NY, 1963.
3. For the origins of the Communist Party see especially W. Kendall, *The*

Revolutionary Movement in Britain 1900–1921, London, 1969, and J. Klug-mann, *History of the Communist Party of Great Britain*, London, 1968, vol. 1.
4. *Workers Weekly*, 4 July 1924.
5. See Pelling, *op. cit.*
6. ILP NAC Documents – Report of the Reorganisation Committee, November 1934.
7. See Ben Pimlott, *Labour and the Left, op. cit.*, chs. 11–14.
8. *New Leader*, 4 September 1931.
9. *New Leader*, 4 October 1935.
10. The argument was still raging forty years later as witness the controversy over Trotskyist 'entrism' into the Labour Party in the 1970s and the tactics of the International Socialists and the Socialist Labour League which had both joined, and subsequently left, the Labour Party in the 1960s.
11. *New Clarion*, 26 November 1932.

CHAPTER 15

1. The major socialist ideas alternative to those of the Left were largely those of Attlee, Evan Durbin, the small but influential group who made up the New Fabian Research Bureau, and R. H. Tawney.
2. Communist Party, *The Road to Victory*, London, 1932, p. 13.
3. See Ben Pimlott, *Labour and the Left, op. cit.*
4. In 1924 the Trades Union Congress had been committed to industrial unionism but with the collapse of the General Strike the unions turned away from all attitudes reminiscent of syndicalism.
5. Labour's Immediate Programme, section 3 – Democracy.
6. In R. S. Cripps *et al., Problems of a Socialist Government*, London, 1935, p. 191.
7. Cripps. *op. cit.*, p. 213.
8. C. R. Attlee, *The Labour Party in Perspective*, London, 1937, p. 160.
9. E. Burns, *The Only Way Out*, London, 1932, p. 74.
10. Burns, *op. cit.*, p. 83.
11. E. J. Strachey, *The Theory and Practice of Socialism*, London, 1936, p. 176.
12. C. R. Attlee, *op. cit.*, p. 152.

CHAPTER 16

1. This wide field has already been surveyed in two doctoral theses: Sam Davis, *British Labour and Foreign Policy 1933 to 1939* (London Ph. D. 1950) and W. R. Tucker, *The Attitude of the British Labour Party towards European Collective Security Problems 1920–1939* (Geneva 1950). See also J. F. Naylor, *Labour's International Policy*, London, 1969.
2. Quoted in C. L. Mowat, *Britain between the Wars*, London, 1955, p. 540.
3. Report of the International Federation of Trade Unions for 1924–26, p. 100.
4. Quoted in B. Braatoy, *Labour and War*, London, 1934, p. 162.

5. Braatoy, *op. cit.,* p. 171.
6. *New Leader,* 22 July 1932.
7. *What the ILP Stands For,* London, 1935.
8. In G. D. H. Cole, *The Intelligent Man's Way to Prevent War,* London, 1934, p. 501.
9. *The Socialist,* September 1935.
10. *Ibid.*
11. H. Morrison, *Labour and Sanctions,* London, 1935, p. 4.
12. *Inprecorr,* 28 September 1935.
13. *Inprecorr,* 12 October 1935.
14. Resolutions of the Seventh Comintern Congress, London, 1935, p. 25.
15. *Op. cit.,* p. 27.
16. G. D. H. Cole, *The Peoples Front,* London, 1937, p. 336.
17. *New Leader,* 25 September 1936.
18. Communist Party, *Sidelights on the Cliveden Set,* London, 1938, p. 17.
19. J. Maxton, *Great Anti-War Speech,* Glasgow, 1938, p. 4.
20. Communist Party, *Statements on Conscription,* 24 May 1939.
21. *New Leader,* 13 October 1939.
22. Communist Party, *Report to the 16th Congress,* London, 1939, p. 23.
23. Communist Party, *The Communist Party in Wartime,* London, 1940, p. 3.
24. Communist League of America, *War and the Fourth International,* New York, 1940, p. 26.
25. *New Leader,* 1 August 1940.
26. Peoples Convention, resolution 7.
27. Reported in *New Leader,* 5 December 1940.
28. *Labour Monthly,* June 1941.
29. *Labour Monthly,* August 1941.
30. *Labour Monthly,* December 1941.

CHAPTER 17

1. See e.g. L. D. Trotsky, *The First Five Years of the Communist International,* New York, 1945 and 1953.
2. Membership figures for the Communist Party are in H. Pelling, *The British Communist Party,* London, 1958 and for the ILP in R. Dowse, *Left in the Centre,* London, 1966.
3. Approximate circulation of exclusively political Left journals in 1939 was:

Daily Worker	80,000 (per day)
Tribune	25,000 (per week)
New Leader	20,000 (per week)
Advance	15,000 (per week)
Challenge	12,000 (per week)

Left News went monthly to all Left Book Club members.
4. The only significant restriction was that affiliates could not send non-members of the Labour Party as delegates to Labour Party meetings and conferences. This rule was probably ignored in many cases.
5. This was the situation in most of Glasgow after the disaffiliation of the ILP.
6. The London Labour Party refused to accept membership applications forwarded to it by the Unity Campaign Committee (*London News* January 1939).

7. See F. W. Craig, *Minor Parties in British Parliamentary Elections 1885-1974*, London, 1975.

8. H. J. Laski, 'The General Election 1935', *Political Quarterly,* January 1936.

9. See M. Hechter, *Internal Colonialism,* Berkeley, Cal., 1975, for a discussion of regional political differences in Britain.

10. In 1931 the ILP won 150,314 of its 279,622 votes in Scotland (53.75 per cent) and in 1935 won 111,256 of its 139,577 (79.7 per cent). In 1931 the CP won 35,618 of its votes in Scotland out of 74,824 (47.6 per cent). In 1935 the CP won 13,462 of its votes in Scotland out of 27,117 (49.6 per cent). Of general and by-election results where either party won more than 10 per cent of the vote in the 1930s the ILP numbered 12 cases in Scotland and Wales between 1932 and 1941 and the CP ten cases between 1931 and 1941. In the English seats they each recorded three such cases only.

11. The most overcrowded wards of Glasgow, in the 1921 Census, nearly all lay in the constituencies of Bridgeton, Gorbals, Camlachie and Shettleston which were represented by the ILP throughout the 1930s. Most of them also returned ILP councillors, even after the disaffiliation of 1932. See M. Kinnear, *The British Voter, op cit.,* p. 133.

12. See Abe Moffat, *My Life with the Miners,* London, 1965.

13. See Arthur Horner, *Incorrigible Rebel,* London, 1960.

14. *Inprecorr,* 9 February 1935.

15. *Inprecorr,* 13 April 1935.

16. The most important influence among Durham miners was Will Lawther, a former Communist, who spoke in favour of Communist affiliation at the 1936 Labour Party conference. One mining village, Chopwell, was a Communist stronghold from the 1920s, but there was virtually no other base for the Communists on the Northeastern coalfields. Ellen Wilkinson records that there were only seven Communists in Jarrow in the 1930s, 'five of whom also held cards in the Labour Party' (E. Wilkinson, *The Town that was Murdered,* London, 1939, p. 193).

17. See H. Pelling, *The British Communist Party,* London, 1958.

18. See A. F. Brockway, *The Bermondsey Story,* London, 1949.

19. Official London Labour Party rallies were held against Fascism, including one addressed by Herbert Morrison in Victoria Park, East London, in June 1936.

20. See L. Minkin, *The Labour Party Conference,* London, 1978 for the mechanics of conference politics.

21. E. Wilkinson, *op. cit.,* p. 206.

22. *Ibid.*

23. See Ben Pimlott, *Labour and the Left, op. cit.,* chs. 11-14.

24. Endorsement was refused in 1937 to W. Mellor at Stockport and to Ben Greene of the Constituency Parties Association at North-West Hull.

25. Several constituency parties were reorganized between 1937 and 1940, the most important being the Manchester City Labour Party. The usual reason was association with the Unity Campaigns.

26. Labour Party Constitution, Clause V, section 1 and Clause VI, section 1.

27. Labour Party Annual Report for 1936, p. 247.

28. *AEU Journal,* October 1936.

29. *Socialist Leaguer,* October 1934.

30. *Manchester Guardian,* 6 October 1937.

31. *Morning Post,* 29 July 1933.

32. In the first weeks of the 1937 campaign, over 20,000 attended meetings, an average of over 1,000 per meeting.

33. *Tribune,* 3 September 1937.

34. For examples and a general discussion of this tactic in British politics see R. Benewick and T. Smith, *Direct Action and Democratic Politics*, London, 1972.
35. See D. Caute, *The Fellow Travellers*, London, 1973 for a general discussion and G. Werskey, *The Visible College*, London, 1978 for an analysis of J. B. S. Haldane, J. D. Bernal and other natural scientists who joined or supported the Communists in the 1930s.
36. *Tribune*, 1 January 1937.
37. Sidney Webb, for example, thought it a mistake 'to bother about a Popular Front when we ought to be busy converting electors and the public at large' (*Tribune*, 15 January 1937).
38. See Pimlott, *op. cit.*

CHAPTER 18

1. Though see J. Stevenson and C. Cook, *The Slump*, especially chapters 1 and 14, for a 'debunking' of the myth of the 'Red Thirties'.
2. See e.g. W. Kendall, *The Revolutionary Movement in Britain 1900–1921*, London, 1969.
3. The Labour Party vote in 1935 was 37.9 per cent of the total and in May 1979 it was 36.9 per cent. For a recent analysis of Labour Party membership see C. Martin and D. Martin, 'The Decline of Labour Party Membership', *Political Quarterly*, 48 (4), Oct–Dec. 1977.
4. Among those active in Left politics in the 1930s Fenner Brockway, Emanuel Shinwell, Jennie Lee, John Gollan, Reg Groves, Ted Willis and Harry McShane were all still alive and politically involved in 1978. Four were in the House of Lords.
5. R. T. McKenzie, *British Political Parties*, London, 1955.
6. See B. Hindess, *The Decline of Working Class Politics*, London, 1971 and Tom Forrester, *The Labour Party and the Working Class*, London, 1976 for conflicting arguments on the social character of contemporary local Labour parties. Unfortunately no such studies were conducted in the 1930s, though Forrester concludes that 'in some senses Labour's relationship to the working class has not changed that much' (Forrester, *op. cit.*, p. 124).
7. See e.g. R. D. Coates, *The Labour Party and the Struggle for Socialism*, Cambridge, 1975 for a recent version of the proposition that the Labour Party cannot bring socialism.

Appendix

Unity Manifesto of the Socialist League, the Independent Labour Party and the Communist Party issued on January 17th, 1937.

'FOR THE ENDING OF RETREAT'

Unity of all sections of the Working Class Movement –

Unity in the struggle against Fascism, Reaction and War, and against the National Government –

Unity in the struggle for immediate demands and the return of a Labour Government as the next stage in the advance to working class power –

Unity through the removal of all barriers between sections of the Working Class Movement, through the adoption of a fighting programme of mass struggle, through democratisation of the Labour Party and the Trade Union Movement –

Unity within the framework of the Labour Party and the Trade Unions –

These are the objectives of those responsible for launching the Unity Campaign – a campaign to revitalise the activity and transform the policy of the Labour Movement.

Today is no time for defeatism or for breakaways; today is no time for retreat or for the abandonment of working-class unity in favour of class collaboration; today is the time for a united challenge and attack.

To weld the power of the workers into an unbreakable front, to advance in the fight for Socialism, we must mobilise for immediate objectives, clear in their appeal and vital in the battle against reaction and Fascism.

On the basis of Unity let the whole Labour Movement declare its determination to oppose Fascism in all its forms, to oppose the National Government as the agent of British Capitalism and Imperialism, to oppose all restrictions upon civil and trade union liberty, to oppose the militarisation of Great Britain.

No Rearmament

Let the Movement declare its implacable opposition to the rearmament and recruiting programme of the National Government, for that Government uses armaments only in support of Fascism, of Imperialist War, of Reaction, and of Colonial Suppression. The fight for Peace demands unbending hostility to a National Government that can in no circumstances be trusted to use armaments in the interests of the working class, of the peoples, or of peace.

To save the peoples of the world from the growing menace of Fascist aggression the working class must mobilise the maximum effective opposition; it must mobilise for the maintenance of peace, for the defence of the Soviet Union and its fight for peace, and for a pact between Great Britain, the Soviet Union, France and all other states in which the working class have political freedom. Working class unity alone can ensure the winning of the battle for peace.

Into the very foreground of political conflict must be brought the demand for the Nationalisation of the Arms industry and for the abolition of the caste and class system within the armed forces.

Down with Imperialism

Let the Labour Movement declare without equivocation that it supports the struggle of the Indian and Colonial peoples against Imperialism; that it is with them in their fight for free speech, a free press, free meeting and organisation, with them in the fight for their immediate demands, in the struggle to alleviate their position of economic and social servitude. Now is the time for the workers, conscious of their power and of the Movement's strength of purpose, to wage incessant struggle, political and industrial alike, for simple things the workers need.

Let the Movement not wait for General Elections but now, by active demonstrations, win and organise support for:

Abolition of the Means Test
T.U.C. scales of Unemployment Benefit
National work of social value for Distressed Areas
Forty hour week in Industry and the Public Service
Paid Holiday for all Workers
High wages, the abolition of tied cottages, for agricultural workers
Co-ordinated Trade Union action for higher wages in industry, especially in Mining, Cotton and Sweated Trades
Non-contributory pensions of £1 at 60
Immediate rehousing of the workers in town and countryside in houses that are homes
Power to get back the Land for the People
Nationalisation of the Mining Industry
Effective Control of the Banks, the Stock Exchanges with their gambling and private profiteering – profiteering accentuated by the armament boom
Making the rich pay for Social Amelioration.

We stand for action, for attack, for the ending of retreat, for the building of the strength, unity and power of the Working-Class Movement.

Bibliography

1. Books on British socialist theory and organizations

ALLEN, V. L., *Trade Unions and the Government* (London, 1960)
ARCHBOLD, E., and LEE, F., *Social Democracy in Britain* (London, 1935)
ARNOT, Robin Page, *The Miners – Years of Struggle* (London, 1953)
⠀⠀⠀⠀⠀⠀⠀⠀⠀⠀⠀⠀⠀⠀*Twenty Years (1920–1940)* (London, 1940)
ASHLEY, M. P., and SAUNDERS, C. T., *Red Oxford* (Oxford, 1933)
ATTLEE, C. R., ⠀⠀⠀*The Will and the Way to Socialism* (London, 1935)
⠀⠀⠀⠀⠀⠀⠀⠀⠀⠀⠀*The Labour Party in Perspective* (London, 1937)
BARKER, B. (ed.), *Ramsay MacDonald's Political Writings* (London, 1972)
BAUMAN, Z., *Between Class and Elite: the Evolution of the British Labour Party*
⠀⠀⠀(London, 1970)
BEALEY, F. (ed.), *The Social and Political Thought of the British Labour Party*
⠀⠀⠀(London, 1970)
BEALEY, F., and PELLING, H., *Labour and Politics 1900–1906* (London, 1958)
BEER, Max, *History of British Socialism* (London, 1948)
BELL, Tom, *The British Communist Party* (London, 1937)
BRAILSFORD, H. N., *Why Capitalism Causes War* (London, 1938)
BRAND, Carl F., *The British Labour Party* (Stanford, 1964)
BRIGGS, Asa (ed.), *Essays in Labour History* (London, 1960)
BRIGGS, Asa and SAVILLE, John, *Essays in Labour History 1918–1939* (London,
⠀⠀⠀1977)
BROCKWAY, A. F., *The Workers Front* (London, 1938)
BURNS, Emile, ⠀⠀⠀*The Only Way Out* (London, 1932)
⠀⠀⠀⠀⠀⠀⠀⠀⠀⠀⠀*Capitalism, Communism and the Transition* (London, 1933)
⠀⠀⠀⠀⠀⠀⠀⠀⠀⠀⠀*What is Marxism?* (London, 1939)
⠀⠀⠀⠀⠀⠀⠀⠀⠀⠀⠀(ed.), *A Handbook of Marxism* (London, 1935)
CATLIN, G. E. C. and others, *New Trends in Socialism* (London, 1935)
CHALLINOR, Ray, *The Origins of British Bolshevism* (London, 1977)
CLINE, C. A., *Recruits to Labour – the British Labour Party 1914–1931* (Syracuse
⠀⠀⠀NY, 1963)
CLINTON, A., *The Trade Union Rank and File: Trades Councils in Britain*
⠀⠀⠀*1900–1940* (Manchester, 1977)
COATES, R. D., *The Labour Party and the Struggle for Socialism* (Cambridge, 1975)
COLE, Margaret, *The Story of Fabian Socialism* (London, 1961)
CRIPPS, Sir R. S. ⠀⠀*Problems of the Socialist Transition* (London, 1934)
and others ⠀⠀⠀⠀⠀⠀*Problems of a Socialist Government* (London, 1935)
CROSSMAN, R. H. S. (ed.), *The God that Failed* (London, 1954)
DARKE, Bob, *The Communist Technique in Britain* (Harmondsworth, 1952)
DOBB, Maurice, *On Marxism Today* (London, 1932)
DOWSE, R., *Left in the Centre* (London, 1966)
DURBIN, E. F. M., *The Politics of Democratic Socialism* (London, 1940)
DUTT, R. Palme, ⠀⠀*Fascism and Social Revolution* (London, 1934)
⠀⠀⠀⠀⠀⠀⠀⠀⠀⠀⠀*The Political and Social Doctrines of Communism* (London,
⠀⠀⠀⠀⠀⠀⠀⠀⠀⠀⠀1938)
FOX, Ralph, *Communism and a Changing Civilisation* (London, 1935)
⠀⠀⠀⠀⠀⠀⠀⠀⠀⠀⠀*The Class Struggle in Britain in the Epoch of Imperialism*
⠀⠀⠀⠀⠀⠀⠀⠀⠀⠀⠀(London, 1933)

FRANCIS, H., and SMITH, D., *South Wales Miners 1926–1973* (London, 1978)
GALLACHER, W., *The Case for Communism* (Harmondsworth, 1949)
GARRATT, G. T., *The Mugwumps and the Labour Party* (London, 1932)
GOLLANCZ, V., and others, *The Betrayal of the Left* (London, 1941)
GRAUBAUD, S. R., *British Labour and the Russian Revolution 1917–1924* (London, 1956)
GROVES, Reg, *The Balham Group: How British Trotskyism Began* (London, 1974)
HAMILTON, Mary Agnes, *The Labour Party Today – What it is and How it Works* (London, 1939)
HARRISON, Martin, *Trade Unions and the Labour Party since 1945* (London, 1960)
HOWELL, David, *British Social Democracy* (London, 1976)
HUTT, A., *The Postwar History of the British Working Class* (London, 1937)
HINTON, J., and HYMAN, R., *Trade Unions and Revolution – the Industrial Politics of the early British Communist Party* (London, 1975)
JANOSIK, E. G., *Constituency Labour Parties in Britain* (London, 1968)
KEMP, A., *The Left Heresy* (London, 1937)
KENDALL, W., *The Revolutionary Movement in Britain 1900–1921* (London, 1969)
KLUGMANN, J., *History of the Communist Party of Great Britain*, vol. 1 The Formative Years 1919–1924 (London, 1968); vol. 2 The General Strike 1925–1927 (London, 1969)
LASKI, H. J.,   *The State in Theory and Practice* (London, 1935)
                 Liberty in the Modern State (Harmondsworth, 1937)
LAWRENCE & WISHART (symposium), *Britain Without Capitalists* (London, 1936)
LEE, Jennie, *Tomorrow is a New Day* (London, 1939)
LEWIS, John, *The Left Book Club: an Historical Record* (London, 1970)
LYMAN, R. W., *The First Labour Government 1924,* (London, 1957)
MACFARLANE, L. J. *The British Communist Party* (London, 1966)
McHENRY, G., *The Labour Party in Transition,* (London, 1938)
McKIBBIN, Ross, *The Evolution of the Labour Party 1910–1924* (Oxford, 1974)
MARTIN, R., *Communism and the British Trade Union Movement: a Study of the National Minority Movement* (Oxford, 1969)
MIDDLEMASS, K., *The Clydesiders* (London, 1965)
MILIBAND, Ralph, *Parliamentary Socialism* (London, 1961)
MINKIN, Lewis, *The Labour Party Conference* (London, 1978)
MITCHISON, G. R., *The First Workers' Government* (London, 1934)
MURPHY, J. T.,   *Preparing for Power* (London, 1934)
                 Modern Trade Unionism (London, 1935)
MURRY, J. M.,   *The Necessity of Communism* (London, 1932)
                 Marxism (London, 1935)
NAYLOR, J. G., *Labour's International Policy: the Labour Party in the 1930s* (London, 1969)
NEWTON, K., *The Sociology of British Communism* (London, 1969)
PEARCE, Brian, *Early History of the CPGB* (London, 1966)
PELLING, Henry,   *The Origins of the Labour Party 1880–1900* (London, 1954)
                   The British Communist Party: A Historical Profile (London, 1958)
                   A Short History of the Labour Party (London, 1961)
                   A History of British Trade Unionism (London, 1963)
PIMLOTT, Ben, *Labour and the Left in the 1930s* (Cambridge, 1977)
POIRIER, P. P., *The Advent of the Labour Party* (London, 1958)
POLLITT, Harry, *Selected Speeches and Articles:* vol. 1 (London, 1953); vol. 2 (London, 1954)

PRIBICEVIC, B., *The Shop Stewards' Movement and Workers Control* (London, 1957)
REDMAN, J., *The Communist Party and the Labour Left 1925–1929* (London, 1957)
REID, J. H. Stewart, *The Origin of the British Labour Party* (Minneapolis, 1955)
SCANLON, J., *The Decline and Fall of the Labour Party* (London, 1932)
        Pillars of Cloud (London, 1937)
        Cast off All Fooling (London, 1939)
SHIPLEY, Peter, *Revolutionaries in Modern Britain* (London, 1976)
SPENDER, Stephen, *Forward from Liberalism* (London, 1937)
STRACHEY, *The Coming Struggle for Power* (London, 1932)
E. J. StL., *The Menace of Fascism* (London, 1933)
        The Nature of Capitalist Crisis (London, 1937)
        What are We to Do? (London, 1938)
        Why You should be a Socialist (London, 1938)
        A Programme for Progress (London, 1940)
        A Faith to Fight For (London, 1941)
THOMAS, H. (ed.), *Tribune 21* (London, 1958)
TORR, D., *Marxism, Nationality and War* (London, 1940)
TSUZUKI, C., *H. M. Hyndman and British Socialism* (London, 1961)
WERTHEIMER, Egon, *Portrait of the Labour Party* (London, 1949)
WILLIAMS, Francis, *Fifty Years March* (London, 1949)
        Magnificent Journey (London, 1954)
WINDRICH, Elaine, *British Labour's Foreign Policy* (Stanford, 1950)
WOOD, N., *Communism and British Intellectuals* (London, 1959)
WUNDERLICH, F., *British Labour and the World* (New York, 1941)
WOODHOUSE, M., and PEARCE, B., *Essays on the History of Communism in Britain* (London, 1975)

2. General history and background

(a) Britain

ADDISON, Paul, *The Road to 1945: British Politics and the Second World War* (London, 1975)
ALDCROFT, D. H., *The Inter-war Economy: Britain 1919–1939* (London, 1970)
BAKKE, E. W., *The Unemployed Man* (London, 1933)
BASSETT, R., *Nineteen Thirty One: Political Crisis* (London, 1958)
        Democracy and Foreign Policy (London, 1952)
BEALES, H. G., and LAMBERT, R. S., *Memoirs of the Unemployed* (London, 1934)
BEER, S. H., *Modern British Politics* (London, 1965)
BENEWICK, R., *The Fascist Movement in Britain* (London, 1972)
BENEWICK, R., and SMITH, T., *Direct Action and Democratic Politics* (London, 1972)
BLYTHE, R., *The Age of Illusion* (London, 1963)
BRANSON, N., and HEINEMANN, M., *Britain in the Nineteen Thirties* (London, 1971)
BUTLER, D. E., and FREEMAN, J., *British Political Facts 1900–1967* (London, 1968)
CAMBRIDGE SCIENTISTS ANTI-WAR GROUP, *Protection from Aerial Attack*, (Cambridge, 1937)

236   *The Radical Left in Britain 1931–1941*

CARR-SAUNDERS, A. M., and JONES, D. C. *A Survey of the Social Structure of England and Wales* (Oxford, 1937)
CAUDWELL, C., *Studies in a Dying Culture* (London, 1938)
COCKBURN, Patricia, *The Years of 'The Week'* (Harmondsworth, 1968)
COLE, G. D. H.   *A Guide to Modern Politics* (London, 1934)
and Margaret,   *The Condition of Britain* (London, 1937)
COLE, G. D. H. and POSTGATE, R., *The Common People 1789–1947* (London, 1948)
COLVIN, Ian, *The Chamberlain Cabinet* (London, 1972)
CONNOR, H. O., *The Astors* (New York, 1941)
COOK, Chris, *The Age of Alignment: Electoral Politics in Britain 1922–1929* (London, 1975)
COWLING, M., *The Impact of Hitler: British Politics and British Policy 1933–1940* (Cambridge, 1975)
CRAIG, F.W.S.(ed.),   *British General Election Manifestos 1900–1974* (London, 1975)
                Minor Parties at British Parliamentary Elections 1885–1974 (London, 1975)
CROSS, Colin, *The Fascists in Britain* (London, 1961)
DAVIDSON, R. C., *British Unemployment Policy* (London, 1938)
DRENNAN, J. (ALLEN, W. E. D.), *BUF, Oswald Mosley and British Fascism* (London, 1934)
GEORGE, Margaret, *The Hollow Men* (London, 1965)
GILBERT, M., and GOTT, R., *The Appeasers* (London, 1963)
GLYNN, Sean, and OXBORROW, J., *Interwar Britain: A Social and Economic History* (London, 1976)
GRANZOW, B., *A Mirror of Nazism: British Opinion and the Emergence of Hitler 1929–1933* (London, 1964)
GREAVES, H. R. G., *Reactionary England* (London, 1936)
HALDANE, J. B. S., *ARP* (London, 1938)
HAMISH HAMILTON (publishers), *Decade 1931–1941* (London, 1941)
HANNINGTON,   *Short History of the Unemployed* (London, 1936)
Wal,   *Unemployed Struggles 1919–1936* (London, 1936)
          The Problem of the Distressed Areas (London, 1937)
          Ten Lean Years (London, 1940)
HAXEY, S., *Tory MP* (London, 1939)
HOGG, Quintin, *The Left was Never Right* (London, 1945)
HYNES, S., *The Auden Generation: Literature and Politics in England in the 1930s* (London, 1976)
KINNEAR, M., *The British Voter: an Atlas and Survey since 1885* (London, 1968)
LINDSAY, T. F., and HARRINGTON, M., *The Conservative Party 1918–1970* (London, 1974)
LIVINGSTONE, Lady, *The Peace Ballot (Official History)* (London, 1935)
MACALPIN, M., *Mr Churchill's Socialists* (London, 1941)
McKENZIE, R. T., *British Political Parties* (London, 1955)
MADGE, C., and HARRISON, T., *Britain by Mass Observation* (Harmondsworth, 1939)
MANDLE, W. F., *Anti-Semitism and the British Union of Fascists* (London, 1968)
MARWICK, A., *Britain in the Century of Total War* (London, 1968)
MONTAGU, Ivor, *The Traitor Class* (London, 1940)
MORRIS, Margaret, *The General Strike* (Harmondsworth, 1976)
MOWAT, C. L., *Britain between the Wars* (London, 1955)
MUGGERIDGE, Malcolm, *The Thirties in Great Britain* (London, 1940)
NICOLSON, Harold, *Why Britain is at War* (Harmondsworth, 1939)

NORTHEDGE, F. S., *The Troubled Giant* (London, 1966)
ORWELL, George, *England, Your England* (London, 1953)
                    The Road to Wigan Pier (London, 1937)
PEELE, G., and COOK, Chris, *The Politics of Reappraisal 1918–1939* (London, 1975)
ROWSE, A. L.,   *The End of an Epoch* (London, 1947)
                    All Souls and Appeasement (London, 1960)
RUDLIN, W. A., *The Growth of Fascism in Great Britain* (London, 1935)
RUSSELL, Bertrand, and others, *Dare We Look Ahead?* (London, 1938)
SEAMAN, L. C. B., *Post Victorian Britain 1902–1951* (London, 1967)
SKED, A., and COOK, Chris, *Crisis and Controversy* (London, 1976)
SKIDELSKY, R., *Politicians and the Slump* (London, 1967)
STEVENSON, J., and COOK, Chris, *The Slump: Society and Politics during the Depression* (London, 1977)
SYMONS, J.,   *The General Strike* (London, 1957)
                    The Thirties (London, 1960)
TAYLOR, A. J. P., *English History 1914–1945* (Oxford, 1965)
THE TIMES, *Official History: vol. 4 The 150th Anniversary and Beyond* (London, 1952)
WILKINSON, Ellen, *The Town that was Murdered* (London, 1939)
WILSON, Trevor, *The Downfall of the Liberal Party 1914–1935* (London, 1966)

(b) Overseas

ALMOND, G., *The Appeals of Communism* (Princeton, 1954)
BORKENAU, F.,   *The Communist International* (London, 1938)
                    European Communism (London, 1953)
BRAATOY, B., *Labour and War* (London, 1934)
BRAUNTHAL, J.,   *The Tragedy of Austria* (London, 1948)
                    History of the Second International 1914–1943 (London, 1967)
BROWDER, Earl, *The Peoples Front in the United States* (New York, 1938)
BURNHAM, James *The Peoples Front, the New Betrayal* (New York, 1937)
CANNON, J. P.,   *The Struggle for the Proletarian Party* (New York, 1943)
                    History of American Trotskyism (New York, 1944)
CATTELL, D. T., *Communism and the Spanish Civil War* (Berkeley, 1956)
CAUTE, David, *The Fellow-Travellers* (London, 1973)
CHURCHILL, W.S.,   *Arms and the Covenant* (London, 1938)
                    The Second World War (London, 1948)
CITRINE, W., *I Search for Truth in Soviet Russia* (London, 1936)
CLAUDIN, F., *The Communist Movement from Comintern to Cominform* (Harmondsworth, 1975)
COLE, G. D. H., *The Intelligent Man's Guide through World Chaos* (London, 1932)
COLE, G. D. H., and Margaret, *The Intelligent Man's Review of Europe Today* (London, 1933)
COLE, Margaret, *Twelve Studies in Soviet Russia* (London, 1936)
CONQUEST, Robert, *The Great Terror* (Harmondsworth, 1971)
DEGRAS, J. (ed.), *Soviet Documents on Foreign Policy 1917–1941* (London 1951–1953)
                    The Communist International 1919–1943: Documents (Oxford, 1965; reprinted Cass, 1971)
DIMITROV, George, *The United Front* (New York, 1938)
EBON, M., *World Communism Today* (New York, 1948)
ECCI, *Fifteen Years of the Communist International* (New York, 1934)

FAINSOD, M., *International Socialism and the World War* (Harvard, 1935)
FISCHER, Ruth, *Stalin and German Communism* (New York, 1948)
GIDE, André, *Back from the USSR* (London, 1937)
GREGORY, J. D., *Dollfuss and his Times* (London, 1935)
IBARRURI, Dolores, *Speeches and Articles* (London, 1938)
INTERNATIONAL ANTI-COMMUNIST ENTENTE, *The Red Network* (London, 1939)
JAMES, C. L. R., *World Revolution* (London, 1937)
JOHNSON, Hewlett, *The Socialist Sixth of the World* (London, 1939)
KUSZYNSKI, J., *The Condition of the Workers in Great Britain, Germany and the USSR 1932–1938* (London, 1939)
LUNN, Sir Arnold, *Revolutionary Socialism* (London, 1939)
McKENZIE, K. E., *Comintern and World Revolution 1928–1943* (New York, 1964)
MOWRER, E. A., *Germany Puts the Clock Back* (Harmondsworth, 1937)
NOEL-BAKER, P. J., *Hawkers of Death* (London, 1934)
ORWELL, G., *Homage to Catalonia* (London, 1938)
PRITT, D. N., *The Moscow Trials* (London, 1936)
RIDLEY, F. A., *Mussolini over Africa* (London, 1935)
THOMAS, Hugh, *The Spanish Civil War* (Harmondsworth, 1965)
TROTSKY, L. D.,   *The Revolution Betrayed* (London, 1937)
                  In Defence of Marxism (New York, 1942)
                  The First Five Years of the Communist International (London, 1953)
VARGA, E., *The Great Crisis and its Political Consequences* (London, 1935)
VINCENT, C., *The Popular Front in France* (London, 1938)
WEBB, S. & B., *Soviet Communism – a New Civilisation?* (London, 1935)
WEISBORD, A., *The Conquest of Power* (London, 1938)
WHEELER-BENNETT, J., *Munich* (London, 1958)
WOOLF, L. and others, *The Intelligent Man's Way to Prevent War* (London, 1933)
WORLD COMMITTEE FOR THE VICTIMS OF FASCISM, *The Brown Book of the Nazi Terror* (London, 1934)
ZILLIACUS, K., *Between Two Wars?* (Harmondsworth, 1939)

3. Biographies, autobiographies and memoirs

ALDRED, Guy, *Essays in Revolt* (Glasgow, 1940)
ANDERSON, M., *Lord Noel Buxton* (London, 1952)
ATTLEE, C. R.,   *As it Happened* (London, 1954)
                 A Prime Minister Remembers (London, 1961)
BALDWIN, A. W., *My Father – the True Story* (London, 1956)
BARR, REV. J., *Lang Syne: Memoirs* (Glasgow, 1949)
BELL, Tom, *Pioneering Days* (London, 1940)
BLAXLAND, G., *J. H. Thomas* (London, 1964)
BROCKWAY, A. F., *Inside the Left* (London, 1942)
                  Socialism over Sixty Years (F. Jowett) (London, 1946)
                  The Bermondsey Story (Dr A. Salter) (London, 1949)
                  Towards Tomorrow (London, 1977)
BROME, V., *Aneurin Bevan (London, 1953)*
BULLOCK, Alan, *The Life and Times of Ernest Bevin* (London, 1960)
CITRINE, W. M.,   *Men and Work* (London, 1964)
                 Two Careers (London, 1967)

CLYNES, J. R., *Memoirs 1924-1937* (London, 1937)
COCKBURN, Claud,   *In Time of Trouble* (London, 1956)
                     Crossing the Line (London, 1958)
COLE, Margaret,   *Growing up into Revolution* (London, 1949)
                     The Life of G. D. H. Cole (London, 1971)
                     The Webbs and Their Work (London, 1949)
                     The Diaries of Beatrice Webb (London 1952 & 1956)
COOKE, Colin, *The Life of Richard Stafford Cripps* (London, 1957)
COOPER, Duff, *Old Men Forget* (London, 1953)
COPEMAN, Fred, *Reason in Revolt* (London, 1948)
CROSS, C. *Philip Snowden* (London, 1966)
DALTON, Hugh, *The Fateful Years 1931-1945* (London, 1957)
DE BUNSEN, V., *Charles Roden Buxton* (London, 1948)
DONOUGHUE, B., and JONES, G. W., *Herbert Morrison: Portrait of a Politician* (London, 1973)
EASTWOOD, Granville, *Harold Laski* (London, 1977)
ESTORICK, E., *Stafford Cripps* (London, 1949)
FEILING, Keith, *The Life of Neville Chamberlain* (London, 1946)
FOOT, Michael, *Aneurin Bevan 1897-1945* (London, 1962)
GALLACHER,   *The Chosen Few* (London, 1940)
  William,   *Revolt on the Clyde* (London, 1941)
                     Rolling of the Thunder (London, 1947)
HALDANE, Charlotte, *Truth will Out* (London, 1949)
HAMILTON, Mary Agnes, *Arthur Henderson,* (London, 1938)
HANNINGTON, W., *Never on our Knees* (London, 1967)
HITLER, Adolf, *Mein Kampf* (First English Edition) (London, 1933)
HOBSON, C. R., *Pilgrim to the Left* (London, 1938)
HYDE, Douglas, *I Believed* (London, 1951)
JACKSON, T. A., *Solo Trumpet* (London, 1953)
JOHNSON, Hewlett, *Searching for Light – an Autobiography* (London, 1968)
JOHNSTON, Tom, *Memoirs* (London, 1952)
KIRKWOOD, David, *My Life of Revolt* (London, 1935)
KOESTLER, Arthur, *The Invisible Writing* (London, 1952)
LANSBURY, George, *My Quest for Peace* (London, 1938)
LAZITCH, Branko, *Biographical Dictionary of the Comintern* (Stanford, 1973)
LEE, Jennie, *This Great Journey* (New York, 1942)
McALLISTER, G., *James Maxton, Portrait of a Rebel* (London, 1936)
McGOVERN, John, *Neither Fear nor Favour* (London, 1960)
McNAIR, John, *James Maxton – the Beloved Rebel* (London, 1955)
McSHANE Harry, *No Mean Fighter* (London, 1978)
MAHON, John, *Harry Pollitt* (London, 1976)
MARQUAND, David, *Ramsay MacDonald* (London, 1977)
MARTIN, Kingsley,   *Harold Laski 1893-1950* (London, 1953)
                     Editor (London, 1968)
MARWICK, Arthur, *Clifford Allen* (Edinburgh, 1964)
MATKOVSKY, N. V., *A True Son of the British Working Class (Harry Pollitt)* (Moscow, 1972)
MORRISON, Herbert, *An Autobiography* (London, 1960)
MOSLEY, Sir Oswald, *My Life* (London, 1968)
MURPHY, J. T., *New Horizons* (London, 1941)
NICOLSON, Harold, *King George V* (London, 1952)
OWEN, Frank, *Tempestuous Journey (Lloyd George)* (London, 1954)
PATON, John, *Left Turn* (London, 1937)

PAUL, L., *Angry Young Man* (London, 1951)
PIRATIN, Phil, *Our Flag Stays Red* (London, 1948)
POSTGATE, R., *George Lansbury* (London, 1951)
POLLITT, Harry, *Serving my Time* (London, 1940)
PRITT, D. N., *Autobiography* (London, 1965 and 1966)
ROLPH, C. H., *Kingsley – the Life, Letters and Diaries of Kingsley Martin* (London, 1973)
SACKS, B., *J. Ramsay MacDonald in Thought and Action* (Albuquerque NM, 1952)
SHINWELL, E., *Conflict without Malice* (London, 1955)
SKIDELSKY, R., *Oswald Mosley* (London, 1975)
SLOAN, Pat, *John Cornford – a Memoir* (London, 1938)
SMITH, Andrew, *I was a Soviet Worker* (London, 1937)
SNOWDEN, Viscount, *An Autobiography* (London, 1934)
SPENDER, Stephen, *World within World* (London, 1951)
      The Thirties and After: Poetry, Politics, People (1933–75) (London, 1978)
STRAUSS, Pat, *Cripps – Advocate and Rebel* (London, 1943)
TEMPLEWOOD, Viscount, *Nine Troubled Years* (London, 1955)
TERRILL, Ross, *R. H. Tawney and his Times: Socialism as Fellowship* (Harvard, 1973)
THOMAS, Hugh, *John Strachey* (London, 1973)
TRORY, Ernie, *Between the Wars* (Brighton, 1974)
'WATCHMAN', *Right Honourable Gentlemen* (London, 1940)
WEIR, L. McN., *The Tragedy of Ramsay MacDonald* (London, 1938)
WILLIAMS, Francis, *Ernest Bevin* (London, 1952)
WILLIS, Ted, *Whatever Happened to Tom Mix?* (London, 1970)
WRENCH, Sir E., *Geoffrey Dawson and our Times* (London, 1955)
YOUNG, G. M., *Stanley Baldwin* (London, 1952)

4. Pamphlets arranged by publishing organization

(a) Official Labour Party and Trade Union Movement

N. B. Only directly relevant Labour publications are included. For a complete list see: *Labour Party Bibliography;* Labour Party, London; 1967
ADLER, F., *The Moscow Trials and the Labour and Socialist International* (London, 1931)
ATTLEE, C. R., *The Betrayal of Collective Security* (London, 1936)
      What We saw in Spain (London, 1937)
      Labour's Aims (London, 1937)
      Labour's Peace Aims (London, 1940)
BAUER, O., *Austrian Democracy under Fire* (London, 1934)
CITRINE, W., *Democracy or Disruption?* (London, 1928)
COMPTON, J., *Hitlerism – Down with Fascism* (London, 1933)
HENDERSON, *Labour and the Crisis* (London, 1931)
Arthur,   *Labour's Peace Policy* (London, 1934)
LABOUR PARTY, *The Labour Party and the Communist Party* (London, 1924)
      The 'New Party' (London, 1931)
      Socialism and the Condition of the People (London, 1933)
      The Socialisation of Industry (London, 1933)
      The Iniquitous Means Test (London, 1933)

The Communist Solar System (London, 1933)
The Proposed United Front (London, 1934)
Fascism, the Enemy of the People (London, 1934)
What is this Fascism? (London, 1934)
Nazis, Nazism and Nazidom (London, 1934)
For Socialism and Peace (London, 1934)
The National Government's Disarmament Record (London, 1935)
Socialism and Social Credit (London, 1935)
Victory for Socialism (London, 1935)
The Agony of Spain (London, 1936)
British Labour and Communism (London, 1936)
Catholics and the Civil War in Spain (London, 1936)
Labour's Immediate Programme (London, 1937)
Party Loyalty (London, 1937)
We Say it Can be Done (London, 1938)
Labour's National Crusade for Peace and Security (London, 1938)
Labour's League of Youth (London, 1938)
Labour and the Popular Front (London, 1938)
For Socialism and Peace (London, 1938)
Labour and Defence (London, 1939)
The Popular Front Campaign (London, 1939)
ARP: Labour's Policy (London, 1939)
Socialism or Surrender (London, 1939)
Unity, True or Sham? (London, 1939)
The Electoral Truce (London, 1940)
Finland (London, 1940)
Stalin's Men – 'About Turn' (London, 1940)
The Communist Party and the War (London, 1942)

LABOUR PARTY SPAIN COMMITTEE, *Spain Campaign Committee* (London, 1937)
LASKI, H. J., *The Labour Party, the War and the Future* (London, 1939)
Is this an Imperialist War? (London, 1940)
The Secret Battalion (London, 1946)
LONDON TRADES COUNCIL, *Memoranda on War* (London, 1935 and 1936)
MINERS' FEDERATION OF GREAT BRITAIN, *The Position of the Coal Miner* (London, 1933)
MORRISON, *A New Appeal to the Young* (London, 1932)
Herbert, *Peace for Whose Time?* (London, 1938)
NATIONAL *British Labour and Communism* (London, 1936)
COUNCIL *Labour and the Defence of Peace* (London, 1936)
OF LABOUR, *International Policy and Defence* (London, 1937)
Help for Russia (London, 1941)
NATIONAL UNION OF GENERAL AND MUNICIPAL WORKERS, *Report on Communists* (London, 1932)
TRADES UNION *The Government Evades its Responsibilities* (London, 1933)
CONGRESS, *The Menace of Dictatorship* (London, 1933)
Workers Control (London, 1933)
Workless – a Social Tragedy (London, 1933)
United against Fascism (London, 1934)
Peace or War? (London, 1935)

                    No United Front with Communism (London, 1936)
                    The Spanish Problem (London, 1936)
TUC and LABOUR PARTY, *Disarm* (London, 1935)
WALL, A. M. and MORRISON, H., *The Labour Movement and Fascism* (London, 1934)
WEBB, M.,   *Labour's Call to Youth* (London, 1933)
                    Youth for Socialism (London, 1934)
WEBB, Sidney, *What Happened in 1931* (London, 1932)

(b) The Labour Left

'ADVANCE' PUBLICATIONS, *Youth Triumphant* (London, 1938)
BEVIN, E., and COLE, G. D. H., *The Crisis* (London, 1931).
COLE, G. D. H., *The Working Class Movement and the Transition to Socialism* (London, 1934)
COLE, G. D. H. and MELLOR, W., *Workers Control and Self-government in Industry* (London, 1932)
CRIPPS, Sir R. S.,   *Can Socialism come by Constitutional Means?* (London, 1932)
                    The Ultimate Aims of the Labour Party (London, 1933)
                    Are You a Worker? (London, 1933)
                    Why this Socialism? (London, 1934)
                    'National Fascism' in Britain (London, 1935)
                    The Unity Campaign (London, 1937)
GROVES, Reg,   *Arms and the Unions* (London, 1935)
                    East End Crisis (London, 1937)
HOME COUNTIES LABOUR ASSOCIATION, *What it is* (Berkhamsted, 1935)
LASKI, H. J.,   *The Crisis and the Constitution* (London, 1932)
                    The Labour Party and the Constitution (London, 1933)
                    Where stands Socialism Today? (London, 1933)
                    Democracy in Crisis (London, 1933)
MARTIN, Kingsley, *Fascism, Democracy and the Press* (London, 1938)
MELLOR, W., *The Claim of the Unemployed* (London, 1932)
NEW FABIAN RESEARCH BUREAU, *Aspects of Socialist Planning,* (London, 1933)
UNION OF DEMOCRATIC CONTROL, *Eyewitness at Olympia* (London, 1934)
SIROCKIN, P., *The Story of Labour Youth* (London, 1961)
SOCIALIST LEAGUE, *Forward to Socialism* (London, 1934)
SSIP, *Facts and Figures for Labour Speakers* (London, 1931)
TREVELYAN, Sir C. P., *The Challenge to Capitalism* (London, 1932)
                    Mass Resistance to War (London, 1934)

(c) The Communist Party

BRAMLEY, Ted, *Bombers over London* (London, 1940)
BURNS, Emile, *Abyssinia and Italy* (London, 1935)
CAMPBELL, J. R., *Peace – but how?* (London, 1936)
                    Spain's Left Critics (London, 1937)
                    Questions and Answers on Communism (London, 1938)
                    Soviet Policy and its Critics (London, 1939)
COMMUNIST   *Class against Class* (London, 1929)
PARTY OF   *The Sedition Bill Exposed* (London, 1934)

GREAT BRITAIN *Sidelights on the Cliveden Set* (London, 1938)
                The Communist Party in Wartime (London, 1940)
CPGB LONDON DISTRICT COMMITTEE, *To the People of London* (London, 1937)
DIMITROV, G., *Dimitrov Accuses* (London, 1934)
                The Working Class against Fascism (London, 1935)
                Communism and War (London, 1939)
DUTT, R. Palme, *Capitalism or Socialism in Great Britain?* (London, 1931)
                The Road to Labour Unity (London, 1938)
                What Next for the Labour Party? (London, 1936)
                We Fight for Life (London, 1940)
GOLLAN, John, *Youth will serve for Freedom* (London, 1938)
                Defend the People (London, 1938)
HALDANE, J. B. S. and others, *The Case for the 'Daily Worker'* (London, 1941)
HORNER, Arthur, *Towards a Popular Front* (London, 1936)
HUTT, Alan, *This Final Crisis* (London, 1935)
KNORIN, V. G., *Fascism, Social Democracy and Communism* (Moscow, 1935)
LITVINOV, Maxim, *The Soviet's Fight for Disarmament* (London, 1932)
LOZOVSKY, A., *What is the Red International of Labour Unions?* (London, 1927)
                The World Economic Crisis (Moscow, 1931)
                Marx and the Trade Unions (London, 1935)
MAHON, John, *Trade Unionism and Communism* (London, 1936)
MANUILSKY, D., *The Revolutionary Crisis is Maturing* (London, 1934)
PIATNITSKY, O., *Unemployment and the Tasks of the Communists* (London, 1931)
                The Bolshevisation of the Communist Parties by Eradicating the Social Democratic Traditions (London, 1932)
POLLITT, Harry, *Which way for the Workers?* (London, 1932)
                The Labour Party and the Communist Party (London, 1935)
                I Accuse Baldwin! (London, 1936)
                Forward! (London, 1936)
                Arms for Spain (London, 1936)
                Austria (London, 1938)
                Can Conscription save Peace? (London, 1938)
                Will it be War? (London, 1939)
                How to Win the War (London, 1939)
POLLITT, H., and DUTT, R. P., *The Truth about Trotskyism* (London, 1937)
RUST, W., *Britons in Spain* (London, 1939)
                The Inside Story of the 'Daily Worker' (London, 1939)

(d) 'Fronts and Ancillaries' of the Communist Party

ADAMS, Harry, *Why Britain Needs a Peoples' Government* (London, 1941)
ANGLO-RUSSIAN
PARLIAMENTARY *The USSR and Peace* (London, 1935)
COMMITTEE, *The Moscow Trials* (London, 1936)
BRITISH YOUTH *The World We Mean to Make* (London, 1936)
PEACE ASSEMBLY *Youth Unite for Peace* (London, 1937)
                Why do we Need a Charter? (London, 1938)
CONNOLLY, J., *An Easy Guide to the New Unemployment Act* (London, 1934)
ELIAS, Sid, *Our Reply to the Royal Commission on Unemployment* (London, 1931)

HANNINGTON,   *The National Hunger March to London* (London, 1930)
Wal,   *Unemployed! To Action!* (London, 1932)
    Crimes against the Unemployed (London, 1932)
    An Exposure of the Unemployed Social Service Scheme (London, 1934)
    Beware! Slave Camps and Conscription (London, 1938)
    Black Coffins and the Unemployed (London, 1939)
INKPIN, Albert, *Friends of the Soviet Union – the Story of the Russia Today Society* (London, 1942)
JONES, V. D., *Conscription? Not for the Youth of Great Britain* (London, 1938)
LABOUR RESEARCH DEPARTMENT, *Mosley Fascism – The Man, his Policy and Methods* (London, 1935)
MARX HOUSE, *The Truth about Trotskyism* (London, 1944)
NUWM, *Who Prevents the United Front?* (London, 1933)
PRITT, D. N.,   *A Call to the People* (London, 1940)
    Forward to a Peoples' Government (London, 1942)
RILU, *The Position of the Minority Movement and its Immediate Tasks* (Moscow, 1932)
RUSSIA TODAY SOCIETY, *Finland – the Facts* (London, 1939)
STUDENT LABOUR FEDERATION, *This is the SLF* (London, 1946)
UNIVERSITY LABOUR FEDERATION, *How we can End the War* (London, 1941)

(e) The ILP, Pacifists, Trotskyists and Anarchists, etc.

ALLEN, R. C., *Effective Pacifism* (London, 1932)
ANARCHO-SYNDICALIST UNION, *Spain – Anarchism* (London, 1937)
BRINTON, H. and others, *Does Capitalism Cause War?* (London, 1938)
BROCKWAY,   *A Socialist Plan for the Unemployed* (London, 1931)
Fenner,   *Socialism at the Crossroads* (London, 1932)
    Pacifism and the Left Wing (London, 1938)
BROWN, H. R.,   *Spain – a Challenge to Pacifism* (Enfield, 1936)
    The War Resisters International (Enfield, 1936)
COMMONWEALTH, *Commonwealth and the Political Parties* (London, 1942)
COMMUNIST LEAGUE OF AMERICA, *War and the Fourth International* (New York, 1940)
COVENANTER, *Labour and War Resistance* (London, 1936)
FOOT, M., and others, *Young Oxford and the War* (Oxford, 1934)
FOURTH INTERNATIONAL, *Manifesto on the War* (New York, 1940)
HUXLEY, A., and SHEPPARD, R., *100.000 Say No!* (London, 1938)
INDEPENDENT LABOUR PARTY, *What the ILP Stands For* (London, 1938)
JOHNSON, F., *The ILP in War and Peace* (London, 1940)
JOWETT, Fred, *The ILP Says No!* (London, 1932)
LONDON FEDERATION OF PEACE COUNCILS, *Rearmament and the Unions* (London, 1937)
LOVESTONE, Jay, *The Peoples' Front Illusion* (New York, 1937)
McGOVERN, John, *Why Bishops Back Franco* (London, 1936)
MARXIST GROUP, *Fight for the Fourth International* (London, 1936)
MAXTON, James, *Great Anti-War Speech* (Glasgow, 1938)
NATIONAL
COUNCIL FOR   *The Thurloe Square Baton Charge* (London, 1936)
CIVIL LIBERTIES *The Record of a Decade of Work 1934–1945* (London, 1945)
NATIONAL PEACE COUNCIL, *Peace and the General Election* (London, 1935)

STRACHAN, J. R., *The War Crisis – the Way Out for the Workers* (London, 1939)
TROTSKY, L. D.,   *The Soviet Union and the Fourth International* (Glasgow, 1934)
        The USSR in War (London, 1939)
WORKERS' INTERNATIONAL LEAGUE, *Transitional Programme of the Fourth International* (London, 1939)

(f) Miscellaneous organisations

ALLEN, Clifford, *Labour's Future at Stake* (London, 1932)
ECONOMIC   *Communism and British Youth* (London, 1936)
LEAGUE,   *The Present Trend of Communism in Britian* (London, 1938)
GODDEN, G. M., *The Communist Attack on Great Britain,* (London, 1935)
JOAD, C. E. M., *The Case for the New Party* (London, 1932)
LIBERAL NATIONAL COMMITTEE, *The Labour Party's Black Record* (London, 1935)
LIBERAL PARTY, *The Liberal Party and the Popular Front* (London, 1937)
NATIONAL CONSTITUTION DEFENCE COMMITTEE, *Series on Extremism* (London, 1937)
NATIONAL LABOUR COMMITTEE, *The Labour Party, the Crisis and the Nation* (London, 1931)

5. Reports, Minutes and official documents

ANNUAL REGISTER OF WORLD EVENTS, *1930 to 1941* (London)
BELLAMY, J. M. and SAVILLE, John, *Dictionary of Labour Biography:* vol. 1 (London, 1972); vol. 2 (London, 1974); vol. 3 (London, 1976)
COMINTERN,   *Communist Policy in Great Britain* (London, 1928)
        XIth Plenum Series (London, 1931)
        XIIth Plenum Series (London, 1932 and 1933)
        XIIIth Plenum Series (London, 1934)
        Program and Statutes Adopted at the Sixth Congress (New York, 1933)
        Fifteen Years of the Communist International (New York, 1934)
        Report of the Seventh World Congress (London, 1936)
COMMUNIST   *Theses of the 1920 Comintern Congress* (London, 1934)
PARTY OF   *Communist Political Education Manual* (London, 1933)
GREAT BRITAIN, *For Soviet Britain* (London, 1935)
        Communist Theory Series (London, 1937)
        On the Thirtieth Anniversary of the Communist Party (London, 1950)
CONGRESS OF PEACE AND FRIENDSHIP WITH THE USSR, *Britain and the Soviets: Verbatim Report* (London, 1936)
COUNCIL OF ACTION FOR PEACE AND RECONSTRUCTION, *Handbook* (London, 1935)
FABIAN SOCIETY, *Annual Reports* (London, 1933–1941)
INDEPENDENT   *Report of Annual Conference* (London 1930–1941)
LABOUR PARTY, *Minutes of the National Administrative Council 1928–1941*
        Documents of the National Administrative Council 1928–1941
        Documents of the London Division 1933–1939
        Report of the Special National Conference (London, 1932)

                    Silver Jubilee Souvenir (London, 1943)
LABOUR PARTY, *Report of Annual Conference* (London, 1920–1942)
                    National Executive Committee Minutes 1931–1941
                    Party Constitution and Standing Orders (London, 1937)
                    Commission of Enquiry into the Distressed Areas (London, 1937)
                    Labour Party Bibliography (London, 1967)
LABOUR AND SOCIALIST INTERNATIONAL, *Fourth Congress Report* (Zurich, 1932)
MINERS' FEDERATION OF GREAT BRITAIN, *Annual Proceedings 1935–1939*
NATIONAL UNITED FRONT CONFERENCE OF ACTION, *Report* (London, 1934)
PEACE PLEDGE UNION, *Peace Service Handbook* (London, 1939)
PEOPLE'S CONVENTION, *Report of the People's Convention* (London, 1941)
POLLITT, Harry, *Road to Victory* (London, 1932)
                    Towards Soviet Power (London, 1934)
SOCIALIST LEAGUE, *Annual Conference Reports 1933–1937*
THE TIMES, *Guide to the House of Commons 1929, 1931 and 1935*
TRADES UNION CONGRESS, *Annual Reports 1929–1939*
TUC AND LABOUR PARTY, *Labour Year Book 1924–1932*

6. Theses

BOWES, N., *The People's Convention* (MA Thesis, University of Warwick, 1976)
CEADEL, M. E., *Pacifism in Britain 1931–1939* (DPhil Thesis, Oxford University, 1976)
DAVIS, S., *British Labour and Foreign Policy* (PhD Thesis, University of London, 1950)
EATWELL, R., *The Labour Party and the Popular Front Movement in Britain in the 1930s* (DPhil Thesis, Oxford University, 1976)
FARRAR, E. M., *The British Labour Party and International Organisation* (MScEcon Thesis, University of London, 1952)
FERRIS, J., *The Labour League of Youth 1924–1940* (MA Thesis, University of Warwick, 1976)
GREENWALD, Norman D., *Communism and British Labour: a study of British Labour Party Politics 1933–1939* (PhD Thesis, Columbia University, 1958)
JONES, C. M., *Crisis of Parliamentary Liberalism: Extremism in Britain in the 1930s* (PhD Thesis, Duke University, 1974)
JUPP, J., *The Left in Britain 1931–1941* (MScEcon Thesis, University of London, 1956)
MACINTYRE, S. F., *Marxism in Britain 1917-1933* (PhD Thesis, Cambridge University, 1976)
SMITH, D., *The Reorganisation of the South Wales Miners' Federation 1927–1939* (PhD Thesis, University of Wales, 1976)
THWAITES, P. J., *The Independent Labour Party 1938–1950* (PhD Thesis, University of London, 1976)
TUCKER, W. R., *The Attitude of the British Labour Party towards European and Collective Security Problems 1920–1939* (Doctoral Thesis, University of Geneva, 1950)

7. Selected Journal articles

ANONYMOUS, 'General Election 1931', *Round Table* (December 1931)

COLLINS, H., 'John Strachey – a Fresh Assessment', *Plebs 59 4* (September 1967)

CRIPPS, Sir R. S.,   'Alternatives before British Labour', *Foreign Affairs (New York)* (October 1934)
'The Future of the Labour Party', *New Statesman* (3 September 1932)

DURBIN, E. F. M., 'Democracy and Socialism in Britain', *Political Quarterly* (July 1935)

EATWELL, R., 'Munich, Public Opinion and the Popular Front', *Journal of Contemporary History VI 4* (1971)

FRANCIS, H., 'Welsh Miners and the Spanish Civil War', *Journal of Contemporary History V 3* (1970)

GOLLAN, John, 'Fifty Years of the Communist Party', *Marxism Today (Special Number) 14* (1970)

GRAINGER, G. W., 'Oligarchy in the British Communist Party', *British Journal of Sociology* (June, 1958)

GREEN, N., 'The Communist Party and the War in Spain', *Marxism Today (Special Number) 14* (1970)

HARRISON, Royden, 'Communist Party affiliation to the Labour Party: transcript of the meeting of 29 December 1921', *Bulletin of the Society for the Study of Labour History 29* (Autumn 1974)

HELLER, R., 'East Fulham Revisited', *Journal of Contemporary History VI 3* (1971)

LASKI, H. J., 'The General Election of 1935', *Political Quarterly* (January, 1936)

JOHNSTONE, M., ROTHSTEIN, A., and others, 'Book Review and Correspondence on Harry Pollitt's Attitude to the 1939 War', *Bulletin of the Society for the Study of Labour History 33, 34 & 35* (Spring, Summer and Autumn, 1977)

MANDLE, W. F.,   'The New Party', *Historical Studies* (October 1966)
'Sir Oswald Mosley Leaves the Labour Party, March 1931', *Labour History 12* (May 1967)

MARWICK, Arthur 'James Maxton: his place in Scottish labour history', *Scottish Historical Review 43* (1964)
'Youth in Britain 1920–1960', *Journal of Contemporary History V 1* (1970)

PARKER, John, 'The constitutional background of the Cripps controversy', *Political Quarterly* (April, 1939)

PIMLOTT, Ben, 'The Socialist League: Intellectuals and the Labour Left in the 1930s', *Journal of Contemporary History VI 3* (1971)

POLLARD, S., 'Trade Union reaction to the economic crisis', *Journal of Contemporary History IV 4* (October, 1969)

PRYNN, D. L., 'Commonwealth – a British "Third Party" of the 1940s' *Journal of Contemporary History VII 1–2* (1972)

ROBERTSON, J. C., 'The British General Election of 1935', *Journal of Contemporary History IX 1* (January, 1974)

ROWSE, A. L., 'Labour Conference at Southport', *Nineteenth Century* (November, 1934)

ROWSE, A. L. and SCANLON, J., 'British Labour in Conference', *Nineteenth Century* (July, 1937)

SAMUELS, S., 'The Left Book Club', *Journal of Contemporary History I 1* (1966)

'The English Left Intelligentsia in the 1930s', *Bulletin of the Society for the Study of Labour History 14* (Spring, 1967)

STANNAGE, C. T., 'The East Fulham by-election 25 October 1933', *Historical Journal 14* (1971)

TAWNEY, R. H., 'The Choice before the Labour Party', *Political Quarterly* (July, 1932)

UPHAM, Martin, 'The Balham Group (a letter)', *Bulletin of the Society for the Study of Labour History 30* (Spring, 1975)

WALKER, P. Gordon, 'The attitude of Labour and the Left to the War', *Political Quarterly* (March, 1940)

WEBB, Sidney, 'What happened in 1931 – a record', *Political Quarterly* (January, 1932)

8. Newspapers and Journals

Adelphi
Advance
AEU Monthly Journal
Bulletin of the Society for the Study of Labour History
Challenge
Civil Liberty
Communist International
Contemporary Review
Controversy
Daily Express
Daily Herald
Daily Mail
Daily Telegraph
Daily Worker
Discussion
Fortnightly Review
Forward
Inprecorr
International Press Correspondence
Journal of Contemporary History
Labour Book Service Bulletin
Labour Magazine
Labour Monthly
Left Forum
Left News
Left Review
London News
Manchester Guardian
Militant
Monthly Bulletin of the Labour League of Youth
Morning Post
New Age

New Clarion
New Europe
New Leader
New Nation
New Statesman and Nation
News Chronicle
Nineteenth Century
Organisational Bulletin of the Labour League of Youth
Party Organiser (CPGB)
Peace
Political Quarterly
Socialist Leaguer
Socialist Review
The Times
Tribune
Worker
World News and Views

Index

Bruce, W., 119
Buchanan, George (1890 – 1955), 23, 95
Bucks Federation of Trades Councils and Labour Parties, 113
Burns, Emile (b. 1889), 132, 160
Busmen's Rank and File Movement, 85; *B. Punch,* 225n

Cable Street. 57, 209; *see also* BUF, Stepney
Callaghan, James (b. 1912), 213
Cambridge University, 99, 169, 211
Campaign for Nuclear Disarmament, 211, 212
Campbell, J.R. (b. 1894), 39, 121, 171
Cannon, James P., 102
Catholics, 61, 87
Cecil, Viscount (1864 – 1958), 219n
Central Board of Conscientious Objectors, 103
Challenge, 78, 94, 228n; *see also* Young Communist League
Chamberlain, Neville (1869 – 1940), 90, 91, 111, 114, 121, 135, 169, 170
Chartists, 17, 203
Chesterfield, 188
Chopwell, 229n
Churchill, Winston S. (1874 – 1965), 58, 90, 113, 116, 202
Citrine, Walter (b. 1887), 12, 58, 65, 89, 192, 209
Clay, Harold, 159
'Cliveden set', 90, 222n
Clydebank, 179; C – side, 2, 148, 171; 'C – siders', 21; C. Valley, 179; C. Workers Committee, 2; *see also* Glasgow
Clynes, J. R. (1869 – 1949), 131
Cockburn, Claud, 222n
Cold War, 204
Cole, G.D.H. (1889 – 1959), 28, 79, 81, 111, 127, 159, 168
Coming Struggle for Power, The, 137
Commons, House of, 144, 169, 226n
Commonwealth, 8, 121
Communist International (Comintern), 13, 19 – 21 *passim,* 26, 30, 31, 36 – 38 *passim,* 44, 45, 47 – 50 *passim,* 68, 70, 77, 78, 96, 121, 127, 138, 149, 164, 167, 170, 174, 196, 203, 217n, 225n; Executive Committee of the CI, 50, 192, 220n;

ECCI eleventh plenum, 31; ECCI twelfth plenum, 41; ECCI thirteenth plenum, 49; Sixth Congress, 13, 30, 216n; Seventh Congress, 27, 50, 60, 72 – 76 *passim,* 144; Twenty-one conditions, 21, 138; *see also* Communist Party of Great Britain, ILP Comintern Affiliation Committee
Communist League, 53
Communist Party of Great Britain, 6, 19, 20, 24 – 27 *passim,* 29 – 33 *passim,* 36, 38 – 41, 43, 45 – 52 *passim,* 54, 63, 66 – 77 *passim,* 79 – 82 *passim,* 86, 88, 92 – 95, 97, 104 – 112 *passim,* 114, 120 – 122, 123, 126 – 128, 131 – 134 *passim,* 136, 138 – 141, 148, 151, 152, 156, 157, 169, 171, 175, 177, 179 – 181, 192, 195 – 197 *passim,* 201 – 203, 205, 207 – 209 *passim,* 216n, 224n, 227n, 228n, 229n; Central Committee, 20, 25, 26, 27, 53, 77, 136, 141, 170; eleventh Congress (1929), 20; twelfth Congress (1932), 26; thirteenth Congress (1935), 75, 76, 179; fourteenth Congress (1937), 93, 94, 168; National Conference (1935) 76; Lancashire District, 181; *see also* Communist International, Communists, Young Communist League
Communists, 9, 12 – 14, 20, 21, 24, 27 – 29, 32, 33, 35 – 38, 40, 42, 44, 46 – 48, 50, 51, 58, 60, 62, 80 – 82, 84 – 86, 90, 96, 99, 101 – 104, 110, 113, 115, 116, 118, 142 – 146 *passim,* 149, 150, 161, 166, 171, 173, 178 – 180, 182, 184, 190, 192, 195, 196, 198, 200, 204, 207, 210 – 212, 226n, 230n; *see also* Communist Party of GB, Communist International, Pollitt
Communist Youth, 78
conscription, 90, 92, 103, 167, 169
Conservative Party, Conservatives, 4, 5, 6, 15, 16, 29, 37, 57, 58, 61, 62, 64, 80, 86, 89, 90, 103, 110, 113, 116, 121, 163, 188, 198, 204, 206, 209, 213, 214, 224n; *see also* National Government
Constituency Parties Association, 83, 108, 153, 154, 176, 181, 189, 193,

Renfrewshire, 179; R. East, 23
revolutionaries, vii, 3, 31, 38, 39, 110,
    136, 138, 140 – 144, 146
Revolutionary Socialist League, 102
Revolutionary Socialist Party, 102
Revolutionary Trade Union Opposi-
    tion, 26
Reynolds News, 79, 111, 112, 127
Rhondda, 59, 93, 179, 180, 202 – 204
    passim, 216n; R. East, 76; *R. Van-
    guard,* 225n; *see also* South Wales
Ribbentrop, J. von, 90
Right Book Club, 129
Riley, Ben, 119
Robeson, Paul, 120
Rothermere, Lord (1868 – 1940), 14, 57
Russian revolution, 3, 21; *see also*
    Bolsheviks, Soviet Union
Rust, William, 36, 50, 128

Saklatvala, Shapurji (1874 – 1936), 21,
    58
Salter, Dr Alfred (1873 – 1945), 22, 163,
    171, 215n
Sandham, Elijah, 48
Sandys, Duncan (b. 1908), 116, 202
Scotland, 2, 3, 10, 16, 21, 25, 35, 53, 67,
    69, 87, 94, 129, 130, 146, 178, 179,
    181, 190, 206, 208, 209, 216n, 225n,
    229n; *see also* Distressed Areas,
    Fife, Glasgow
Scottish Labour Party (1880s), 179
Scottish Socialist Party, 35, 53, 54, 176,
    181
Seaham election of 1935, 58
Second International, 19, 21, 31, 44,
    163; *see also* Labour and Socialist
    International
Second World War, 1, 8, 91, 92, 103;
    declaration of, 85, 91
Sheffield, 178
Shepherd, G.R. (1881 – 1954), 98, 119
Shinwell, Emanuel (b. 1884), 22, 58,
    230n
Shop Assistants, Warehousemen and
    Clerks, National Union of, 192
Snowden, Philip (1864 – 1937), 8
social democracy, 18, 20, 31, 37, 41, 45,
    49, 137, 138, 187
Social Democratic Federation, 6, 130,
    132, 148, 155, 202
'social fascism', 20, 21, 30, 31, 33, 41, 50,

55, 72, 73, 134, 138, 149, 160, 211;
    see also Communist International
    – Sixth Congress
Social Service Centres, 25
socialism, -ists, 11 – 13, 17 – 19 *passim,*
    21, 29, 34, 35, 49, 60, 65, 75, 78, 81,
    89, 99, 110, 117, 120, 125, 126, 129,
    131, 133, 136 – 140 *passim,* 144,
    145, 147 – 150, 152, 154, 155 – 162
    passim, 186, 187, 191, 197, 200, 201,
    212 – 214, 230n; S. Common-
    wealth, 112, 214; s. movement, 16;
    s. societies, 6, 100, 173, 191, 226n
*Socialism and the Condition of the
    People,* 12, 43, 70
Socialism in Our Time, 22, 24, 157
Socialist Labour League, 227n
Socialist Labour Party, 130
Socialist League, 12, 28, 35, 42, 46, 47,
    53, 54, 59, 66, 70 – 72 *passim,* 74,
    75, 81, 94, 104 – 107, 125, 128, 131,
    134, 143, 144, 155, 157, 159, 164,
    166, 168, 176, 181, 182, 191, 192,
    197, 200, 218, 224n, 225n; confer-
    ence of 1935, 71, 74; conf. of 1936,
    81; *Socialist Leaguer,* 70
Socialist Party of Great Britain, 132
Society for Socialist Inquiry and Propa-
    ganda, 28,.42, 125, 215n, 217n
Soldiers' Voice, 141
South East England, 10, 83, 176, 181;
    South of England, 11, 84, 175; *see
    also* London
South Wales, 1, 2, 3, 10, 16, 25, 28, 67,
    87, 94, 129, 130, 146, 148, 178 – 181
    passim, 190, 206, 208, 209, 229n;
    SW Council of Action, 180; SW
    Miners Federation, 30, 179, 180;
    see also Distressed Areas, Rhond-
    da
Southwark, 182
Soviet Union (USSR), 13, 20, 53,
    60 – 62 *passim,* 67, 87 – 90 *passim,*
    92, 106, 111, 118, 122, 125, 132,
    133, 138, 144, 145, 156, 160, 164,
    167 – 171 *passim,* 195, 198, 201,
    202, 205, 207, 213; Communist
    Party of the SU, 19, 50, 132; Five
    Year Plans, 61, 132; government
    of, 86, 101, 113; Stalin constitu-
    tion, 62, 145; *see also* Bolsheviks,
    Friends of the SU, Moscow, Rus-
    sian revolution, Stalin